THE RADICAL PAPERS: READINGS IN EDUCATION/RE

Edited by
HAROLD W. SOBEL
and
ARTHUR E. SALZ
Queens College
The City University
of New York

the Radical

NGS IN EDUCATION / READINGS IN EDUCATION / READINGS

Papers

EDUCATION / READINGS IN EDUCATION / READINGS IN EDU

Harper & Row, Publishers
New York   Evanston
San Francisco   London

99207

ACKNOWLEDGMENTS

Joan Baez, excerpt from *Daybreak.* Copyright © 1966, 1968 by Joan Baez. Reprinted by permission of the publisher, The Dial Press. "Farewell Angelina" by Joan Baez. Copyright © by Joan Baez. Reprinted by permission of Folklore Productions, Inc.

Roland S. Barth, "So You Want to Change to an Open Classroom," *Phi Delta Kappan,* October 1971. Reprinted with permission.

Richard Brautigan, "Gee, You're so Beautiful That It's Starting to Rain," from *The Pill Versus the Springhill Mine Disaster* by Richard Brautigan. Copyright © 1968 by Richard Brautigan. A Seymour Lawrence Book/Delacorte Press. Reprinted by permission of the publisher.

James Cass, "A School Designed for Kids." Reprinted with permission from *Saturday Review,* March 21, 1970. Copyright 1970 Saturday Review, Inc.

Walter R. Coppedge, "What the World is Coming To," *Phi Delta Kappan,* October 1970. Reprinted with permission.

Alice de Rivera, "On De-Segregating Stuyvesant High." Reprinted with permission from *Sisterhood Is Powerful,* Robin Morgan, ed. (New York: Random House, Vintage Books, 1970). Copyright © 1969 by Alice de Rivera.

George Dennison, Paul Goodman, Nat Hentoff, John Holt, and Jonathan Kozol, "New Nation Seed Fund." Reprinted with permission of the New Nation Seed Fund, Box 4026, Philadelphia, Pa. 19118.

THE RADICAL PAPERS: READINGS IN EDUCATION

Connie Dvorkin, "The Suburban Scene." Reprinted with permission from *Sisterhood Is Powerful,* Robin Morgan, ed. (New York: Random House, Vintage Books, 1970). Copyright © 1970 by Connie Dvorkin.

Herbert J. Gans, "Report from the Center for Urban Archaeology," *The Urban Review,* a publication of the Center for Urban Education, Vol. 3, No. 2 (November 1968), pp. 16–17. Reprinted by permission.

Ira Glasser, "Are Children People?" Reprinted with permission from *Civil Liberties in New York,* March 1968, p. 4.

James D. Greenberg and Robert E. Roush, "A Visit to the 'School Without Walls.'" This paper was condensed from an article entitled "A Visit to the 'School Without Walls': Two Impressions." Readers wishing to have the two authors' complete reactions to the Parkway Program should refer to the *Phi Delta Kappan,* Vol. 51, No. 9 (May 1970), pp. 480–484.

Beatrice and Ronald Gross, "A Little Bit of Chaos." Reprinted with permission from *Saturday Review,* May 16, 1970. Copyright 1970 Saturday Review, Inc.

John Guernsey, "Portland's Unconventional Adams High." Reprinted with permission from *American Education,* U.S. Dept. of Health, Education, and Welfare, Office of Education, Vol. 6, No. 4 (May 1970), pp. 3–7.

Carol Stolley Hastie, "Sesame Street: The Establishment Easy Street." Reprinted with permission from *New Schools Exchange Newsletter,* No. 57 (April 1, 1971), p. 15.

Ivan Illich, "Abolishing Schools," *The New York Times,* May 3, 1971, p. 37, and May 4, 1971, p. 47. © 1971 by The New York Times Company. Reprinted by permission.

Christopher Jencks, "Education Vouchers," *The New Republic,* Vol. 163, No. 1 (July 4, 1970). Reprinted by permission of *The New Republic,* © 1970, Harrison-Blaine of New Jersey, Inc.

Jonathan Kozol, "Look, This System Is Not Working," *The New York Times,* April 1, 1971. © 1971 by The New York Times Company. Reprinted by permission.

Liberation News Service, cartoon (frontispiece). Reprinted with permission of Liberation News Service, 160 Claremont Avenue, New York, N.Y. 10027.

Peter Marin, "Children of the Apocalypse," *Saturday Review,* September 19, 1970. Reprinted by permission of Peter Marin, c/o International Famous Agency. Copyright © 1970 by Peter Marin.

Richard Martin, "Anything Goes," *The Wall Street Journal,* December 1, 1970. Reprinted by permission of *The Wall Street Journal.*

New Schools Exchange Newsletter, "LEAPschool." Reprinted with permission from *New Schools Exchange Newsletter,* No. 54 (March 1971), p. 7. "We Have Created a School Where . . ." Reprinted with permission from *New Schools Exchange Newsletter,* No. 41 (June 1970), pp. 2–3.

New York Civil Liberties Union, "Hot Time in a Cold Town." Reprinted with permission from *Civil Liberties in New York,* March 1968, p. 5.

ACKNOWLEDGMENTS (Cont'd.)

Neil Postman, "The Politics of Reading," *Harvard Educational Review,* 40, Spring 1970, 244–252. Copyright © 1970 by President and Fellows of Harvard College.

Everett Reimer, "An Essay on Alternatives in Education." This essay was originally published in *Interchange,* Vol. 2, No. 1. These extracts in later draft appear in *School Is Dead: Alternatives in Education,* copyright © 1970, 1971 by Everett Reimer. Reprinted by permission of Doubleday and Co., Inc.

Wallace Roberts, "No Place to Grow." Reprinted with permission from *Saturday Review,* March 21, 1970. Copyright 1970 Saturday Review, Inc.

Michael Rossman, "Declaration on the Birth of the Child Lorca." Reprinted with permission from *New Schools Exchange Newsletter,* No. 47, n.d., pp. 2–3. Copyright © 1970 by Michael Rossman. Included in his book, *The Wedding Within the War* (New York: Doubleday, Anchor Books, 1971).

Peter Schrag, "Growing Up on Mechanic Street," from *Out of Place in America,* by Peter Schrag. Copyright © 1970 by Peter Schrag. Reprinted by permission of Random House, Inc.

Harvey B. Scribner, "What Needs Reforming?" *The New York Times Annual Education Review,* January 11, 1971; originally titled "Restructuring Deemed An Urban 'Imperative.' " © 1971 by The New York Times Company. Reprinted by permission.

Mark R. Shedd, "Decentralization and Urban Schools," *Educational Leadership,* Vol. 25, No. 1 (October 1967), pp. 32–35. Reprinted with permission of the Association for Supervision and Curriculum Development and Mark R. Shedd. Copyright © 1967 by the Association for Supervision and Curriculum Development.

Bonnie Barrett Stretch, "The Rise of the Free School." Reprinted with permission from *Saturday Review,* June 20, 1970. Copyright 1970 Saturday Review, Inc.

Arthur J. Tobier, "The Open Classroom: Humanizing the Coldness of Public Places," *The Center Forum,* a publication of the Center for Urban Education, Vol. 3, No. 6 (May 15, 1969). Reprinted by permission.

Charles Weingartner, "Communication, Education, and Change." This article appeared in slightly different form in *Education Synopsis,* Vol 13, No. 2 (Spring 1968). Reprinted by permission of the author.

where it's at

we must be doing something wrong

someone's doing something right

where do we go from here?

Ten forty-three.
In exactly TWO MIN-
UTES I'll ring the
FIRST BELL and
they'll all
stand still!

All, that is, except
your potential DEVIATE!
Your fledgling REBEL!
Your incipient BOAT-
ROCKER! THEY'LL try
to move all right!
THEY'LL have to
learn the HARD
way not to move!

So I'll SCREAM at 'em
and take their NAMES
and give them FIVE
DETENTIONS AND EXTRA
HOMEWORK! NEXT time
they won't move
after the first
bell!

They'll grow up to accept
TAXES! HOUSING DEVELOP-
MENTS! INSURANCE! WAR!
MEN ON THE MOON! LIQUOR!
LAWS! POLITICAL SPEECHES!
PARKING METERS!
TELEVISION!
FUNERALS!

Because when they've
learned not to question
the FIRST BELL, they'll
learn not to question
their TEXTS! Their
TEACHERS! Their
COURSES!
EXAMINATIONS!

Non-movement
after
the first
bell is
the
backbone
of Western
Civilization!

Liberation News Service

your head while all those around

Sobel and Salz, in this collection of statements about education and the schools, are trying to help us to understand the situation. The situation is the problem that the schools comprise.

Nobel prize-winner Albert Szent-Gyorgyi tells us:

> We live in a new cosmic world which man was not made for. His survival now depends on how well and how fast he can adapt himself to it, rebuilding all his ideas, all his social and economic and political structures. His existence depends on the question of whether he can adapt himself faster than hostile forces can destroy him. At present, he is clearly losing out.
>
> We are forced to face this situation with our caveman's brain, a brain that has not changed since it was formed. We face it with outdated thinking, institutions, and methods, with political leaders who have their roots in the old, prescientific world and think the only way to solve these formidable problems is by trickery and double talk. . . .[1]

As Szent-Gyorgyi points out, all that is at stake in our attempts to solve this problem of educating ourselves to the "new cosmic world" is our survival. But in order to *do* anything about a problem we must first be aware that it exists. If that seems too obvious to be worth stating, you have simultaneously missed the point and illustrated it.

Charles Silberman, in his thorough (and by no means radical) report on the Carnegie Foundation supported study of the schools entitled *Crisis in the Classroom,* attributed most of the crisis to "mindlessness." He meant by this that it was virtually impossible to find anyone in the schools *thinking* about what they were doing and why they were doing it. Mostly, people in the schools—teachers, administrators, and students—are just doing what they are told. They are "just following orders." What Silberman's study reveals, then, is that there is little awareness in the schools themselves that *they* are a problem.

It is tempting to elaborate on the curious staff subculture in the schools. Perhaps just one observation is appropriate at this point—that schools are psychopathically devoted to trivia. They reveal an incredible devotion to the task of elevating the trivial to the level of the crucial, and then go on to expend most of their energy and resources on the witless task of enforcing the "rules and regulations" that derive from this self-sterilizing process. In the midst of

[1] Albert Szent-Gyorgyi, *The Crazy Ape* (New York: Grossett & Dunlap, 1970), p 17.

you are losing theirs, maybe you just

don't understand the situation

several simultaneous problems of catastrophic dimensions, including among the more obvious: the erosion of traditional institutions and values, universal ecological destruction, increasing urban implosion, the civil rights revolution, economic chaos, epidemic anomie, and rampant drug addiction, what "problems" do the schools spend their time and energy solving? Two of the most consuming in recent years have been (and still are) the length of boys' hair and the shortness of girls' skirts!

The function of this book, however "impractical" and "romantic" it seems to those whose intellectual capabilities confine them to cutting right through to the surface of most problems, is to help us to become aware of the schools as a problem, and then to *think* about that problem in a way that produces some possible solutions.

And even this modest and reasonable intention is jeopardized by an insidious sub-problem: inertia. It turns out that there is no agency, person, or process in the schools at large that is devoted mostly, much less exclusively, to inventing and instigating institutional change. There are isolated exceptions, and some of them are noted in this book. Generally, teachers do not think of themselves as responsible for such a function. They feel already overburdened with the tasks of "covering the required material," and "enforcing rules and regulations." Administrators, most commonly, see their mission primarily as that of *resisting* change. The last thing an administrator will do is "upset the community." This leads, predictably, to their working to maintain the status quo.

So, who is there to assume the responsibilities of the role of change agent in the schools? If you say "the students," think about that for a bit, especially about what it would *really* take to make it so. In any case, this role certainly won't be taken on by anyone who denies that the problem exists, or who won't *think* about it at the very least. It won't be taken on by anyone who automatically rejects new ideas.

Charles Kettering, who specialized in new ideas, said that new ideas are almost impossible to get into practice because 99 out of 100 people immediately start cataloging what is wrong with them, and pointing out why they won't work. Sobel and Salz have put together a book for the one person in a hundred who is "romantic" enough to think about what might be right in a new idea about schools.

CHARLES WEINGARTNER

SCHOOL IS NOT HEALTHY FOR CHILDREN AND OTHER LIVING THINGS

PREFACE

"Beginning with school, if not before, an individual is systematically stripped of his imagination, his creativity, his heritage, his dreams, and his personal uniqueness, in order to fit him to be a productive unit in a mass technological society. Instinct, feeling, and spontaneity are suppressed by overwhelming forces." Most, if not all, of the contributors to this book would probably agree with this verdict from Charles Reich's *The Greening of America*.

This anthology presents the ideas of contemporary educational critics. After citing what is wrong with American education, it offers examples of model schools. The final section looks to the future and contemplates some ways change may be brought about. Most of the contributing authors are left of center on the educational spectrum, and a few fall right off the end. The essays are impressionistic, romantic, and idealistic, all of which makes them highly commendable from our point of view. They are not scholarly, i.e. dull, nor empirical, i.e. full of masses of data signifying nothing. Those readers who thrive on hard evidence have (to borrow a phrase from Postman and Weingartner) "just finished reading this book." We fear that those who need proof that "freedom works" are not the most likely candidates to human-ize education. We hope that our readers have, at least, the insight of the teacher who, watching her young open classroom student smear paint, turned to a visitor and said "I know that child is learning something, but I'm not sure what it is."

The reader will note that the essays do not touch upon such frequently discussed topics as team teaching, differentiated staffing, performance contracting, computer-based instruction, or behavioral objectives. We also leave out the equally important subject of air-conditioned schools with carpeted classrooms. If we consider these less than important for the teaching-learning act, what do we deem significant? In a few words—kids, teachers, roles, human encounters, school atmosphere, societal values, politics, and the culture—the stuff of which education and life are made. We, therefore, do include pieces on students' rights, the abolition of schools, indoctrination on Sesame Street, the educational voucher plan, high school women's liberation, the politics of reading, the free school movement, and the open classroom. We contend that if our schools are to be saved, these must be the areas of our concern.

In recent years, much has been written about school problems such as overcrowding, underfinancing, drugs, and discipline. The radical critics in this work focus on other problems—institutional rigidities, archaic role conceptions, and underlying politico-economic factors that explain much about American education. They argue that our schools today resemble prisons and pickle factories more than centers of learning. They agree with Charles Silberman when he says that our schools have lost sight of their goals and become "mindless." The solutions offered by the critics will seem alarmingly simple to some, and simply alarming to others. To us, they seem "just right."

One of the sad facts about school practices is that they don't change very readily. In spite of virulent criticism and endless recommendations for improvement there doesn't seem to be any effective vehicle or strategy for change. We know that the school system is geared more to self-preservation than self-renewal and that if schools don't self-renew quickly they will self-destruct. (For example, 60 percent of more than 1,000 principals questioned by the National Association of Secondary School Principals reported that their schools experienced some kind of student protest during 1969). We have the feeling that most school people, to use W. H. Auden's phrase, are "lecturing on navigation while the ship is going down." That is to say, they are concentrating on the wrong solutions to the wrong problems in the wrong places.

Fortunately, some people are engaged in the work of renewal. These persons fall into two categories—reformers and revolutionaries. Reformers wish to make the system work. They are often found in public schools; they advocate the open classroom, believe in reduced emphasis on competition and grading, and take a humanistic approach to learning. They are the intellectual and spiritual heirs of the progressive education movement. Persons associated with this position whose works are included in this collection are Neil Postman, Charles Weingartner, Harvey Scribner, and Mark Shedd. The second species of change-agents—the revolutionaries—see little hope for the schools as currently structured, and in one case, would abolish schools altogether. Revolutionaries talk about alternative modes of education and free schools. Their radical critiques are related to criticism of the society at large. Like Salli Rasberry and Robert Greenway they ask: "How long has it been since you taught in a culture in which you fully believed?" Peter Marin, Michael

Rossman, Carol Stolley Hastie, and Ivan Illich are the authors in this work who represent this position.

It is not necessary for the reader to agree with every judgment rendered by the contributors to this book. Radicals, like other mortals, are guilty of hyperbole and even error. What is hoped is that the reader will come away with a new vision, a different perspective, possibly with the ability Robert Burns wrote of—"to see ourselves as others see us."

Some readers may wish to know in advance whether they will be sympathetic to the points of view expressed in this book. To make this determination, we have devised a questionnaire that yields a Radical Pedagogical Quotient (RPQ). By giving yourself ten points for each correct answer, you arrive at your score. The pass mark is 60 percent. Anyone scoring below should ask the bookstore proprietor for his money back.

RADICAL PEDAGOGICAL ATTITUDINAL TEST

Instructions: To the left of each statement, in the space provided, place the letter *A* next to the statement if you agree, and the letter *D* next to the statement if you disagree. If in doubt, we recommend cheating.

—— 1 / Every child knows that in going to school, he is interrupting his education. (*Marshall McLuhan*)

—— 2 / Play is the serious business of childhood. (*Jean Piaget*)

—— 3 / The public schools—those "killers of the dream" are the kind of institutions one cannot really dislike until one gets to know them well. (*Charles Silberman*)

—— 4 / I am in general for the total abolition of high schools. (*Paul Goodman*)

—— 5 / That school was just too big and too hard to move. You couldn't move the desks, and you couldn't move the blackboard, and the teacher—you couldn't move her either. (*Free school student describing her experience in a public school first-grade class.*)

—— 6 / If we taught children to speak, they'd never learn. (*Bill Hull*)

—— 7 / It seems to me that anything that can be taught to another is relatively inconsequential and has little or no significant influence on behavior. (*Carl Rogers*)

—— 8 / Most commonly the authoritie of them that teach, hinders them that learne. (*Montaigne, 1540*)

—— 9 / I believe that education is a process of living and not a preparation for future living. (*John Dewey*)

—— 10 / Life is a banquet—and too many sons of bitches are starving to death. (*Auntie Mame*)

Pencils down. Please pass all papers to the front of the room. Score ten points for each statement with which you agreed.

At this point, some of you may be feeling as Dorothy Parker did when she quipped in a review: "This is not a book to be tossed aside lightly, but thrown away with great force." If, on the other hand, you are still with us, let us begin our journey into the Alice in Wonderland of the schools. Try to forget that you were once incarcerated within their walls, and therefore have probably been brainwashed into accepting their operative norms. Pretend, if you will, that you are the proverbial visitor from Mars, objective and open-minded. Think about the life-space carved out by schools, the human (and inhuman) encounters that take place therein. Speculate as to whether you would enjoy attending the "good schools" described in the third part and whether you would like your children to have this opportunity. Hopefully, as you end this voyage, you will agree with us that there is a job to be done, that the system is savable, and that the future, dear readers, is in your hands. *Venceremos!*

HAROLD W. SOBEL
ARTHUR E. SALZ

where it's at

There was so much
handwriting on the wall
That even the wall fell down.

CHRISTOPHER MORLEY

REPORT FROM THE CENTER FOR URBAN ARCHAEOLOGY

This report describes the preliminary findings of excavations conducted by the Center for Urban Archaeology in a suburban American settlement of the Early Atomic Age (*circa* 1950 to 2100). The year's 'dig' was highly successful, for we uncovered a large building approximately 900 years old, probably erected at the beginning of the E.A. Age. Detailed analyses to determine the purpose of this structure are now underway.

The building consisted of nearly 50 rooms, all on one floor, with a central wing and two long perpendicular wings to form the letter H. Except for some large rooms in the central wing, almost all rooms were uniformly of the same size. In two of these, part of the flooring has been sufficiently preserved to suggest that a group of people gathered there frequently. We think that these people were arranged in rows facing toward an inside wall, where a special person or machine may have stood to lead the group in a common activity.

The very largest room was built on an incline, sloping down toward a smaller room with a raised floor. Another large room contained remains of primitive wood and metal

Herbert J. Gans

working tools; in yet another we found three metal casings, on which we believe the inhabitants started fires with the aid of a gas. Three rooms held fragments of what must have been scientific equipment, but of an earlier era and no longer used by the scientists of the period. One such room was littered with fish skeletons, the bones of small domesticated birds and animals, and large numbers of glass fragments.

The most interesting of the large rooms had a very high ceiling, and large metal rings and bars of various sizes were evidently attached to the walls. Immediately adjacent we uncovered two identical smaller rooms, probably encased in porcelain, in which a liquid was dispensed from metal pipes in the ceiling.

The building was entered from the central wing; its wall construction suggests many doors, as if masses of people had normally come in at the same time. Nearby were a number of smaller rooms. In one we found an almost perfectly preserved table; the fact that it was made of mahogany, even then a rare wood, suggests that an important functionary occupied the room. An antechamber contained a small locked metal case which held a few coins; its cover was inscribed in raised letters. The only letters still identifiable were 'Pt' and 'Csh'.

As far as we can tell, the building was not in full use at the time of its destruction, for we found parts of only three skeletons, male, probably 13–17 years of age, all of them in the room with the metal rings and bars.

Because of the sparsity of skeletons and artifacts, we can only guess at the purpose of this structure, and the team is currently considering a number of hypotheses to guide the analysis. Some team members believe the building was a prison, the series of uniform rooms housing groups of prisoners, each overseen by a guard. The rooms with the metal rings and pipes could have been used to torture prisoners. The advocates of this hypothesis also support their argument by the location of the structure on a large open space some distance from other buildings as if to isolate it from the rest of the settlement.

This writer doubts that the structure was a prison, for we found no evidence of the barred windows and towers used in this era to prevent prisoners from escaping; and preliminary chemical analyses have indicated no trace of human blood anywhere, thus ruling out torture. It is, of course, possible that the building was an institution to rehabilitate young prisoners, for we know that the elders of this culture were enmeshed in bitter conflict with their young. It may be that the various instruments we excavated were used for milder, nonlethal forms of torture.

Other team members believe that the structure served the community as a meeting place, either for religious or political functions. The big room with the sloping floor may have been used by priests or tribal leaders for community-wide gatherings or rites; the uniform rooms, for meetings of clans or other subgroups. The proponents of the religious hypothesis suggest that the room with the metal rings was designed for orgiastic exercises; the metal pipes may have supplied alcohol, a liquid depressant widely used by this culture for mind-expansion. They also speculate that the letter H may have had a sacred meaning. The avocates of the political explanation argue that the fire-making artifacts and the animal bones point to the serving of food, a popular practice at community gatherings of the culture. They add that the metal box contained 'Political Cash', used to reward leaders for making the desired public decisions.

I find neither hypothesis persuasive. We know that the religious and political rituals of this culture did not involve wood or metal working tools, and its political ideology was egalitarian, so that the community could not have been segregated into nearly 50 subgroups.

Two younger team members think that the building was used to educate the age group represented by the skeletons we excavated. They suggest that the young people were required to assemble in the uniform rooms each day where they were taught by an elder specially trained for this purpose, and that the other rooms were devoted to special schooling in the use of tools, scientific instruments, methods of food preparation and animal killing. It is thought that the room with the metal rings provided muscular training to prepare young people for hand-to-hand combat in intertribal wars.

Although this theory offers explanations for almost all the finds uncovered by our dig, I frankly find it indefensible. For example, since the outside walls of the uniform rooms were evidently constructed of window glass, it is hard to believe that the young people would have paid much attention even to a specially trained elder; they must have spent most of their time watching the activities going on outside. Moreover, it seems highly unlikely that the relatively advanced culture of the Early Atomic Age would have instructed its young people in the use of tools and scientific instruments already anachronistic at the time.

However, my main objection to this hypothesis is that no archaeological studies of yet earlier cultures have ever found a special building devoted to educating the 13–17 age group. In these earlier cultures, as in our own, young people of that age were educated by involvement in the life of the community, by working in various productive and public service activities to learn how the community functioned, what work opportunities were available to them, and what types of work they found most suitable to their own personalities. In preindustrial cultures, where occupational roles were limited, they were simply fitted into a slot and then learned the traditional ways of filling it. This contrasts with our own era, in which the work experience, combined with a couple of hours of daily reading and discussion, helps them learn to understand themselves and adult society, and prepares them for benefiting maximally from the general education and specialized occupational training of the universities when they are 18.

It is simply inconceivable to me, therefore, that the Early Atomic Age would have used special educational institutions which segregated, physically and socially, this alert and vital age group from the everyday life of the community. Surely the culture was sophisticated enough to know that Man learns best by doing and problem solving in an ongoing enterprise, that the 13–17 age group is much too energetic to spend its days cooped up in training rooms, and that youngsters of any age learn best from each other, and not from an elder, who, by necessity, must impose his own ways on them.

The young team members argue, and rightly so, that one cannot assume other cultures to have cherished the values that we consider rational. They also suggest that the building was similar to our own childhood training laboratories for instruction in graphic, visual, oral and mathematical modes of communication. I feel, however, that the differences outweigh the similarities. Our laboratories may segregate young people for educational purposes, but only from ages 4 to 12. During these years, they are best able to learn communication skills, but are still too inexperienced in social living to benefit materially from social studies and other academic methods for understanding self and society. Moreover, the laboratories use teaching machines, informal learning groups and individual tutoring; they certainly do not force youngsters, who are still quite asocial, into formal groups for instructional purposes.

My own hypothesis is that the building was a relic from the Machine Age which immediately preceded the Early Atomic Age. Probably built as a prison, it no longer served a regular purpose in the settlement and may even have stood empty. After all, despite its size, the structure contained only three skeletons and just a handful of the millions of artifacts extant in this period. We know that the culture preserved outdated buildings as part of its worship of history; we also know that its young people often had to isolate themselves in unused structures for sexual rites and other forms of play which were outlawed by the elders.

There is not enough evidence to prove this, or any other, hypothesis, and further excavations of similar structures are needed. If we can obtain the necessary research grants, we shall look for other American communities of this period that are better preserved. If only Nuclear War I had not so completely obliterated so many of these settlements.

WHAT THE WORLD IS COMING TO

WALTER R. COPPEDGE

In the lifetime of the middle-aged and older, the ability to remember Pearl Harbor has provided a continental divide for the twentieth century. Those too young or unborn then were casualties of history, without the peculiar historical consciousness of my age group. "Over 30" really means that one remembers Pearl Harbor; under 30, one doesn't and one refuses to make many of the quarrels of parents the cause of youth.

Last year [1969] a very significant thing happened. The Apollo 11 moonshot voyage made 1969 a major reference point in history, like 44 B.C., 1066, 1492, and 1776. The voyage of Columbus divided the Middle Ages from modern times; 1969 will separate terrestrial man from space man, earth history from cosmic history.

This extraordinary feat symbolizes aptly and dramatically what is now commonly acknowledged to be a revolutionary age, for the change this century has experienced and is yet to witness must be considered exponential. The foundations of Western culture were severely shaken by two world wars; the Scopes trial and the diffusion of Freudian investigation destroyed for modern man the authority of the past. The seamless cloak of Western culture is now a crazy patchwork quilt which existential man gathers about his nakedness.

In our time there have been the political revolutions of the Soviet Union, Southeast Asia, Latin America, and China. But in a very real sense today in Western Europe and the United States, the most dramatic revolutionaries are not necessarily political, they are cultural. They are in our colleges and high schools.

"Revolution" in this sense means a profound shift in the values of a society as it undergoes basic economic and cultural changes. The militant young, perhaps a statistically inaccessible minority, have been an advance guard; they have signaled in the fashions, styles, and politics the radicalness of the change. As in most revolutions, the authorities are confused as to the meaning of events around them and are unsure of their own values. These uncertain attitudes have created permissive concessionism and ambiguities in ruling or administering, thus enabling the exploitation of a revolutionary situation.

About this revolution—in which only a tiny fraction are political revolutionaries—there are some interesting generalizations I will audaciously offer:

Today, as in no other time, the young are their own model. The rites of passage with which we are most familiar—the donning of togas, ordeals of pain, presentation at deb parties—have no modern symbolic equivalent, since the young do not aspire to (and perhaps even condemn) the sense of experience of the older generation.

Manifesting such sincere and remarkable indifference and equipped with a brash and unreflecting confidence, the young are now in a position (particularly since the Sixties) to impose their own styles on the older generation so that the pattern is reversed: The old aspire to be like the young and the ambivalence of older generation values is heightened.

A few examples will instance this obvious truth. Mini-skirts, sideburns, and mod clothes are directly the result of the Beatles phenomenon—all fashions introduced by the young and now adopted by the middle-aged (or "wrinklies," as over-thirties are sometimes known). Popular music is now largely dominated by the beat Elvis and the Beatles introduced to a very unappreciative older generation just a few years ago. The dance form now dominant is the tribal gyration which "wrinklies" watched uncomprehendingly in 1960; tangoes, waltzes, rhumbas, and the sedate fox-trot are relegated to the discard heap of minuets, lavoltas, and fandangoes. Our language has been similarly affected by the laconic simplicities of the younger style, whose idiom has derived from music ("groovy") and drugs ("hippy").

Given the lack of aspiration for such middle-class American staples as a mortgage on a home in Meadowfarm Estates, 36-month payments on a Buick, and a membership in Kiwanis, it is no wonder that there is increasing dissatisfaction with more substantial symbols of bourgeois America: capitalism or "plastics!" (the advice encapsulating the system which Benjamin rejects in the 1968 film *The Graduate*). The flag now becomes a symbol of conscription as well as "imperialist aggression"; conventional manners are thought to mask insincerely the real indifference we feel toward one another as well as to camouflage racial hostility; traditional institutions like the church have seemed increasingly irrelevant and irritatingly hypocritical. (Benjamin, again in *The Graduate*, rescues his girl from a meaningless marriage and bars the narthex door with a cross to lock up the enraged congregation.) At the university, the assault on American and Western culture has been frontal. Perpetuating both the technocracy which enables capitalism to flourish and the traditional liberal and humanitarian values, the university is our most revered American institution, our most sacred intellectual refuge. To defecate in Grayson Kirk's wastebasket is to commit the ultimate secular blasphemy.

That action summarizes all the gross-outs, obscenities, and contempt for the establishment which student radicalism has displayed from the days of the Free Speech Movement at Berkeley in 1964 to the takeover at Cornell in April of 1969.

The sense of past—never truly apprehended by a generation which has learned far more from television than from books—is superseded by the urgency of the present. Whether the problem is black separatism or Vietnamese withdrawal, the young are involved *now* in problems for which they want immediate answers. Involvement is the issue in two recent movies which portray the ethos of the young. The city discovered by the "Midnight Cowboy" in the film of that name is a viciously competitive sexual and economic jungle which produces such symbolic cripples as Ratso. In *Medium Cool* (a richly ironic title), the message is even clearer: We live in a land of violence, and we who ignore the confrontations we must daily encounter—the simple ones of human need and suffering as well as the more complex issues of politics and race—we who ignore these problems do so by a slow hardening of the heart, by the atrophying of concern, but purchasing detachment with the coin of indifference.

History appears to have little relevance for so romantic and visceral a generation. What is real and immediate is sensation and its quest, as evidenced in underground movies, drugs, op art, and rock music. Blowing one's mind—i.e., experiencing a nonrational emotional high—is desirable. Fueled by adrenalin, militants from Paris to Tokyo, Stockholm to Mexico, have stormed the university, saying that they want to make life new, that they want Revolution. (There was an extraordinary oppositeness in a wall slogan during the May riots in Paris: "The more I make revolution, the more I want to make love; the more I want to make love, the more I want to make revolution." Such a graffito epitomizes the emotional intoxication of making common cause in revolt.)

Perhaps the most salient phenomenon of the youth is the uniqueness of their communication. Although the underground press in the United States claims a readership of over 600,000, the written word is not the primary vehicle by which the young express themselves to one another. Mammoth youth assemblies are something history has not seen since the Children's Crusade. The Washington moratorium drew 250,000, but the Woodstock music festival attracted 300,000 young people who, in the midst of squalor and rain, generously shared their food and drink and displayed a kindly affection to outsiders which amazed the local constabulary. Rock music is indeed a prime vehicle for wordless but powerful transmission of feeling and attitude. This most interesting form of music in 50 years has been virtually ignored by the university.

Perhaps because in the past a sensitive exchange of viewpoints between the young and the establishment has not been possible, the violent communication of the platform take-over has become almost a pattern on the national scene; let us only cite radical action in the last two years among such diverse but august groups as the American Medical Association, the American Bar Association, the National Conference on Social Welfare, the American Political Science Association, and even the Modern Language Association. The young who seize the microphone may not have all the ideas, but they do have ideas—fresh, inventive, fertile, challenging ideas which are energizing and often redirecting the social purposes of these professional groups. If the group is not responsive, a splinter group of the young is formed; thus the Free University became for a while a free-wheeling splinter institution whose existence radically criticized what went on in the halls of academe.

Nowhere is the impact of the young on American society more serious than in advertising, where the old "reason why" ad has been replaced by an unconventional, whimsical, or shocking presentation. One oberver of the trade noted that at the age of 33 a man may be getting a little senior, and employers favor a man in his early twenties to one nearing the magical dividing line. If advertising is a direct agent of change in society, then we would do well to contemplate the awesome power for changing our lives possessed by the under-thirties. A glance at the language of the young will also show the difference: It is desirable to be "loose," because the loose are not rigid or "hung-up" like the old. "It" means action of all kinds, commercial or artistic, although the word "action" originally described easy but interesting sexual activity; hence in recent slang it was very important to be "where it's at" or to be "with it."

These changes have two principal implications for education. The first is a word so familiar as to have become cant in educationese: relevance.

Too often in the past we have insisted on *instruction* rather than *education*, on that mode of teaching which piles up facts (the root meaning of the Latin *in* + *struere*) instead of that which educes or draws forth, brings out, develops from a latent condition. We have expected the student to extract from a mass of unrelated materials, called a curriculum, something which he will find pertinent to the pursuit of life or a livelihood. In college the student must reach the level of the instructor or fail, fall in that race course, originally called the Circus Maximus, from which the word *curriculum* derives. In the future, it will be increasingly the business of the educator to begin with the experience of the student, to reach down to his level so that curiosity is teased, provoked, stimulated, engaged to build and proliferate.

No one of course ever proposed an irrelevant education, relevance being entirely subjective. But we teach ancient history as if it *were* irrelevant, Latin as if it were dead. The fact is that a study of Periclean Athens has quite a lot to say about the urban crisis in the second half of the twentieth century, and some knowledge of Latin is of immense value in equipping the student with the ability to manipulate symbols which we call verbal skill. If we really knew Thucydides, as Henry Steele Commager observed . . ., we would never have engaged in the Peloponnesian War we call Vietnam. For the educator, the principle should be clear: begin with what *interests* the student, moving from the specific to the general. Sylvia Ashton Warner found that she could not teach Maori children about life in an English village, but she could open their minds to reading by building on such emotive words as *knife, kiss, cold, volcano, blood*. Similarly every student wants to know about love, sex, war, and so on—for these forces touch his life.

A student unable to master the intricacies of Galbraith or Adam Smith might nevertheless come to an understanding of the complexity of the marketplace if he can observe what happens in the department store or filling station where he works. I have found my own imagination taxed in attempting to answer my six-year-old's extraordinarily interesting questions: What is fire? Why are there burglars? The able teacher could develop mini-courses, for questions such as these, intelligently and sensitively answered, produce precisely that multiplier effort which Rousseau noted in his *Émile* 200 years ago.

We don't acquire our really important learning in packages. As interested explorers we are not concerned about boundaries which mark those august empire states called disciplines—separating literature from history, sociology from psychology, chemistry from biology, and so on. But as educators we begin to be concerned about passports, visas, and entry and exit permits, failing to realize that the student wants to explore life in its mysterious wholeness, rather than in the exclusive little principalities of subject areas.

The second quality we must recover in education is the sense of mystery: of selves and worlds not palpable to the cognitive mode. We are concerned with life, we say. Therefore we organize the study of biology, but somehow we never apprehend the miracle of motion when we dissect a frog, or the truth of a flower when we count stamens and pistils. We talk about the spiral nebulae but how seldom do we, as Whitman suggested, look up "in perfect silence at the stars."

We teach as if the only realities were those captured at two removes in those rivers of ink which are words. We ignore the psycho-physical relationship of mind and body, feeling and language.

We teach children to add, but we are indifferent to whether or not they can smell. We are concerned that they discriminate between red and green but we are oblivious to their sense of the tactile differences in stones, woods, fabrics, and metals. We care about their distinction of some kinds of sound, but we care nothing about whether they know by taste a kumquat from a cantaloupe. These immemorial modes of knowing are atrophying under our overwhelmingly verbal educational system. The off-Broadway youth musical *Salvation* is fascinatingly corroborative of this indictment: Two song titles, "Let's Get Lost in Now" and "Tomorrow Is the First Day of the Rest of My Life," reveal the sensory significance of the present.

Our system is also overwhelmingly rational and cognitive, and in the last few decades it has either ignored or sacrificed the intuitive or affective. That kind of teaching which advocates dispassion, disinterest, and detachment is disastrous to a generation calling for commitment. The analytical professor will not speak to this generation who are crying for professors who profess.

Disenchantment with siccative rationalism, with that settled lowest common denominator of experience called common sense, manifests itself in the pursuit of the occult. Free Universities across the nation sponsor classes in Eastern thought; the ancient Chinese book of fortune-telling, the *I-Ching*, has become a best seller on progressive college campuses. Psychedelic paraphernalia— black light posters, incense, Oriental art—are obvious household equipment throughout student apartments. The intense interest in astrology epitomizes the fascination with the occult.

It is pertinent to remark here the enthusiasm for nature observable in the hippie communes of the West and New England. Young people may be smoking pot but they are also making bread, perhaps coarse and lumpy, but certainly unlike the styrofoam product we settle for in supermarkets. For adolescents, camp directors have noted the new enthusiasm for really primitive camps with tents set in bare fields and food foraged in the wilderness.

The sense of the mystery of life will perhaps never come to us as educators until we develop what Wordsworth called a "wise passiveness"—that gift which Blake suggested enables the untutored child and the mystic "To see a world in a grain of sand / And a heaven in a wild flower, / Hold infinity in the palm of your hand / And eternity in an hour."

Any retrospect of the Sixties must convince us that the younger generation (and here again I mean the cadre of the committed fringe) have richly contributed to American life. Substantial gains in civil rights, a new dynamism to American culture, the general liberation of films, new explorations in the arts, an increasing relevance and vitality in college curricula, growing dissatisfaction with the multitudinous hypocrisies of our lives, and the slow and painful reappraisal of our national values—these contributions have been real and positive. But the momentum of change is producing a period of crisis. To be sure, our lives continue in comfortably familiar routines. But we are living in a time of storm, and the beleaguered crew is required continually to jettison cargo. Only those articles will be retained to which we assign high value.

Among the things which are to go, I suspect, will be Junior-League-Georgian suburbs and Eisenhower-ranch houses, big cars and combustion engines; billboards and main streets of Hardees and used car lots; Mantovani music and furniture reproductions; nondisposable beer cans and bottles; J. Edgar Hoover and the Mafia; the inanities of situation comedy on commercial TV; DDT, of course, prohibitions against birth control as well as against death control; religious fundamentalism of all kinds and much of established institutional Christianity as we now know it. People will be educated to think ecologically—to realize that one man's waste is literally another man's poison—and to think systematically so there will be decreasing distinction between public and private sectors. Sexual practices will become far more permissive and more and more people will question the value of the family unit. The examples of Sweden and England indicate that unmarried motherhood will become acceptable in most communities. Society will find a more efficient mind-transformer than alcohol. If no better substitute than marijuana is invented or discovered, it will become the favored mode of social intercourse.

As for education, if we can accept my notion that relevance requires our reaching down to the experience of the student, then the relevant school of the future will minimize the self-contained classroom. Talking to the young today means addressing them as individuals. The teacher will become increasingly democratic, recognizing that in education as in ethics the means shape the ends. The teacher will be reaching out to the students, increasingly using not the school so much as the city for primary learning resources.

A Unitarian seminary now in New York may point the pattern. Eschewing survey courses, classroom lectures, examination cramming, and the whole system of degrees and credits, the faculty instead are directing their students to live, work, and study in the city, developing specializations such as the dance for public worship. Oriental religions, poverty programs, or drug and alcohol therapy. Independent study through the study of great books—with supplemental learning in tutorials and seminars—forms the basis of an approach which internalizes learning and converts it to principle, insuring an enduring relevance to the whole educational process.

What I have attempted to do is to provide evidence for the assertion that we are living in a revolution, by which is meant a time of radical change. In times when we are no longer sure of anything, we must, privately and socially, create our own values and observe them lest we betray ourselves.

In the context of the new age signaled by the moonshot, why—once we grasp its awesomeness—should we continue the murderous struggles between Catholics and Protestants in Ireland, between Walloon and Fleming in Belgium, between Arab and Jew in Palestine, between Ibo and Yoruba in Nigeria? How long can human beings with a cosmic consciousness permit racism, whether in South Africa or South Carolina? Or the subjugation of peoples in Czechoslovakia or Tibet?

In 1928, Yeats predicted that this civilization would be coming to a close, and a new man of a higher spiritual consciousness would displace the earth man of materialistic interests and absorptions. I find such a vatic prophecy interesting now. Arnold's lines about "wandering between two worlds, the one dead, and the other powerless to be born" no longer have the meaning today which gave them relevance before 1960.

. . .

Growing Up on Mechanic Street

PETER SCHRAG

It is impossible to think of those adolescents without a strange mixture of affection, apprehension, and fear. To imagine them at all, it becomes necessary to shoulder aside the black /white clichés of youth-talk—about middle-class revolt and ghetto rebellion—and to perceive a grayer reality. I am not writing here of affluent suburbs or what others have called blacktown, but about the children of those whom Americans once celebrated as workingmen. Again sociology fails us; there are no definitions or statistics. If there were, the matter would be better understood.

Phrases like "the forgotten man" and "the silent majority" are too political to serve as normative descriptions, but there is no doubt that there are forgotten kids who are, indeed, genuine victims: children of factory workers and truck drivers, of shop foremen and salesclerks, kids who live in row houses above steel mills and in ticky-tacky developments at the edge of town, children who will not go to college, who will not become affluent, who will not march the streets, who will do no more, no less, than relive the lives of their parents.

We have all seen them: the kids on the corner with their duck-tail haircuts; the canvas-bag-toting types, lonely and lost, lining up at induction centers; kids in knocked down cars

that seem to have no springs in back, whose wedding announcements appear daily in the newspapers of small towns (Mr. Jones works for the New York Central Railroad—no particular job worth mention—Miss Smith is a senior at Washington High) and whose deaths are recorded in the weekly reports from Saigon—name, rank, home town. On the south side of Bethlehem, Pennsylvania, just above the mills, there is an alley called Mechanic Street; once it was the heart of the old immigrant district—the first residence of thousands of Hungarians, Russians, Poles, Mexicans, Germans, Czechs, and Croats. Most of them have now moved on to materially better things, but they regard this as their ancestral home. Think of the children of Mechanic Street; think of places called Liberty High and South Boston High, of Central High and Charlestown High, and of hundreds of others where defeat does not enjoy the ironic distinction of the acknowledged injustice of racial oppression.

They exist everywhere, but convention has almost wiped them from sight. They are not supposed to be there, are perhaps not really supposed to believe even in their own existence. Thus they function not for themselves but to define and affirm the position of others: those who are very poor, or those who are affluent, those who go to college. In visiting the schools that they attend, one must constantly define them not by what they are, but by what they are not, and sometimes, in talking to teachers and administrators, one begins to doubt whether they exist at all.

The fact that defeat is not universal makes the matter all the more ugly. The record of college placement and vocational success, which schools so love to celebrate, and the occasional moments of triumphant self-realization, which they do not, obscure—seem, in fact, to legitimate—the unexpressed vacancy, the accepted defeat, and the unspoken frustration around and beyond the fringe. When we see a growing number of students from blue-collar families going to college we begin to assume that they all go, and that they will all be happy and successful when they get there. Yet it is still a fact—as it always was—that the lower ranks of the economic order have the smallest chance of sending their children on, and that those who fall below the academic middle in high school tend to represent a disproportionate percentage of poor and working-class families. It seems somehow redundant to say all this again; but if it isn't said there will be no stopping the stories of blissful academic success.

The social order of most white high schools—the attitudes that teachers and students have about other students—is based (in proper democratic fashion) on what people do in school, on their interests, their clubs, their personalities, their accomplishments. (Students from blue-collar families with serious college ambitions associate with the children of white-collar professionals, and share their attitudes, styles, and beliefs, which tend to be more liberal —politically and personally—than those of their parents. A few participated in the Vietnam moratorium last fall [1969], and a handful, unknown to their fathers, have gone to the local draft counselors. But they represent a minority.) It is possible to leave Mechanic Street through school achievement—to community and state colleges, to technical schools, to

better jobs—yet it is hardly universal. Fewer than half actually go. What kids do in school tends, as always, to be predetermined. The honors class is filled with the children of professionals, kids whose parents have gone to college. The general course (meaning the dead end) and the vocational track are composed of the sons and daughters of blue-collar workers. The more "opportunity," the more justified the destiny of those who are tagged for failure. The world accepts the legitimacy of their position. And so do they. Their tragedy and the accompanying threat lie precisely in their acceptance of the low esteem in which school, society, and often their parents regard them, and in their inability to learn a language to express what they feel but dare not trust.

Imagine, says a school counselor, that you could become an animal, any animal. What species would you choose? The secret heart would choose freedom: Eagles soaring over mountains, mustangs racing across the plain, greyhounds loping through fields. Freedom.

Dreams are to be denied. The imagined future is like the present without parents. Jobs, domesticity, children, with little joy, seen in shades of gray. Coming out of school in the afternoon, the boys already resemble their fathers when the shifts change, rows of dark, tufted mail order house jackets, rows of winter hats with the ear flaps laced above the head, crossing the road from the plant to the parking lot, from the high school to the waiting buses and the bare-wheeled Chevies. The girls, not yet stretched by pregnancy, often trim in short skirts and bright sweaters, will catch up with their mothers, will be married at eighteen or twenty,

23

will often be engaged before the tedium of school is at an end. "Unwanted kids," says a school administrator, "kids of guys who got girls in trouble, kids of Korean War veterans and veterans of World War II who didn't want the first child, and before they knew it they had two or three. All their lives their kids have been told to get out of the way, to go watch television. They don't have anybody to talk to. There was a recent survey that indicated that 72 per cent of the first children of this generation were unwanted. These are the kids."

They sit in rows of five, five by five in the classroom, existing from bell to bell, regurgitating answers, waiting for the next relief. The mindless lessons, the memory and boredom, and the stultifying order of cafeterias and study halls—no talking, sit straight, get a pass—these things need not be described again. From bell to bell: English, mathematics, history, science—and, for some, release to the more purposeful and engaging activities of the shop: auto mechanics, data processing, welding, wiring, carpentry, and all the rest—some relevant, some obsolete, but all direct. There is an integrity, even joy, in material behavior —a sharp tool, an engine repaired, a solid joint—that the artificial world of the conventional academic course rarely allows. Material things respond; theory is applicable and comprehensible—either the thing works or it doesn't; it never prevaricates or qualifies, while words and social behavior, metaphors and politics remain cloudy, elusive, and distant. You see them wiring an electric motor or turning a machine part on a lathe, or fixing a car: pleasure, engagement, or, better, a moment of

truth. The Big Lie, if there is one, will be revealed later ("No," says the director of a vocational school in an industrial city, "we don't tell the students that the construction unions are hard to join; it would discourage them in their work. They'll find out soon enough that it helps to know someone, to have a father or an uncle in the union. . . . But after a kid manages to break in, he's proud of what he learned in the school of hard knocks, and he'll do the same thing to the new guys.")

From class to class, from school to home and back, there is a sort of passing-through. What is learned is to defer—to time, to authority, to events. One keeps asking, "What do they want, what do they do, what do they dream about?" and the answer is almost always institutional, as if the questions no longer applied: They go to school; they have jobs—in the candy factory, at the gas station, in a little repair shop, in a diner—and they ride and repair their cars. Many of them live in a moonlight culture, a world where people have second jobs, where mothers work, where one comes home and watches whatever is on television, and no longer bothers to flip channels in search of something better.

Some distinctions are easy and obvious. Schooling certifies place; it selects people, not only for social class, but also for geographic mobility. The college-bound students speak about moving somewhere else—to the larger cities, to the West Coast, wherever events still permit the fantasy of a better future, or at least of change; the more national the college, the more likely they are to move. Among those who don't go to college there is little talk (except in depressed towns) of moving on. Academic losers stay put. "I know this is a dreary place," said a high school senior in Bethlehem. "But I like dreary places." It wasn't meant to be a joke. Big cities, they tell you again and again, are dangerous. (And in the cities they talk about protecting the neighborhood, or about how they still live in a good neighborhood.) Some places, they say, you can't walk the streets without getting knifed—by you know who. You hear it from sixteen-year-olds.

The instrument of oppression is the book. It is still the embodiment of the Great Mystery; learn to understand its secrets and great things will follow. Submit to your instinctive and natural boredom (lacking either the skills to play the game or the security to revolt), and we will use it to persuade you of your benighted incompetence: "I didn't want to write a term paper, but the teacher said it would be good if I did; when I handed it in she made fun of it; so I quit school." The family knows that you should stay in school, that you should go to college and "get an education," but it does not know that often the school doesn't work, or that it works principally at the expense of its own kids. One of the tragedies of the black revolt is that it frequently confused the general incompetence of schools with racism, thus helping to persuade much of the blue-collar community that its children were in fine shape, that the educational system was basically sound, and that complaints came either from effete intellectuals or ungrateful, shiftless blacks. Teachers who purported to represent genuine intellectual achievement (The Book) were thus allowed to continue to conceal their contempt for both kids and brains behind their passion for conformity and order,

and to reaffirm the idea—already favored among working-class parents —that schooling was tough, boring, vicious, and mindless.

The school is an extension of home: In the suburbs it is rated on college admissions, on National Merit winners, and similar distinctions; in the working-class neighborhood of the city it tends to be judged on order and discipline. Either way, the more talk there was nationally about the need for technologically trained people, the more the school was able to resist challenges to its own authority. "Technological complexity" replaced naked authority as the club of conformity in the school.

What the school did (and is doing) was to sell its clients, young and old, on the legitimacy of the system that abused them. Of course there were exceptions—students, teachers, schools—and even the drearier institutions are sufficiently equipped with the paraphernalia of *fun*—sports, bands, clubs—to mitigate the severity and enlist community support. It is hard to find schools that do not arrogate to themselves some sort of distinction: the state championship marching band, league leadership in football or track, a squad of belles who twirl, hop, bounce, or step better than anyone else in the county. A girl makes her way from junior pompom girl to cheerleader or majorette; a boy comes from the obscurity of an ethnic neighborhood to be chosen an all-state tackle. There is vitality and engagement and, for the moment, the welding of new common-interest groups, new friendships, new forms of integration. It is the only community adolescents have, and even the dropouts sometimes sneak back to see their friends. And yet, many of these things come to a swift and brutal end: a note in the yearbook, some clippings, a temporary sense of value and distinction convertible into an early marriage, a secretarial job, an occasional scholarship. The most prestigious activities of high school have no lasting value; next year, or the year after that, there will be no band, no football, no pep club. Too often life reaches its highest point at seventeen.

It may well be that even white working-class parents are becoming more suspicious of the mediocrity of their schools, more aware of their crimes, and less taken by the joys they offer. The imperious contempt of large-city administrators is not limited to the complaints of the black community, and the increase in number of defeated school bond issues and tax overrides is hardly a sign of growing confidence in the school people who propose them. And yet, the things that have been preached by the best people for a hundred years (and which many of them no longer believe)—order, hard work, self-denial, and the general legitimacy of schooling—these things die hard, or die not at all.

It is too easy to forget the faces, too hard to forget the crowd. American youth, Edgar Friedenberg wrote, are "already deeply implicated in the deeds and values of their culture. . . . They go along with it and sincerely believe that in doing so they are putting down trouble makers and serving the best interests of their community." That was, of course, before Berkeley and Columbia, before revolt had reached sufficient mass to be called a "counterculture." For the children of Mechanic Street, however, nothing changed, except that it added yet another demon to the many others that could not be faced. The kids of the lower middle in the order of the school had always known that they don't have much to say about anything; they have been put down most of their lives by parents, contemptuous teachers, and by fellow students. (The blue collar is still stigmatized; in the school the vocational students are fender-benders, and occasionally a particularly nasty remark is answered with sudden, explosive violence: "He called us grease monkeys, so we pushed him right through that glass door. We stick up for our rights.") What they do have to say is often directed against the most threatening invitations to independence and the most obvious examples of freedom, which constitutes the secret dream. They would—most of them—not permit demonstrations against the Vietnam War, would prefer that their teachers maintain the very order that puts them down, are resentful of anyone that can be called a hippie. ("It's not the parents that cause that," said a student radical, "it's the school. It teaches people to be uptight.") If the war continues at the present rate, several in each of their high school classes will be dead before they ever have a chance to live; of course, they would rather not have the war—and a few have joined peace marches and demonstrations—but, they tell you (in tones of a text they wish they could remember with more confidence), we have to Resist Communism, have to stand up for our rights. What about Mylai; what about the massacre of women and children in Vietnam? Most of them aren't much disturbed, haven't thought about it, or been asked about it, and haven't discussed it. You hear about someone's cousin or brother, over in "Nam," who talked about how those crazy people even had kids throwing grenades at our convoys. It's war, and you never know who's going to try and kill you. But the agony of the reply, the painful speech, in class after class, makes it impossible to press too many questions; the Hard Line plays back no better than a Shakespearean sonnet or a Euclidean theorem never worth learning. You do what you're told. Propaganda and schooling are the same thing. You ought not, you tell yourself, to pick on kids.

There is no place to go. No place now, no place ever. For the lower half of the school population—the general course, the voc-ed course, the yet to be certified losers with their low-C grades, the high school is like a refugee camp, a camp for displaced persons waiting for something to happen. The central fact of existence is not school or home or the great institutions of American rhetoric, but the automobile, the one place where life can proceed apart from those institutions, the one place where the stunted remains of the dream of freedom can grow. We have heard all this many times before—the drag racers, the hot rods—sometimes in amusement, sometimes in indignation, but we haven't come close to understanding how much it means. The car, quite simply, is everything. It is the only place where adult experimentation is tolerated: experiments with sex, with self-realization, with independence, with courage, with change, with death. The car shuttles within the city limits, sometimes to McDonald's or the Burger King, sometimes to the drive-in movie (Clint Eastwood, John Wayne, *Easy Rider*), but rarely beyond, rarely even to the next town.

There is no place to go, except to

the car itself. The radio—and the heater—thus become essential accessories, and parking becomes an all-purpose word for sex. It is the thing you do on a date. For the affluent, who have large houses and some privacy—and parental tolerance—to entertain, it may also be an invitation to turn on; sex at home, pot in the car. For those who are not rich, the car represents almost every level of reality. It is something you work on, something useful (or superpowered) that you maintain, it is a place to live, it is escape, it is privacy. It is hard to get through high school without at least one accident, perhaps even harder to become a man without being able to claim one close call—out on the spur route, or in the empty parking lot of a shopping center late on a Saturday night. Someone pulls alongside, you give the engine everything, and for a few brief moments you feel speed and power and triumph. People don't grow up with cars; they grow up in them.

There is much talk, in town after town, about having places for "young people to go," about teen centers and recreation halls (the chaperoned dances having been abandoned by all but junior high students), but that concern seems to reflect a deeper despair about the community, about *place*, and about the future itself. As the old ethnic and regional culture breaks up, the culture of aspiration—what we used to call the mainstream—should grow in its power to attract and hold. But often, needless to say, it does not. In the smaller towns and in the hyphenated neighborhoods of cities, traditional patterns and institutions—food, family, the church, the Ukrainian Hall, the Polish-American Club—become increasingly tenuous; church membership grows older, the

27

neighborhood more bland, the swimming hole more distant, the culture more thin. The local mill, the mine, the plant, once ferocious and mythic in its demands on men, in its economic unpredictability, in its brutality, is tamed by unions, by government, and by corporate management itself. The kids don't remember the last strike, the last layoffs, let alone the last fight with the Pinkertons, the National Guard, and the company dicks. Every year a few more landmarks disappear, another memory dies, another set of roots is destroyed.

For most parents, there is still the hope of a better place, and almost every one of them does his best to get his kid to go. But the ebullient romance, the Alger myths, the dream of adventure and enterprise—all those things have been inundated by size and technology, and abandoned by the very people who invented them in the first place. The fact that things are less manageable, that the country and the world no longer respond the way we once imagined they should (or that they have become unmanageable altogether) may not be as traumatic for the ethnic and social underclass that had never controlled much of anything anyway—but it does reduce the interest and the fun of trying to join. One of the striking things is that many kids are not ambitious for power or possessions. "My parents," said one, "never had what they wanted; they couldn't get along on what they had. But we can." And yet the life that he and many others imagine is almost identical to the life of the present. As today opens up a little—a better home, a car, a television set, and a steady job—tomorrow seems to close down. Modesty in achievement and ambition is matched by an inability to visualize anything richer—in experience or possessions, or in the world at large. The generation gap—for rich, for poor, for all—is precisely this: that many kids, for the first time, are growing up without a sense of the future. And that, for America, is new.

They are people who have lost one country and haven't yet found another. Some of them are at least marginal participants in the counterculture; the hair on the boys grows longer, the hard rock is universal, and drugs (pot and pills), now prevalent among the swingers—college prep, affluent, or black—are beginning to infiltrate the middle, often with the tacit acquiescence of the cops who know that they have lost some of their troublesome adolescent clients to the euphoria of pot, and who are, in any case, powerless to stop it. There may still be high schools in America where drugs aren't traded, but they are probably scarcer than dry towns. At the same time, the potential for revolt, for repression, for violence, random and directed, remains. In one high school, a senior—long hair, mustache, articulate—speaks about his plans: When he graduates he will join the Marine Corps, go to Vietnam "where the action is," then return home and become a state cop. "I'll cut my hair before *they* get to it," trading one form of expression for another. Perhaps there are few alternatives left. Perhaps Vietnam remains one of the viable ways to become a man, or to become anything at all.

"Maybe," said a sophisticated high school teacher, "we better leave everything alone. If these kids ever become politically conscious, who knows whether they'll join the SDS or the brown shirts." There are signs that they could do either, just like anyone else. Some of them have harassed peace demonstrators, heckled civil rights marchers, and have beaten up black kids in integrated schools or on the periphery of changing neighborhoods, and have been beaten up in return. And while middle-class, college-oriented students—and blacks— have made the papers with their activism, there also have been, in some of the inner cities, self-styled protofascist gangs hunting blacks, hippies, and other signs of vulnerable liberalism. In the 1968 election, the major support for George Wallace within the labor movement came from younger members—the older brothers of the kids now finishing school.

Who is to say how things are learned? For the children of Mechanic Street—as for all others—the classroom has rarely been more than a marginal place. Except for minimal literacy and a few tricks picked up in a home-ec course, the girl who marries at eighteen was educated at home, though she may well have used the school to find her husband. Except for the certification that schools bestow on good behavior and acceptable habits, the boy who takes a job immediately after graduation (or who, with a fifth of his peers, never graduates at all) takes little from his school, except perhaps a vaguely unexpressible sense of defeat.

And yet, something is learned— perhaps from television, perhaps from the school community itself. The well-publicized tension between generations seems to have given language and content to the specific tensions between parents and children. Which is to say that "student revolt" or "youth revolt" seems to be applicable even where there are no students and no "youths" who identify with larger causes. Even politically conservative and/or apathetic kids now seem able to articulate differences with their parents. Many of them revolve around nothing newer than the company they keep, the people they date, and the time they have to be home at night. Nonetheless, the atmosphere of revolt provides new strategies for all (long hair, for example), opens new possibilities, and offers new ways of rationalizing old ones.

Marshall McLuhan's notion of the global village may still be more vanity than reality; yet it is accurate in one major respect: The media— television, radio, and records—are creating communities where none existed before. Media are creating bonds of style, age, and interest that transcend the particularities of locality and background. The surface manifestations of a style may themselves satisfy the longing for place and identity, providing alternatives for neighborhoods, rituals, and traditions that no longer exist. In this sense "revolt" is the opiate of the masses. High school reform and protest may never go beyond the abandonment of the dress code. But the media may also be creating the possibilities both of the development of new forms of consciousness and culture and (for the same reason) centralized political management and control. Unless Americans are prepared to revolutionize their educational system—providing far more intellectual and cultural freedom and diversity than they are currently willing to allow—the high school will, in fact, be no more than a huge amplifier for the signals that the media are willing (or permitted) to transmit. Considering the unbelievable boredom of the slow track in the

29

average high school, and the treatment accorded its students, no "educator" can berate TV without being laughed off the stage. If there is any escape from that boredom, it is in the car and in television itself. The children are moving away from Mechanic Street. But where will they go?

No Place to Grow

WALLACE ROBERTS

Winnetka, Illinois, is bounded on the west by Eden's Expressway, I-94, a concrete, one-dimensional line; on the east by Lake Michigan, a body of water in another time zone; on the north by Glencoe, a canyon of wealthy anonymity; and on the south by Kenilworth, an island of exclusivity. The boundaries of Winnetka are only a particular set of synapses. It is a suburb of the mind.

New Trier Township, in which Winnetka is located, is no less unreal, being in fact not a municipality nor any similar delineation of space, but a figment of the collective imaginations of some long-dead Cook County politico's intent on devising an easily graftable means of collecting taxes.

New Trier Township, however, serves another function, which some think should be less grubby and more cosmic: the education of high school students. Not surprisingly, New Trier's two high schools are named East and West, for there is no need to gild the lily in a community that can afford to landscape a new school with fully grown trees and shrubs.

Not surprisingly either, New Trier's East and West perform their function well, meaning that they annually funnel more than 90 per cent of their graduates into college, many into the most prestigious institutions. This is not surprising because formal education is in its essence a middle-class preoccupation, and the residents of New Trier Township are middle-class with a vengeance. In fact, it is that state of mind, and not the extra wealth, or the sculptured lawns, or the country clubs, that makes the villages of New Trier Township *upper* middle-class.

Winnetka, for instance, where New Trier Township High School East is located, has a population of about 15,800, a median income of $27,300 compared to a national figure of $7,300, a foreign-born population of about 15 per cent, extremely few blacks, a few Jews, not many more Democrats, two stations for the Chicago and North Western Railroad to handle the commuter crush, 6,000 elms gradually falling victim to disease, a zoning limitation of three stories in the business district, no liquor sales, several stately mansions on subdivided lots, a few genuine estates on undivided land, and many white stucco homes trimmed with heavy, brown-stained beams.

It also has such a broad and thorough agreement about community life that there is no need for political parties or even factions on local issues; town government is controlled by The Caucus, a group of about sixty self-appointed guardians who choose the always unopposed candidates for public office. The most controversial issue to arise at the annual town meeting last January (which had a turnout of about 300) was whether a dog leash law should be adopted. It's a chronic question; ten years ago the Winnetka town fathers even hired sociologist Scott Greer to sample public opinion on leash laws and the quality of municipal services. There was a 50–50 split on dog control and widespread satisfaction with services and with the town in general: 93 per cent said they could think of no other place in the country where they would prefer to live, although the town is stamped out of the same mold as perhaps fifty others, including the three other villages in the township—Glencoe, Kenilworth, and Wilmette—and such other spiritual enclaves as Newton, Scarsdale, Bronxville, Great Neck, Greenwich, Bryn Mawr, Silver Spring, Grosse Pointe, Shaker Heights, Clayton, Webster Groves, and Palo Alto.

Greer also said in his survey that there was a "high degree of loyalty and commitment to community" in Winnetka and that it was a "community in more than name." It is pure hype, a gigantic PR job, a manic attempt to build boundaries, and to define a life that should be. Greer noted that, as with the Philadelphia *Bulletin*, "nearly everyone reads the Winnetka *Talk* regularly." The newspaper (owned by Time-Life) serves three major purposes: to carry real estate (the town's biggest industry after education) advertising; maid and baby sitter want ads; and announcements—of business promotions, engagements and weddings, art exhibits, women's club speakers, school lunch menus, the fact that Winnetka is real. That last announcement must be made twice weekly in the Winnetka *Talk* because there is a secret suspicion that it is nothing more than the wish-fulfilled fantasy of a generation that beat the Depression soundly.

Not here to knock the idea of fantasies. I may have run from my own Winnetka—from my own white stucco home trimmed with brown stained beams, from my own high school, which was just as competitive and as academically oriented as New Trier, and from that world where I met no blacks on a personal basis, other than our cleaning lady, until after college—I may have run from that fantasy, but I have since merely replaced it with another that serves the same purpose: to shield me from the realities I find disturbing, distasteful, threatening, frightening, and denying my life of purpose, meaning, and continuance. It's a lousy world, no matter how you look at it, and we must create imaginings that allow us both to function in society and to be protected from it. But Winnetka has outlived the fantasy of itself.

Winnetka is a world that people say they have adopted for the sake of their children: the schools, both the high schools and the elementary schools—such as Crow Island, designed by Eero Saarinen and an early showpiece of progressive education—the golf and tennis lessons provided by the town recreation department, the boating on the lake, the Skokie Playfield, the Cook County Forest Preserve, and the Fourth of July foot races on the town common.

"There is no unpleasantness here," was the way one mother put it. Winnetka is what any parent would want for his children because he didn't have it so well or in such abundance when he was growing up. It's the kind of world that any parent would give to his children if he could. It's the kind of world that, even if it's not within immediate reach, it will be grasped for anyway. "The atmosphere is good here," said one father and long-time public official. "There's room to move. There's also a lot of wealth here, but there's a lot of poverty, too, because people move here for the school but can't really afford it."

Poverty does exist in Winnetka, but it's hard to find, as are the hints that the comforts may be ambiguous, that security may have its victims as well as its beneficiaries. There are, however, voices from the corners of the mind which speak half-believed thoughts, ideas that, if fully believed, would create intolerable tensions.

"It has a lot of conveniences," the thirty-six-year-old lawyer said. "I can't fault it, really. Except it is a one-class town. That's not important to us, but it is to the kids unless we make it a point to expose them to others. We go back home to West Virginia in the summers, and our kids are exposed to people of a different class there."

A doctor with one daughter in college and two other children in New Trier East: "The kids have warped ideas about what life is like. There's no way to expose them to it except in artificial ways. They see that CBS show on hunger. Do they know what that's really about? They don't understand." His wife added, "Yes, Winnetka offers a sense of security, but maybe that doesn't mean much anymore in a world like this."

The conversation ended at that point. There didn't seem to be anything else to say. It was a dry, Midwestern-cold Saturday afternoon, my second day in Winnetka. On the day before, I had stopped by New Trier East for about an hour and had wandered the corridors. Students were moving about without any visible restraints, talking in neither shouts nor whispers, fooling around a little bit here and there. Obviously there was no carefully enforced pass system nor any strictly enforced rules about behavior.

I walked toward a lot of noise and discovered the cafeteria littered with brown bags, sandwich wrappers, milk cartons, and juice cans. Rock music blared out of several speakers, and a number of banners were hanging from the walls announcing the wrestling, gymnastic, and basketball events for the weekend. Five black students, the only five to be seen (there are thirty-five in a school of 3,564 students), sat at one table without any whites.

Just outside the cafeteria there were about two dozen kids standing or sitting on the floor of a short, wide hallway between the cafeteria and the auditorium. Some were just talking, waiting for the lunch period to end, but others were playing boy-girl type games, flirting rather awkwardly it seemed.

Nearly all the kids were neatly, fashionably dressed and clean. They were very clean-looking. The outfits broke down into basic categories: miniskirts and sweaters, dress shirts and slacks, bellbottoms and body shirts, and jeans and work shirts. Every now and then there was an odd combination of this basic pattern, and about as often a green and white NT-E letter sweater. A lot of long, straight, 100-strokes-a-night hair on the girls, and a lot of medium-long, but very carefully razor-cut hair on the boys. Again, exceptions but not many, not many at all.

Despite the lack of any visible hobbles, their movements were somehow restrained, not from a Waspish sense of decorum or good manners or obedience to rules, reactions that are too cerebral. It was as if each student were regulated by some internal device, the way the speed of a car can be controlled by a governor so that the throttle cannot be fully depressed. Any inclination they had to take a deep breath was checked by a gut feeling that they seemed unable to understand and were not even aware of.

My expectations had been different. My hopes had been that the tone of the school would be alive and exciting, that the kids would be groovy, aware, cynical. I wanted them to be different from what my friends and I had been eleven years ago. I wanted them to tell me at least that they might not be going to college or coming back to a Winnetka or planning to have straight careers.

These kids were supposed to be the alienated products of affluent America. They were the ones who, if they haven't already closed down their high schools, would close down their colleges next year or be living in communes. These were the kids who are supposed to be making the "counterculture," who are demanding political changes and who are bringing about changes in life-styles and culture. In my own mind, I had created an image that things were changing, that they had to be changing, that they couldn't go on as before, yet what I felt at that first glance and throughout the week was

that nothing had changed because the kids of Winnetka are scared, not afraid, but scared, scared to move, to breathe, to live.

Not of the bomb, population explosion, famine, black riots, pollution, political repression, Vietnam, or even the draft. They are scared of what they know in the pit of their guts, something that has never been taught them in school or at home: that for them there is no comfort, that continuance is only one possibility, that survival is no longer a matter of personal challenge but of depersonalized threats, that the molds into which they are being forced by parents, schools, and community simply will not fit, that Winnetka, careers, the country club life, the volunteer service with the Junior League, none of that will allow them the same comfort it has afforded their parents.

As I left the doctor and his wife and drove over to the Hubbard Woods section of town, I recalled the previous evening's conversation with Louis, a graduate of New Trier West, now a senior at Northern Illinois University.

"People expect more, a lot more from you, if they know you're from New Trier, so I don't talk about it. I'm not really ashamed I'm from New Trier. It's not my fault; it's not anyone's fault, but I just don't talk about it. The school just has so much of everything. The photography lab at West is much better equipped— rugs and everything—than the one at college. Everyone expects much more from you because they think that, since everything has been handed to you, you can do it. You have to go to college—there's no question, even, about that—and to the best possible college. If you don't, you feel . . .

33

well, you feel as if you've broken a covenant with God. . . .

"I know I got a good education there. It was tough, really hard work. No exam I've taken in college has been harder than the New Trier May (senior finals) exams, but goddamn, the competition. I hated it, I really hated it. The funny thing is that now I love it, too. Art (his college major) is very competitive, and I love it, in a way."

About forty small children were skating on the floodlighted ice rink in front of the railroad station, made by the town's recreation department in a small park. At the corner of Green Bay Road, a group of ten boys, about twelve years old, their skates lying on the sidewalk, were gaily flinging snowballs at the cars and trucks moving slowly through the lightly falling snow.

I wandered over to The Bookmark nearby with some vague idea of seeing if this bookstore was any different from the one in the main section of town that had displayed many expensive art books on the table nearest the door. I went in and began to look over a rack of paperback current nonfiction when I heard a girl's voice ask the clerk for Robert Heinlein's *Stranger in a Strange Land*. I turned to look. She was no more than fifteen, wearing a blue parka and black ski pants tucked into red wool socks that came above her boots. Her skates were hung over her shoulders, one in front and one in back. A red, knitted stocking cap was perched on top of her long black hair.

The clerk said he was all out, but it bounced right off her. "No," she said, without either apology or condescension, "I ordered it special and received a card that it had arrived." She gave the clerk her name, and he

bent down to check a row of books under the counter. I looked at her and wondered about this girl and that book, a pleasant science fiction story about the Second Coming, the Messiah being a human child of human parents raised by highly cerebral beings on Mars before being brought back to Earth.

Three or four years ago, *Stranger* was truly a book of the underground culture, and since then it's been made a reference point in the song "Triad" by the Jefferson Airplane, and its Martian vocabulary has been adopted in the press. It has passed through the bookstores of the culturally with-it campuses and is now becoming a full-scale youth culture fad, comparable to *Catcher in the Rye, The Lord of the Rings* trilogy, and Hesse's *Steppenwolf* and *Siddhartha*. The difference is that those books read like Job, Ecclesiastes, and Jeremiah. Not only is the plot of *Stranger* similar to the Gospels, its tone of hope, of the possibility of brotherly love, is also similar. There is, however, no talk of salvation or redemption, but only of the necessity of keeping up the struggle. After the girl had paid for her copy, she went over to the hardcover, nonfiction section and spent ten minutes skip-reading Eugene McCarthy's *The Year of the People*, and then left without buying it.

Toward the end of the basketball game that night between New Trier East and Highland Park, I noticed a student with longish, casually combed hair, dressed in blue jeans, lace boots, and a rumpled brown corduroy jacket that had a green and white WORK FOR PEACE button on it. He was interested in the game but detached. The close score and consequent excitement of the last few minutes did not reach him as it did most of the other stu-

34

dents. It was as if he were watching a complex piece of machinery. His name was Kurt, and we got to talking and continued after the game over coffee and ice cream at Hubbard's Cupboard.

"It hurts me to see kids always putting off living for the future. I think college will be just as much of a drag as high school and that the kids who say, 'Just wait until I get into college, then I'll really be able to be free,' are kidding themselves because then there's a job and marriage and things that you get tied to.

"My father's a salesman of high-grade varieties of papers, and he's done very well at it. He started off with nothing, and he's done really well, but he's not happy. He doesn't say so, but I can tell. Now he's looking forward to his retirement so he can do what he wants, finally. He thought that once he got enough money he could do that, but he can't. He goes to the beach and tries to relax, but he can't be still. He has to be thinking about his job and doing something with his hands, and now he hopes to be able to do what he wants when he retires. He is happiest when he's working with his hands. He's always fixing up the house, tearing down walls, putting up new ones and things like that. When he retires he wants to run a marina in northern Michigan. He should be doing it now.

"The thing is, though, our parents want us to be doctors or lawyers or something like that. We don't want to disappoint them and drop down socially, but what's the point? I'm not sure I want to be a lawyer or a doctor. I'm not sure I want to go to college because that means I'm accepting the social system. Yet, I can't drop out, but that may be the one

way I can survive. I feel like I'm in between, but I don't know how long I can go on that way."

The next day I met Dave, an intense, unsmiling senior, respected by both his fellow students and his teachers. He began describing the depth of his hatred of the town, of his parents, his teachers, his fellow students, the security, cleanliness, and emptiness of Winnetka, its shoddy and shallow values, and his love of danger and dirt—the whole existential rap of fascination with death and filth. I thought I was listening to a parody of an intellectual New York magazine writer, until he told me about his "sin" as he called it, that he "hustled" men at a YMCA.

My first reaction, of course, was that he was putting me on, but too many other things fit: the realistic detail, his general outlook, and the match with the logic of the rest of his conversation. Besides, as a teacher, I had known kids from exactly the same kind of community who were overt homosexuals and whose embrace of it had nothing to do with pubescent play.

Dave's hatred of New Trier and Winnetka may have been a justification for his own behavior rather than a cause, but the sequence is unimportant. What counts is that he was an anguished, tormented kid who hated himself more than anything else.

That's it, essentially. Sure, there are hundreds of facts about New Trier East: its 168 different courses; its track system; its superabundance of activities ranging from an FM radio station to a falconry club that existed for several years; its lavish array of equipment and facilities; its high-powered, highly intelligent, and sometimes creative and sensitive teachers; the liberal and even oc-

35

casionally humanistic attitude of the administrators; its elaborate advisory system and large college guidance staff; the lack of any substantial dress code; the freedom given to juniors and seniors to leave school during their study halls; last year's widely attended symposium on drugs; the opportunity to take ungraded courses; the student-run study halls; the honor system; the uncensored student paper; "the long history of student responsibility," as principal Ralph McGee put it. All the sound, liberal educational innovations.

But there is also the numbers game, in which low grades in high-level courses can be multiplied by a certain factor to give their equivalent standing on a normal curve, the fact that many students say they engage in the hyperactivities not for their intrinsic value but so their participation will look good on their records, that there are also boobs on the faculty, such as the one who chased three giggly girls out of the telephone booth in the main entranceway and told them they couldn't use that one because they were supposed to use another one.

And the student council meeting that finally had to be adjourned because no one, not even the president, the sponsor of the bill, nor the faculty advisers, had any clear idea of what exactly was being debated. A chief participant in that Wonderland scene was one member of a small group of radicals who got themselves elected to the council, some say to destroy it, some to reform it. I had not sought out these kids because I didn't want to hear a long rap that had been lifted from an underground newspaper from some other school, for the left-wing underground paper at New Trier was woefully short of any original analysis (some said this was

because the school was so liberal there was nothing to complain about; New Trier also has an underground *right*-wing press, but it was no better).

Another kind of student I deliberately tried to avoid was the professional New Trier Liberal Student and Spokesman for the Younger Generation. I wasn't entirely successful; one of them cornered me and delivered himself of a long, sincere, but hopelessly mawkish description of his fellow students—how they were really becoming concerned with "the problems of the environment," what the Moratorium Day protest had been like, how many were "working" in the Chicago slums, and how responsible they all were.

Finally, too, the college guidance office looks like a travel bureau with photo murals of campuses covering the walls and scores of catalogues scattered over tables and piled in the bookcases, and the head of the guidance staff could not or would not give me a direct answer to the question of what they did for the kids who should not or could not go to college.

Coming of age in Winnetka is an agonizing experience. It is not intended to be; it is supposed to be challenging and difficult—no *rite de passage* can fail to be so. But the basic assumptions of the process were made before 1950, when *Life* did a euphoric cover story on this model school system, and those assumptions were drawn from a different world.

Mrs. Mitchell Dawson, a psychiatric social worker with the Family Counseling Service of Glencoe: "There is no hiding place down here anymore. There is nothing to resist, no limits within which it is safe to rebel. There is no place that is secure from the relentless intrusion of the world. Young people in the past had illusions that protected them, but there is no comfort in illusions now. . . .

"There are not very many without problems, even the ones who appear to accept it all. The questioning of values is almost a fad; you're just not with it if you don't question values. And they do, and they're left alone, helpless to find their own values, with nothing certain to strengthen them."

The kids of New Trier may be the most brilliant, aggressive, and competitive collection of youths in the country. They may be able to do differential calculus, expound upon DNA, and perform sophisticated analyses of Dostoyevsky, James, Locke, Rousseau, and Proust, but they are pressure-cooked, intellectual combatants who have been force-fed highly complex and abstract ideas about life and death, good and evil, power and virtue. Through the media they see it all in "real life" happening outside those filmy lines of the mind, but they have no conscious way to make the connections between those ideas calmly discussed in the classroom and what they are going to have to deal with sooner or later. They can discuss the subtleties of Conrad intelligently, but they can have no visceral understanding that life may be a "choice among nightmares." Their feeling of fears is vaguely defined but strong, and eventually they are going to do more than simply regurgitate answers to essay questions on exams.

Adolescent identities are formed by stumbling and falling, by creating a personalized set of survival techniques, but only one set is really offered in Winnetka, and it is obsolete.

The kids of Winnetka are not really allowed to find the skills that fit their needs. They are forced to think they must accept those of their parents. Those skills may have worked for food gathering and hunting societies, but existence in this one is problematic at best for entirely other reasons than physical needs. Survival now is primarily an intellectual and emotional struggle, of creating different fantasies, different dreams.

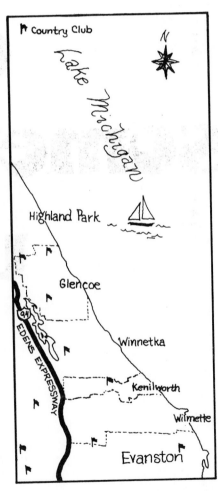

we must be doing something wrong

"*Do you like getting A's?*" *asked*
Dr. Sunshine.

"*Sure. They're nice when they*
come along. Show 'em to Mom and
stuff."

My blood was up. "Jesus, it makes
me burn when you start talking about
grades. Here's this magnificent little
person, you know? She looks as if
she has half a chance of finding out
what life's all about, and you're going
to tell her to try and get A's. A's kill
people."

Dr. Sunshine wavered and looked
fuzzy and then decided to take me on.
He told me about how it all goes back
to the infant mortality rate, and how
in order to conquer plague bacteria
there have to be X number of people
getting A's in trigonometry. He said
that in order ever to change the
course of history we had to have
learned the history we got in school.
I told him that the history we got in
school had nothing to do with real
history, past or present, that we
would be better off finding out the
truth. I agreed that everything went
back to the infant mortality rate, and
that the reason babies kept dying was
that nobody gave a damn about them
and that one reason nobody cared
about them was that the school sys-
tems neglect ever to mention anything
about life, truth, decency, love, aware-
ness or kindness. He shook his head
and said no, stopping babies from
dying had nothing to do with caring,
it had to do with getting A's in trigo-
nometry. I told him he was crazy.

JOAN BAEZ
Daybreak

CHILDREN OF THE APOCALYPSE

To oppose Fascism, we need neither heavy armaments nor bureaucratic apparatuses. What we need above all is a different way of looking at life and human beings. My dear friends, without this different way of looking at life and human beings, we shall ourselves become Fascists. —Silone

Peter Marin

am not really interested in "education" as a subject. What moves me more are the problems of the young. At best, questions about education should be treated topically: as a way of living with the present, of *making* do. But there is something beyond that too, a way of looking at men and women, a visionary expectation, that keeps us seeking the most human ways of making do. But the most human ways of making do these days have to do with our rhetoric about the public schools, and we forget in the midst of it what we really owe the young.

But knowing what we owe them means knowing what is going on, and it is hard to get a fix on that. Whatever happens is shrouded in folds of propaganda and rhetoric, abstraction and fantasy. *Revolution, Repression, The Age of Aquarius, The Counter-Culture, Law and Order, The Great Society, The Death of Reason, The Psychedelic Revolution.* . . . It goes on and on—a vast illusion comprised of banners and winking neon meanings that fog the frantic soup in which we swim: the mixture of innocent yearning and savagery, despair and exhilaration, the grasping for paradise lost, paradise *now,* the reaching for a sanity that becomes, in frustration, a new kind of madness.

If this is not the kingdom of apocalypse, it is at least an apocalyptic condition of the soul. We want the most simple human decencies, but in our anguish we are driven to extremes to find them. We reach blindly for whatever offers solace. We yearn more than ever for some kind of human touch and seem steadily less able to provide it. We drift in our own confusion, chattering about the "future": at once more free and more corrupt, more liberated and bound, than any others on the face of the earth.

In the midst of it, adrift, the young more than ever seem beautiful but maimed, trying against all odds to salvage something from the mess. With daring and luck many seem to survive, and some few thrive, but too many others—more than we imagine—already seem destined to spend their lives wrestling with something very close to psychosis. Despite all our talk we have not adequately gauged their suffering. Theirs is a condition of the soul that marks the dead end of the beginnings of America—a dreadful anomy in which one loses all access to others and the self: a liberation that is simultaneously the most voluptuous kind of freedom and an awful form of terror.

Merely to touch in that condition, or to see one another, or to speak honestly is to reach across an immense distance. One struggles with the remnants of a world-view so pervasive, so perverse, that everyone must doubt whether it is possible to see anything clearly, say it honestly, or enter it innocently. The tag ends of two dozen different transplanted foreign cultures have begun to die within us, have already died, and the young have been released into what is perhaps the first true "American" reality —one marked, above all, by the absence of any coherent culture.

The problem is not merely that the "system" is brutal and corrupt, nor that the war has revealed how savage and cynical a people we are. It is, put simply, that "social reality" seems to have vanished altogether. One finds among the young a profound and befuddled sense of loss—as if they had been traumatized and betrayed by an entire world. What is release and space for some is for the others a constant sense of separation and vertigo—a void in which the self can float or soar but in which one can also drift unmoored and fall; and when one falls, it is forever, for there is nothing underneath, no culture, no net of meaning, nobody else.

That is, of course, what we have talked about for a century: the empty existential universe of self-creation. It is a condition of the soul, an absolute loss and yearning for the world. One can become anything—but nothing makes much sense. Adults have managed to evade it, have hesitated on its edges, have clung to one another and to institutions, to beliefs in "the system," to law and order. But now none of that coheres, and the young seem unprotected by it all, and what we have evaded and even celebrated in *metaphor* has become, for a whole generation, a kind of daily emotional life.

The paradox, of course, is that the dissolution of culture has set us free to create almost anything—but it also deprived us of the abilities to do it. Strength, wholeness, and sanity seem to be functions of *relation,* and relation, I think, is a function of culture, part of its intricate web of approved connection and experience, a network of persons and moments that simultaneously offer us release and bind us to the lives of others. One "belongs" to and in culture in a way that goes beyond mere politics or participation, for belonging is both simpler and more complex than that: an immersion in the substance of community and tradition, which is itself a net beneath us, a kind of element in which men seem to float, protected.

That is, I suppose, what the young have lost. Every personal truth or experience puts them at odds with the "official" version of things. There is no connection at all between inner truth and what they are expected to be; every gesture demanded and rewarded is a kind of absolute lie, a denial of their confusion and need. The "drifting free" is the sense of distance; it is distance—not a "generation" gap, but the huge gulf between the truth of one's own pain and possibilities and the world's empty forms. Nothing supports or acknowledges them, and they are trapped in that gulf, making the best of things, making everything up as they go along. But that is the most basic and awful task of all, for it is so lonely, so dangerous, so easily distracted and subverted, so easily swayed. The further along one gets the more alone one is, the more fragile and worried, the deeper into the dark. It is there, of course, that one may need help from adults, but adults have no talent for that at all; we do not admit to being in the dark—how, then, can we be of any use?

If all this is so, what sense can one make of the public schools? They are stiff, unyielding, microcosmic versions of a world that has already disappeared. They are, after all, the state's schools, they do the state's work, and their purpose is the preservation of things as they were. Their means are the isolation of ego and deflection of energy. Their main structural function is to produce in the young a self-delusive "independence"—a system of false consciousness and need that actually renders them dependent on institutions and the state. Their corrosive role-playing and demand systems are so extensive, so profound, that nothing really human shows through—and when it does, it appears only as frustration, exhaustion, and anger.

That, of course, is the real outrage of the schools: their systematic corruption of the relations among persons. Where they should be comrades, allies, equals, and even lovers, the public schools make them "teacher" and "student"—replaceable units in a mechanical ritual that passes on, in the name of education, and "emotional plague"; a kind of ego and personality that has been so weakened, so often denied the experience of community or solitude, that we no longer understand quite what these things are or how to achieve them.

Whatever one's hopes or loves, each teacher is engaged daily in that same conspiracy to maim the young. But I am talking here about more than the surface stupidities of attendance requirements, grades, or curriculum. Those can be changed and updated. But what seems truly untouchable is what lies behind and beneath them: the basic irredeemable assumptions about what is necessary, human, or good; the treatment of the person, time, choice, energy, work, community, and pleasure. It is a world-view so monolithic and murderous that it becomes a part of us even while we protest against it.

I remember returning one fall to a state college in California after a summer in the Mexican mountains. I had been with my friends, writing, walking, making love—all with a sense of freedom and quietude. That first day back I felt as I always did on campus, like a sly, still undiscovered spy. After all, what was it all to me? I walked into my first class and began my usual pitch: They would grade themselves, read what they wanted or not at all, come to class or stay home. It was all theirs to choose—their learning, their time, their space. But they were perplexed by that. Was it some kind of trick? They began to question me, and finally one of them asked, exasperated: "But what can we do if we don't know what you *want?*"

It was a minimal satori. I could not speak. What ran through my mind was not only the absolute absurdity of the question but the lunacy of our whole charade: the roles we played, the place we met, the state's mazelike building, the state's gigantesque campus, and, beyond all that, what we mean by "schooling," how we had been possessed by it. I knew that whatever I answered would be senseless and oppressive, for no matter how I disclaimed my role, whatever I said would restore it. So I stood there instead in silence, aware that what I had taken lightly to be mad was indeed mad, and that one could never, while there, break through those roles into anything real.

Well, almost never. The most human acts I have ever found in our colleges and high schools are the ones most discouraged, the surreptitious sexuality between teachers and students. Although they were almost always cramped and totally exploitive, they were at least some kind of private touch. I used to imagine that one fine afternoon the doors of all the offices would open wide with a trumpet blast, and teachers and students would emerge to dance hand in hand in total golden nakedness on the campus lawns in a paroxysm of truth. In a sense, what I imagined then is close to what sometimes happens more realistically in the student strikes and demonstrations. One finds in the participants a sense of exhilaration and release, a regained potency and a genuine transformation of feeling: the erotic camaraderie of liberation. There is an immense and immediate relief at the cessation of pretense. It is one's role, as well as the rules, which is transgressed, and one somehow becomes stronger, more real—and suddenly at home.

But that doesn't happen often, and usually only in the colleges, and the young are left elsewhere and almost always to suffer in silence the most destructive effect of the schools—not their external rules and structure, but the ways in which we internalize them and falsify ourselves in order to live with them. The state creeps in and gradually occupies us; we act and think within its forms; we see through its eyes and it speaks through our mouths—and how, in that situation, can the young learn to be alive or free?

We try. We open the classroom a bit and loosen the bonds. Students use a teacher's first name, or roam the small room, or go ungraded, or choose their own texts. It is all very nice; better, of course, than nothing at all. But what has it got to do with the needs of the young? We try again. We devise new models, new programs, new plans. We innovate and renovate, and beneath it all our schemes always contain the same vacancies, the same smells of death, as the schools. One speaks to planners, designers, teachers, and administrators; one hears about schedules and modules and curricular innovation—new systems. It is always "materials" and "technique," the chronic American technological vice, the cure that murders as it saves. It is all so smug, so progressively right—and yet so useless, so far off the track. One knows there is something else altogether: a way of feeling, access to the soul, a way of speaking and embracing, that lies at the heart of all yearning or wisdom or real revolution. It is that, precisely, that has been left out. It is something the planners cannot remember: the living tissue of community. Without it, of course, we shrivel and die, but who can speak convincingly about that to those who have never felt it?

I remember talking to one planner about what one wants from others.

"Respect," he said, "And their utmost effort."

"But all I want," I said, "is love and a sense of humor."

His eyes lit up. "I see," he said. "You mean positive feedback."

Positive feedback. So we debauch our own sweet nature. I don't want positive feedback, nor do the young. What they need is so much more important and profound—not "skills" but qualities of the soul; daring, warmth, wit, imagination, honesty, loyalty, grace, and resilience. But one cannot be taught those things; they cannot be programmed into a machine. They seem to be learned, instead, in activity and communion—in the *adventurous presence of other real persons.*

But there is no room in the schools for that. There is no real hope of making room there. Those who want to aid the young must find some other way to do it. Yes, I know, that is where most of the young still are. I can hear the murmurs protesting that only the demented, delinquent, or rich can go elsewhere. But that is just the point. This is the monolithic system of control that must be broken. We have wasted too much time and energy on the state's schools, and we have failed to consider or create alternatives. Now it is time to cut loose from the myth. We must realize once and for all that, given the real inner condition of the young, the state's schools are no place to try to help them.

But if that is the case, my friends ask, what *do* you do? I have no easy answers. There are cultural conditions for which there are no solutions, turnings of the soul so profound and complex that no system can absorb or contain them. How would one have "solved" the Reformation? Or first-century Rome? One makes accommodations and adjustments, one dreams about the future and makes plans to save us all, but in spite of all that, because of it, what seems more important are the private independent acts that become more necessary every day: the ways we find as *private persons* to restore to one another the strengths we should have now—whether to make the kind of revolution we need or to survive the repression that seems likely.

What I am talking about here is a kind of psychic survival: our ability to live decently beyond institutional limits and provide for our comrades enough help to sustain them. What saves us as men and women is always a kind of witness: the quality of our own acts and lives. This is the knowledge, of course, that institutions bribe us to forget, the need and talent for what Kropotkin called "mutual aid"—the private assumption of responsibility for others.

I remember talking one evening with a student who was arguing the need for burning things down. Her face was a stiff, resisting mask of anger and grief.

"But what else," she said, "can I do?"

I wasn't sure. "Try to get to the bottom of things. Try to see clearly what we need."

"But when I see clearly," she said, "I freak out."

"That's why we need friends," I said.

"But I have no friends."

And she began to cry. That is it precisely. How does one really survive it? There is nothing for such pain save to embrace it, to heal it with warmth, with one's own two hands. One comes to believe that what each of us needs is an absolute kind of lover—not for the raw sex, but for what is sometimes beneath and intrinsic to it: a devoted open presence to perceive, acknowledge, and embrace what we are.

That is the legitimacy which comes neither from the ballot nor the gun, a potency, resilience, and courage that one can learn only by feeling at home in the world. But how can the young feel that? There are few such lovers, and the other old ways are gone. Once upon a time one had a lived relation to culture, or place, or the absolute. But God has vanished and the culture is tattered and savage and "place" has become the raw, empty suburb or the ghetto.

What else is left? Not much. Only others: those adrift in the same dark, one's brothers and sisters, comrades and lovers—the broken isolate bits of a movable kingdom, an invisible "community" that shares, inside a particular fate. It is only in their eyes and arms, in their presence and affection, that one becomes real, is given back, and discovers the extent of one's being.

What we are talking about here are really acts of love, the gestures by which one shares with others the true dimension and depth of the world. Those gestures are a form of revelation, for they restore to others a sense of what is shared. But one can only make them when one feels free, when the space we inhabit is our own, an open environment, a "field" in which we can begin to see clearly, act freely—and be real.

I know that this is shaky ground. How can one explain what one means by real? It is experiential and subjective: a quality and condition of some kind of deeply inhabited moment. We talk about ecstasy and ego-death and peak experience, but those seem equally imperfect ways of describing the experience of *being in the world*. One *is*. That is all. Our chronic sense of isolation dissolves; there is a correspondence, an identity, between inner and outer, world and world. It is a making whole; it knits together the self at the same time that the self is felt to be a part, the heart, of what surrounds it.

What it is, always, is a reclamation of our proper place in the world—and those who want to help the young must realize that it cannot happen in the schools. Perhaps, after all, it doesn't really matter whether we transgress their limits by leaving them or while staying within them, so long as we learn to ignore them wherever we are. Can one do that while still in the state's schools? I don't think so. But perhaps some teachers want to try—and why not? Perhaps it *is* worth the effort and anguish—as long as one always remembers that one's primary obligation is not to the system, not the state, but to the young—and not as a teacher, but as an equal and ally. That obligation—like a doctor's or lawyer's—is absolute; more important than our own comfort or job, and it can be satisfied only when one is willing to refuse, point-blank, to do anything that really damages the young—no matter who programs or asks for it. One must be willing to suspend the rules, refuse one's role, reject the system—and live instead with the young—wherever you find them—as the persons we really are. If that is impossible in the schools, then one must be willing to leave the schools and take the young, too—into the street, into one's own home—wherever we can live sensibly together.

Perhaps what schools need are "escape committees" of resistance devoted, like the draft resistance, to discovering alternatives for the young. We have plenty of working models, places such as the First Street School in New York or Berkeley's Other Ways; the "free schools" scattered on either coast; community day-care centers and ghetto storefront schools; female liberation groups; communes of all kinds; free clinics; therapeutic centers like Synanon; experimental colleges; the hard-edged courage of the Panthers and Young Lords. All of these function in different ways as an education in liberation: the attempts of people to move past institutions and do for themselves what the state does not.

Not everyone can do it, of course. It is a scary idea. Our heads are heavy with a fear of "dropping out." The institutional propaganda convinces too many of us that there is one world here and another there, and that there is some kind of illegitimate limbo where our actions dissolve in the air. But *there* is simple private life, the life of the street, the free relations between persons, and it is only there, these days, that one can be free or real enough to serve the young. But if it is dangerous out there, it is also incredibly lovely at times, full of learning, full of freedom, and only those who have lived or traveled with the young in those open fields know just how exhilarating, if exhausting, it is.

But what about the future? When I talk with my friends these days the sugarplum visions dance in their heads, and they tell me about their systems and salvations, or the dawning age of Aquarius and the new consciousness. Well, I want to believe it. But these days there is also the cop at the door with his gun, and the new mechanical men, and also something in me, the old Adam, the old father, whispering *not yet, not yet.* I remember a man I knew in New York who ate nothing but bologna and cheese sandwiches, and when he broke his jaw and had to sip through a straw he dumped bologna and cheese and bread in his blender, added milk, and had his usual sandwich.

Which is to say, the future changes, but we may not. Whatever there is on the other side of this confusion will be, at best, not so different from what we already have now, on occasion, in our best moments. No new senses, no third sexes, no cosmic orgasms, no karmic rebirths. No, if we are daring and lucky, what will be "revolutionary" will simply be that more of us, all of us, will have more of a chance for a decent human life—good comrades and lovers, a few touches of ecstasy, some solitude and space, a sense of self-determination.

I once asked a student what she would do if she awoke in paradise.

"Walk around," she said. "Get something to eat."

I don't have any other answer. We will do what we do now—but we will do it better. We will sit talking with friends around a table, do some decent work, hold one another guiltlessly in our arms, touch a bit more softly, more knowingly. We will understand a bit more and dance a bit more and breathe a bit more and even think a little more—and all, perhaps, a bit more intelligently, more bravely.

That isn't much, but it is also almost everything, and what we are forced to do now is learn how to do all that for ourselves. There is no one to show us how—no program, no system. One can only have such lives by trying to live them, and that is what the young are trying to do these days, all on their own, whether we help them or not. The few real teachers I know, those really serving the young, are simply those who try to live such lives in their company, as freely and humanly as they can. The rest of "education" is almost always rhetoric and nonsense.

Declaration on the Birth of the Child Lorca

Michael Rossman

We will not send our child to a public school, or even to a private one in the usual sense. Together we have managed to learn much the schools couldn't teach us, and unlearn some of what they did. The heart of our knowledge is ours now, and it tells us we must be responsible ourselves for the conditions of our child's growth. This is no romantic hippy daydream. It is a full political act: grounded in theory, chosen as strategy, implemented with all the skills of our consciousness.

We choose to move on the future by freeing our child from the control of the present State. We declare independence from its essential instrument, the System of Education. We will not give our young over to be conditioned in obedience with its programs by any of its representatives, however unofficial, informal and liberal. *We will grow our own.* And we will grow them as free as we can manage, in situations where we have only to contend with what is in ourselves of the lives we are trying to leave behind.

Several years ago we left the Educational System, where we were cut off from our many selves. We sidestepped the institutions that continue it in society, and began to come together. Now we know that other lives of learning are possible. We can name them. Crippled as we are, we can create their initial conditions: we understand what is involved, and have the skills and the power. For we have been learning to be what we imagine: to live in our bodies, make art with our lives, realize cooperation, and fight Fascism by any means necessary, including the creation of alternate realities, guerrilla enclaves of Life in the State of Death.

Good life learning means understanding is integrated in action. We display our knowledge of the culture of specialized roles, with its destructive systems of education, competition and authority, by how we manage to be each other's teachers, siblings and lovers, parents and children, by how we tend and heal and share each other's growth. We must focus at home through this if we are to focus anywhere else and into the future. *We will grow our own.* And we ourselves must be directly involved in what and how our children learn, for no one else can represent our interest in the future.

For this we must make our lives over: rearrange the ways we work, the styles of our play, the priorities of our time and our love; and move beyond the roles that still bind us from within. To replace what we reject, we must learn anew what we have to share, and grow to make it adequate. The price of making of our lives a school for our children is our own transformation. We believe it is possible, because it is already begun.

Our parents were forced to abandon their children to the part-time uses of the State because they were integrated into its economy and culture, because they saw no alternative, because they were isolated in marriage and privacy and could not organize their lives to be also a school. We know now that no couple can cope alone with even their own relation. We learn in a larger community. To free our young many must come together, to share their powers in critical mass and intimacy. We believe it involves all entering equal as children into the school of a larger Family.

It also means learning economic cooperation, to free space and resources. And it means committing ourselves to political identity and struggle. At present here, one elementary credential can front for up to fifty kids, leaving us with only our own limitations. But when many choose to use this freedom it will be curtailed and that will be only the beginning. For Fascism is rising softly in this land, you have seen its sign in the black headline of the sky.

The State registered our son with a number at his birth, and designs to own him. Our growing up prepared us for integration into its army, its civil and industrial bureaucracies, its systems of consumption and exploitation, decision and power. It cannot afford us to let our son grow unprepared, let alone prepared for something else. It will not give him over to the gropings of our freedom without a deadly struggle. This will take many forms. To meet them, we must realize together who we are and the politics of our necessities and choices. And prepare to resist, to fight for the cradle of our future, and to flourish in and beyond our resistance.

Learning Power to the People.

Five years ago, when many of us began to write and speak about the problems of the public schools in cities such as Boston and New York, it seems to me that we were more than innocent in one regard. We would point out that schools in the United States were not encouraging children to think freely and to question bravely, to fight for justice and to cry for those in pain. We would point out that schools contained and silenced, muted and anesthetized our children. We would point out that this was not the way to turn out honest souls like Thoreau or good men like Gandhi or brave men like Malcolm X or Martin Luther King. We would complain like children standing by a huge and slightly obsolete machine. "Look," we would say, "this system is not working."

The innocence of this approach now seems quite overwhelming. Public school was never in business to produce Thoreau. It is in business to produce a man like Richard Nixon and, even more, a population like the one which could elect him. It does not require the attribution of sinister motives, but only of the bare survival-instincts, to know that an interlocking network of industrial, political and academic interests does not exist to subsidize the demolition of its methods.

Businessmen are not in business to lose customers, and schools do not exist to free their clients from the agencies of mass persuasion. School and media possess a productive monopoly upon the imagination of a child.

It is not bizarre, it is not unexpected, it is entirely logical, that public schools should serve the public interest in this fashion. That we can continually lose sight of the indoctrinational function of the public school is only perhaps the more persuasive evidence that we ourselves are well indoctrinated.

We are a rich nation living well at the expense of others. It is of the essence that schools should teach us how to live at peace with an uneasy sense of conscience. Just children are a terrible danger to an unjust nation unless they can be etherized successfully. It is the major function of the public schools to offer us that ether.

Often we hear each other speaking in frustrated or in disappointed tones about a particular school or a particular school system that seemed to us for a little while to be moving industriously outward in the direction of some kind of new and promising "wide-open freedom," where the kids might probe into the activities of their own school board, examine the

working? 99

Jonathan Kozol

motives of big business and the Department of Defense, scrutinize chauvinism, condemn false offerings in press and television, take sides with the powerless against the dominant and strong. When it does not turn out to be like this at all, we grow enraged and bitter, and protest the great deception that we were so willingly led into.

There is, I now believe, a terrible innocence about the character of our reiterated disappointment. Schools are not intended to lead children into avenues of ethics, candor or dissent. Children are not expected to come anywhere close to speculations of this order. They are intended to think *about* not *into.* They are intended to acquire information *regarding,* not leverage *upon.*

They are intended to conceive themselves to be free people by the exercise of unimportant liberties and semblances of ineffective options.

The walls that stand around the flag and chalkboard of the U.S. public school will not be leveled by the sound of trumpets or by another research-project sponsored by the Ford Foundation. We should not fool ourselves about the nature of the task before us. There is a terrible yearning in us all, as I believe, for almost any variety of warm, placating and believable deception: anything, it seems, no matter of what shape or origin, so long as we shall not be forced to put our bodies on the line or stake our lives for something we believe in. We turn in desperation to complex technologies (called systems), new phantasies of "open schools" within closed buildings, new phrases ("Discovery," "The Integrated Day") for old deceptions. What is the realistic meaning of alternatives "within the system," if the system is the primary vehicle of state control?

A school that flies the flag and conscientiously serves the interest of that flag it flies, cannot serve those of justice. School cannot at once both socialize to the values of an oppressor and toil for the liberation and the potency of the oppressed. If innovation is profound, it is subversive. If it is subversive, it is incompatible with the prime responsibility of public school. The public schools may be inept, archaic, old and unattractive, but they are not suicidal.

Indoctrinational schooling and the mandatory practice of a twelve-year house arrest are the keystone of a mighty archway in this nation. It will not be taken out without grave consequences for the structure it supports; nor will it be taken away without the kind of struggle and the kind of sacrifice for which young people in this nation are now only beginning to prepare themselves.

NEIL POSTMAN

the Politics of Reading

An earlier version of this article was presented as the keynote address at the Lehigh University Reading Conference, January 24, 1970.

Teachers of reading comprise a most sinister political group, whose continued presence and strength are more a cause for alarm than celebration. I offer this thought as a defensible proposition, all the more worthy of consideration because so few people will take it seriously.

My argument rests on a fundamental and, I think, unassailable assumption about education: namely, that all educational practices are profoundly political in the sense that they are designed to produce one sort of human being rather than another—which is to say, an educational system always proceeds from some model of what a human being *ought* to be like. In the broadest sense, a political ideology is a conglomerate of systems for promoting certain modes of thinking and behavior. And there is no system I can think of that more directly tries to do this than the schools. There is not one thing that is done to, for, with, or against a student in school that is not rooted in a political bias, ideology, or notion. This includes everything from the arrangement of seats in a classroom, to the rituals practiced in the auditorium, to the textbooks used in lessons, to the dress required of both teachers and students, to the tests given, to the subjects that are taught, and most emphatically, to the intellectual skills that are promoted. And what is called reading, it seems to me, just about heads the list. For to teach reading, or even to promote vigorously the teaching of reading, is to take a definite political position on how people should behave and on what they ought to value. Now, teachers, I have found, respond in one of three ways to such an assertion. Some of them deny it. Some of them concede it but without guilt or defensiveness of any kind. And some of them don't know what it means. I want to address myself to the latter, because in responding to them I can include all the arguments I would use in dealing with the others.

In asserting that the teaching of reading is essentially a political enterprise, the most obvious question I am asking is, "What is reading good for?" When I ask this question of reading teachers, I am supplied with a wide range of answers. Those who take the low ground will usually say that skill in reading is necessary in order for a youngster to do well in school. The elementary teacher is preparing the youngster for the junior high teacher, who prepares him for the senior high teacher, who, in turn, prepares him for the college teacher, and so on. Now, this answer is true but hardly satisfactory. In fact, it amounts to a description of the *rules* of the school game but says nothing about the purpose of these rules. So, when teachers are pushed a little further, they sometimes answer that the school system, at all levels, makes reading skill a precondition to success because unless one can read well, he is denied access to gainful and interesting employment as an adult. This answer raises at least a half-

dozen political questions, the most interesting of which is whether or not one's childhood education ought to be concerned with one's future employment. I am aware that most people take it as axiomatic that the schooling process should prepare youth for a tranquil entry into our economy, but this is a political view that I think deserves some challenge. For instance, when one considers that the second most common cause of death among adolescents in the U.S. is suicide, or that more people are hospitalized for mental illness than all other illnesses combined, or that one out of every 22 murders in the United States is committed by a parent against his own child, or that more than half of all high school students have already taken habit-forming, hallucinogenic, or potentially addictive narcotics, or that by the end of this year, there will be more than one-million school drop-outs around, one can easily prepare a case which insists that the schooling process be designed for purposes other than vocational training. If it is legitimate at all for schools to claim a concern for the adult life of students, then why not pervasive and compulsory programs in mental health, sex, or marriage and the family? Besides, the number of jobs that require reading skill much beyond what teachers call a "fifth-grade level" is probably quite small and scarcely justifies the massive, compulsory, unrelenting reading programs that characterize most schools.

But most reading teachers would probably deny that their major purpose is to prepare students to satisfy far-off vocational requirements. Instead, they would take the high ground and insist that the basic purpose of reading instruction is to open the student's mind to the wonders and riches of the written word, to give him access to great fiction and poetry, to permit him to function as an informed citizen, to have him experience the sheer pleasure of reading. Now, this is a satisfactory answer indeed but, in my opinion, it is almost totally untrue.

And to the extent that it is true, it is true in a way quite different from anything one might expect. For instance, it is probably true that in a highly complex society, one cannot be governed unless he can read forms, regulations, notices, catalogues, road signs, and the like. Thus, some minimal reading skill is necessary if you are to be a "good citizen," but "good citizen" here means one who can follow the instructions of those who govern him. If you cannot read, you cannot be an obedient citizen. You are also a good citizen if you are an enthusiastic consumer. And so, some minimal reading competence is required if you are going to develop a keen interest in all the products that it is necessary for you to buy. If you do not read, you will be a relatively poor market. In order to be a good and loyal citizen, it is also necessary for you to believe in the myths and superstitions of your society. There-

fore, a certain minimal reading skill is needed so that you can learn what these are, or have them reinforced. Imagine what would happen in a school if a Social Studies text were introduced that described the growth of American civilization as being characterized by four major developments: 1) insurrection against a legally constituted government, in order to achieve a political identity; 2) genocide against the indigenous population, in order to get land; 3) keeping human beings as slaves, in order to achieve an economic base; and 4) the importation of "coolie" labor, in order to build the railroads. Whether this view of American history is true or not is beside the point. It is at least as true or false as the conventional view *and* it would scarcely be allowed to appear unchallenged in a school-book intended for youth. What I am saying here is that an important function of the teaching of reading is to make students accessible to political and historical myth. It is entirely possible that the main reason middle-class whites are so concerned to get lower-class blacks to read is that blacks will remain relatively inaccessible to standard-brand beliefs unless and until they are minimally literate. It just may be too dangerous, politically, for any substantial minority of our population *not* to believe that our flags are sacred, our history is noble, our government is representative, our laws are just, and our institutions are viable. A reading public is a responsible public, by which is meant that it believes most or all of these superstitions, and which is probably why we still have literacy tests for voting.

One of the standard beliefs about the reading process is that it is more or less neutral. Reading, the argument goes, is just a skill. What people read is their own business, and the reading teacher merely helps to increase a student's options. If one wants to read about America, one may read DeToqueville or *The Daily News;* if one wants to read literature, one may go to Melville or Jacqueline Susann. In theory, this argument is compelling. In practice, it is pure romantic nonsense. *The New York Daily News* is the most widely read newspaper in America. Most of our students will go to the grave not having read, of their own choosing, a paragraph of De Toqueville or Thoreau or John Stuart Mill or, if you exclude the Gettysburg Address, even Abraham Lincoln. As between Jacqueline Susann and Herman Melville—well, the less said, the better. To put it bluntly, among every 100 students who learn to read, my guess is that no more than one will employ the process toward any of the lofty goals which are customarily held before us. The rest will use the process to increase their knowledge of trivia, to maintain themselves at a relatively low level of emotional maturity, and to keep themselves simplistically uninformed about the social and political turmoil around them.

Now, there are teachers who feel that, even if what I say is true, the point is nonetheless irrelevant. After all, they say, the world is not perfect. If people do not have enough time to read deeply, if people do not have sensibilities refined enough to read great literature, if people do not have interests broad enough to be stimulated by the unfamiliar, the fault is not in our symbols, but in ourselves. But there is a point of view that proposes that the "fault," in fact, *does* lie in our symbols. Marshall McLuhan is saying that each medium of communication contains a unique metaphysic —that each medium makes special kinds of claims on our senses, and therefore, on our behavior. McLuhan himself tells us that he is by no means the first person to have noticed this. Socrates took a very dim view of the written word, on the grounds that it diminishes man's capacity to memorize, and that it forces one to follow an argument rather than to participate in it. He also objected to the fact that once something has been written down, it may easily come to the attention of persons for whom it was not intended. One can well imagine what Socrates would think about wire-tapping and other electronic bugging devices. St. Ambrose, a prolific book writer and reader, once complained to St. Jerome, another prolific writer and reader, that whatever else its virtues, reading was the most anti-social behavior yet devised by man. Other people have made observations about the effects of communications media on the psychology of a culture, but it is quite remarkable how little has been said about this subject. Most criticism of print, or any other medium, has dealt with the content of the medium; and it is only in recent years that we have begun to understand that each medium, *by its very structure*, makes us do things with our bodies, our senses, and our minds that in the long run are probably more important than any other messages communicated by the medium.

Now that it is coming to an end, we are just beginning to wonder about the powerful biases forced upon us by the Age of the Printed Word. McLuhan is telling us that print is a "hot" medium, by which he means that it induces passivity and anesthetizes almost all our senses except the visual. He is also telling us that electronic media, like the LP record and television, are reordering our entire sensorium, restoring some of our sleeping senses, and, in the process, making all of us seek more active participation in life. I think McLuhan is wrong in connecting the *causes* of passivity and activity so directly to the structure of media. I find it sufficient to say that whenever a new medium—a new communications technology—enters a culture, *no matter what its structure*, it gives us a new way of experiencing the world, and consequently, releases tremendous energies and causes people to seek new ways of organizing their institutions. When Gutenberg announced that he could manufacture books, as he put it, "without the help of reed, stylus, or pen but by wondrous agreement, proportion, and harmony of punches and types," he could scarcely imagine that he was about to become the most important political and social revolutionary of the Second Millennium. And yet, that is what happened. Four hundred and fifty years ago, the printed word, far from being a medium that induced passivity, generated cataclysmic change. From the time Martin Luther posted his theses in 1517, the printing press disseminated the most controversial, inflammatory, and wrenching ideas imaginable. The Protestant Reformation would probably not have occurred if not for the printing press. The development of both capitalism and nationalism were obviously linked to the printing press. So were new literary forms, such as the novel and the essay. So were new conceptions of education, such as written examinations. And, of course, so was the concept of scientific methodology, whose ground rules were established by Descartes in his *Discourse on Reason.* Even today in recently illiterate cultures, such as Cuba, print is a medium capable of generating intense involvement, radicalism, artistic innovation, and institutional upheaval. But in those countries where the printed word has been pre-eminent for over 400 years, print retains very few of these capabilities. Print is not dead, it's just old—and old technologies do not generate new patterns of behavior. For us, print is the technology of convention. We have accommodated our sense to it. We have routinized and even ritualized our responses to it. We have devoted our institutions, which are now venerable, to its service. By maintaining the printed word as the keystone of education, we are therefore opting for political and social stasis.

It is 128 years since Professor Morse transmitted a message electronically for the first time in the history of the planet. Surely it is not too soon for educators to give serious thought to the message he sent: "What hath God wrought?" We are very far from knowing the answers to that question, but we do know that electronic media have released unprecedented energies. It's worth saying that the gurus of the peace movement—Bob Dylan, Pete Seeger, Joan Baez, Phil Ochs, for instance—were known to their constituency mostly as voices on LP records. It's worth saying that Viet Nam, being our first television war, is also the most unpopular war in our history. It's worth saying that Lyndon Johnson was the first president ever to have resigned because of a "credibility gap." It's worth saying that it is now commonplace for post-TV college sophomores to usurp the authority of college presidents and for young parish priests to instruct their bishops in the ways of *both* man and God. And it's also worth saying that black people, after 350 years of bondage, want their freedom—now. Post-television blacks are, indeed, our true *now* generation.

Electronic media are predictably working to unloose disruptive social and political ideas, along with new forms of sensibility and expression. Whether this is being achieved by the structure of the media, or by their content, or by some combination of both, we cannot be sure. But like Gutenberg's infernal machine of 450 years ago, the electric plug is causing all hell to break loose. Meanwhile, the schools are still pushing the old technology; and, in fact, pushing it with almost hysterical vigor. Everyone's going to learn to read, even if we have to kill them to do it. It is as if the schools were the last bastion of the old culture, and if it has to go, why let's take as many down with us as we can.

For instance, the schools are still the principal source of the idea that literacy is equated with intelligence. Why, the schools even promote the idea that *spelling* is related to intelligence! Of course, if any of this were true, reading teachers would be the smartest people around. One doesn't mean to be unkind, but if that indeed is the case, no one has noticed it. In any event, it is an outrage that children who do not read well, or at all, are treated as if they are stupid. It is also masochistic, since the number of non-readers will obviously continue to increase and, thereby, the schools will condemn themselves, by their own definition of intelligence, to an increasing number of stupid children. In this way, we will soon have remedial reading-readiness classes, along with remedial classes for those not yet ready for their remedial reading-readiness class.

The schools are also still promoting

the idea that literacy is the richest source of aesthetic experience. This, in the face of the fact that kids are spending a billion dollars a year to buy LP records and see films. The schools are still promoting the idea that the main source of wisdom is to be found in libraries, from which most schools, incidentally, carefully exclude the most interesting books. The schools are still promoting the idea that the non-literate person is somehow not fully human, an idea that will surely endear us to the non-literate peoples of the world. (It is similar to the idea that salvation is obtainable only through Christianity —which is to say, it is untrue, bigoted, reactionary, and based on untenable premises, to boot.)

Worst of all, the schools are using these ideas to keep non-conforming youth—blacks, the politically disaffected, and the economically disadvantaged, among others—in their place. By taking this tack, the schools have become a major force for political conservatism at a time when everything else in the culture screams for rapid reorientation and change.

What would happen if our schools took the drastic political step of trying to make the new technology the keystone of education? The thought will seem less romantic if you remember that the start of the Third Millennium is only 28 years away. No one knows, of course, what would happen, but I'd like to make a few guesses. In the first place, the physical environment would be entirely different from

what it is now. The school would look something like an electric circus— arranged to accommodate TV cameras and monitors, film projectors, computers, audio- and video-tape machines, radio, and photographic and stereophonic equipment. As he is now provided with textbooks, each student would be provided with his own still-camera, 8 mm. camera, and tape casette. The school library would contain books, of course, but at least as many films, records, video-tapes, audio-tapes, and computer programs. The major effort of the school would be to assist students in achieving what has been called "multi-media literacy." Therefore, speaking, filmmaking, picture-taking, televising, computer-programming, listening, perhaps even music playing, drawing, and dancing would be completely acceptable means of expressing intellectual interest and competence. They would certainly be given weight at least equal to reading and writing.

Since intelligence would be defined in a new way, a student's ability to create an idea would be at least as important as his ability to classify and remember the ideas of others. New evaluation procedures would come into being, and standardized tests— the final, desperate refuge of the print-bound bureaucrat—would disappear. Entirely new methods of instruction would evolve. In fact, schools might abandon the notion of teacher instruction altogether. Whatever disciplines lent themselves to packaged, lineal, and segmented presentation would be offered through a computerized and individualized program. And students could choose from a wide variety of such programs whatever they wished to learn about. This means, among other things, that teachers would have to stop acting like teachers and find something useful to do, like, for instance, helping young people to resolve some of their more wrenching emotional problems.

In fact, a school that put electric circuitry at its center would have to be prepared for some serious damage to all of its bureaucratic and hierarchical arrangements. Keep in mind that hierarchies derive their authority from the notion of unequal access to information. Those at the top have access to more information than those at the bottom. That is in fact why they are at the top and the others, at the bottom. But today those who are at the bottom of the school hierarchy, namely, the students, have access to at least as much information about most subjects as those at the top. At present, the only way those at the top can maintain control over them is by carefully discriminating against what the students know—that is, by labelling what the students know as unimportant. But suppose cinematography was made a "major" subject instead of English literature? Suppose chemotherapy was made a "major" sub-

ject? or space technology? or ecology? or mass communication? or popular music? or photography? or race relations? or urban life? Even an elementary school might then find itself in a situation where the faculty were at the bottom and its students at the top. Certainly, it would be hard to know who are the teachers and who the learners.

And then perhaps a school would become a place where *everybody*, including the adults, is trying to learn something. Such a school would obviously be problem-centered, *and* future-centered, *and* change-centered; and, as such, would be an instrument of cultural and political radicalism. In the process we might find that our youth would also learn to read without pain and with a degree of success and economy not presently known.

I want to close on this thought: teachers of reading represent an important political pressure group. They may not agree with me that they are a sinister political group. But I should think that they would want to ask at least a few questions *before* turning to consider the *techniques* of teaching reading. These questions would be: What is reading good for? What is it better or worse than? What are my motives in promoting it? And the ultimate political question of all,

"Whose side am I on?"

Sesame Street

THE ESTABLISHMENT EASY STREET / Carol Stolley Hastie

Once upon a time, in the peaceable urban kingdom of Media-city, there was a place known far and wide as Sesame Street. Ruled over in benevolent hard-sell by Gordon, Susan and the Childrens' Television Workshop, everyone dwelled in happy co-optation. Mr. Hooper never sold rotten vegetables in his grocery store and Big Bird never flew a fix or left an acid drop-ing. The Monsters were always well-controlled and not in the least terrifying. And the children always did what was expected of them, for this was a carefully designed and thoughtfully structured place. □ For the past year some six million children between the ages of three and five, and at least as many brothers and sisters, have been watching Sesame Street, learning their letters and numbers and, more importantly, learning what was expected of them. A survey of articles and reviews written in the past year reveals almost complete unanimity and uncritical acclaim for the program. In a characteristically effusive and unrestrained promotion of Sesame Street, a report in the February 1970 issue of *Nations Schools,* a journal for educators and administrators, ended with these words: "In almost every respect, Sesame Street is revolutionary in its use of television for mass education—with some profound implications if it is successful." And how is this success to be measured? . . . "If kids can learn to count to ten, the program will have proved itself." □ Despite this stated simplicity, the success of the program is more than counting to ten and learning the alphabet, and the implications are both profound and pervasive. When Gordon gives cookies to the Cookie Monster, putting them in and taking them out of the paper bag, the message is indeed the familiar and comforting message. More cookies equals "More Happy!!" less cookies elicits "Less Happy," and even the untutored and inarticulate Cookie Monster has learned that material acquisition brings pleasure and happiness. And since paper bags break, and sharing is not on the prescribed vocabulary list, he learns also it is best to eat all the cookies right away. But if sharing is not encouraged, neither is open and free interaction between the children and the adults. As Sedulus, writing in *The New Republic,* observed: ". . . everything that happens on Sesame

Street is planned in advance by adults who stick to the lesson no matter what children around them do or say. . . . Grownups initiate everything. And their concerns are trivial." In the McLuhan "classroom without walls" as in the classroom, these trivial concerns are precisely the concerns that prevail and take precedence. Least important among them is the opportunity to judge, to question, to seek information, to analyze and to evaluate.

□ In this context, outrageous distortion is commonplace in the paradoxical wonderland of Sesame Street. The deteriorating habitability of our cities is parodied by Oscar, living in a garbage can singing "I Love Trash," and ideological conflict is always pleasantly resolved by Ernie and Bert in lived-happily-ever-after superficiality. Yet this paradox too is reflective of the adult world that created it. Overwhelmed by the magnitude of our social and economic ills, we turn to the variegated magic of the media— a potent soporific on our sensibilities. Dr. Benjamin Spock, speaking to (and perhaps for) mothers in the July 1970 *Redbook,* summed up our faith in the dream-machine solution by stating: "If such a program can accomplish anything appreciable in improving the educability of the young, it will be worth billions of dollars a year in terms of better trained citizens, fewer unemployables in the next generation, fewer people on welfare, smaller jail populations." In a society where even the best trained and educated of its citizens are unemployed (aerospace engineers) and in jail (priests, professors, at times baby doctors), one cannot help but question any educational program that fails to deal with these contradictions and inconsistencies. Yet over $8 million has already been funded to Sesame Street, considered a "revolutionary innovation," where such failures have become part of its success. □ To understand this "double-think" and "new-speak" context, one should examine the list of the program's financial backers. Of the initial funding, half came from the federal government, primarily Office of Education and Project Head Start. The other half came as contributions from such formidable philanthropies as the Carnegie Corporation, the Ford Foundation and the Corporation for Public Broadcasting. Markle Foundation, fortunes amassed from bituminous coal mining, has currently been supplanted by Post Cereals, a non-nutritive subsidiary of General Foods. The government and big business, who have conspired frequently in the past to pollute the atmosphere, destroy natural resources and maintain the economic disparities which permit malnutrition, inadequate prenatal and child health care and a high incidence of infant mortality are together once again in another vaudeville act titled "suffer unto us little children and we will trample them for good this time!" This burgeoning merger of government and big business in the field of early childhood education deserves more than a cursory glance. Nixon's childcare program, part of the highly touted Family Assistance Plan, opens the way to profit-making daycare centers on government subsidies. Big business concerns that have indicated interest in the daycare "business" include United Fruit, Standard Oil of New Jersey and U.S. Steel. At a recent exploratory meeting attended by these large companies, they were invited to participate in a session called "fleecing the pre-school sheep." Former teachers Ann Cook and Herb Mack, in an incisive article in the journal *Social Policy,* Sept./Oct. 1970 warn: "Sesame Street must be understood, therefore, as yet one more example of the trend. . . . Skills, not children are emphasized; how the child performs, not who he is, or how he thinks becomes the focus. Symptoms, not causes are treated." There is great need at present ". . . (to) examine the relationship between our educational institutions and conditions in our society." □ Sesame Street, not to minimize its innovative and imaginative feature, represents at best a program of limited, skill-oriented objective, offering traditional pedagogy done up in McLuhanesque trappings. It is not a fairyland that these little lambs are led to but a slaughterhouse, where love of each other, of life and of learning is patently and painstakingly destroyed on a network of profit, capital gain and Nielson ratings. For in a capitalist society, even the natural capacity of children to want to learn—to acquire knowledge and explore the world of ideas—becomes a marketable commodity and fair game in the all-but-free enterprise system.

ABOLISHING SCHOOLS

By Ivan Illich

CUERNAVACA, Mexico—The entrenchment of institutionalized schooling in the U.S. social structure was recently checked by the Supreme Court in *Griggs et al. v. Duke Power Company.*

Chief Justice Warren Burger, speaking for a unanimous Court, held that the requirements—as a condition of employment—of either a high-school diploma or of success in a standardized general education test are prohibited under certain conditions by the Civil Rights Act of 1964. This case may set us on the road to the legal recognition that schooling requirements, in and of themselves, constitute a discrimination which hampers social advancement and thus violates public policy.

Tests relevant to job competency are not prohibited by the act, but the employer has to prove that any given standard is necessary for his business. The Court extends the application of the concept of "job relevance" which appears in the legislative history of the 1964 Civil Rights Act to the requirement of a high-school diploma as well. The Court rules that any tests used "must measure the person for the job, not the person in the abstract."

This decision encourages those of us who refuse to believe in the benefits of schooling. It sustains our argument that an individual's economic or social advancement should not be made to depend on his ability or willingness to attend age-specific small-group meetings, under the authority of a teacher, for 500 to 1,000 hours every year. This constitutes the hidden curriculum of schooling which seems irrelevant both to the goals of a liberal educator and to preparation for any specific job.

The Court in *Griggs* tells us that "diplomas and tests are useful servants, but Congress has mandated the common-sense proposition that they are not to become masters of reality." This mandate has now received a big assist from the Court itself. It was gravely needed. The proponents of compulsory schooling have taught us that diplomas and, more recently, general tests are indeed the masters of reality. Americans take this mastery for granted.

I rejoice in *Griggs* because the present Court headed by and spoken for by so American a Chief Justice as Burger has seen fit to demolish this myth. But I rejoice even more, because I see in this decision and in the reasoning on which it is based, implications far wider than the Court had any occasion, in this context, to consider. The decision represents an exemplary breakthrough in the present, worldwide crisis of schools. It is the first juristic step towards the disestablishment of the school—a move as necessary today as the separation of church and state was in 1789.

Employers will find it difficult to show that schooling is a necessary prerequisite for any job requirement. It is easy to show that it is necessarily antidemocratic because it inevitably discriminates.

I believe it can be shown that almost the entire American structure of schooling is irrelevant for gaining competence in the vast majority of American jobs. I also believe it can be shown that our open-minded structure of schooling is inherently discriminatory. It is evidently so for those who are denied a fair part in the school budget because of their color. It is equally discriminatory for anyone who does participate in it without climbing the very last rung.

Michael Crichton worked for his doctorate at the Harvard Medical School with the rather specialized purpose of qualifying to write about the medical profession. He claims that being trained as a medical scientist, as all medical schools train their pupils, has little relevance to medical practice.

Everybody knows that some of the most successful practitioners of the law, present as well as past, have achieved their success without the benefit of any legal schooling whatever. It is even more significant that the legal schooling of some of the greatest jurists of our time (Hugo Black, the late Robert Jackson) was negligible. Justice Story, the father of American legal schooling, had none at all. We also know of cases—Caryl Chessman is just one example—where the confinement, discipline and leisure provided inmates of penitentiaries with unusual opportunity to become competent lawyers. Schooling may perhaps be a useful servant, but not when, as today, we have let it become the master of reality and of ourselves.

CUERNAVACA, Mexico—The hidden curriculum of compulsory schooling discriminates by its very nature. It serves as a means to apportion scarce resources and jobs to the person who qualifies for them through the largest consumption of public funds. It makes out of the loser a failure. Compulsory schooling establishes the presumption that the person who has consumed more professional treatment under the supervision of certified teachers is therefore socially more useful—and unquestionably entitled to the choice privileges society has to offer.

The social structure as a whole has organized itself into operating departments, fitting various levels of dropouts. Persons who have failed, for whatever reason, to accumulate a certain number of packaged units of schooling are automatically excluded from positions whose level within the structure provides money, power, and social prestige in an ascending order. This happens, no matter how irrelevant the prescribed schooling may be to the jobs in question.

One of the diabolic features of this system is that it teaches the individual who is caught up in it to discriminate against himself. He is taught to disqualify himself as incompetent, uneducable or unworthy of a job for which he has no formal credentials. The hidden curriculum of schooling trains him to know his place. The discriminatory nature of certified schooling as the puberty rite of a technological tribe can be neatly illustrated by the organization of school itself. No one may teach in a public grade school or high school, no matter how great his abilities as a teacher, or what his mastery of his subject, unless he has been certified as schooled in the theory of teaching and the bureaucracy of schools.

If this structure is not in fact designed to assign privilege, disqualify the self-learner, and train clients for an economy based on increasing dependence on futile service but instead meant to serve the communication of skills and the awakening of political discernment and critical judgment, then it has ceased to be a useful servant. It has become the master of reality.

In yesterday's article I expressed optimism as to the impact of the Supreme Court's decision in the *Griggs* case. This optimism might seem extreme to some people, even to people favorably inclined to my over-all view of the need to de-school society. They may question the foundation of my hope that *Griggs* set us on our way to the legal recognition of the inherently discriminatory nature of schooling or of tests which are calibrated by it.

True, *Griggs* is limited to the problem of discrimination against certain clearly definable classes. True, it is limited to the application of a particular statute. But an earlier Court, in *Brown v. Board of Education*, managed to prohibit a clearly undesirable discrimination without the aid of a statute, on the basis of constitutional guarantees of due process, and due process is guaranteed to all citizens, not just to those who belong to particularly vulnerable classes. May we not hope that a Court as daring as the Burger Court may extend its present ruling further to diminish the discrimination inherent in our system of publicly established and compulsory schooling? May we not hope Congress together may eventually abolish the mastery over contemporary reality of an overgrown institution of past centuries?

If I were of a less sunny disposition, I should worry more about social scientists who will be employed in the meantime to "prove" the relevance of schooling requirements that employers may see fit to impose on prospective employees.

HIGH SCHOOL WOMEN: TWO VIEWS

THE SUBURBAN SCENE by Connie Dvorkin

I was born March 4, 1955, in Doctor's Hospital in New York City. All my life I have lived in an unincorporated area of the town of Greenburgh, though my mailing address is Scarsdale and the school district is Edgemont, Greenburgh Union Free District No. 6. I am in the eighth grade and have been a pacifist and a vegetarian since October 1968. I live in a Republican stronghold and the conservatism that usually goes along with that is very evident here. My prison's name is Edgemont Junior–Senior High School, grades 7–12, with approximately 850 inmates. I am the so-called secretary of Edgemont Students for Action to which all the activist radicals and more radical liberals more or less belong.

I think I first heard of the Women's Liberation Movement on WBAI (Radio Free New York), most likely on "Radio Unnameable." Like Eldridge Cleaver in *Soul on Ice,* I never realized how oppressed I was until someone brought it into the open. I wrote a letter asking for some literature on the Women's Liberation Movement that I could read. It was for a Social Studies report that never materialized. But that is irrelevant like school is. The important thing is that I read the stuff and immediately agreed with everything. Ironically the very night I was reading it I was babysitting and watching TV. The show, "I Love Lucy," was an episode where the two women were to be equal to the men for one night—no courtesies "due to a woman," no shit like that for *one* night, eating out at a restaurant—and they couldn't do it. They *had* to depend on their husbands. They couldn't face life out in front, they had to hide behind their husbands' names and souls. The kids I was sitting for laughed their asses off, and I realized that I would have, too, five months earlier.

Now, with awakened eyes, I could see all the brainwashing of my sisters that goes on at school. It starts almost the instant they are born, by their mothers, and by fathers encouraging the boys to take an interest in cars, baseball, etc., and discouraging girls. A girl I know who was always a "tomboy," now, in the compulsory intramural volley ball we have with the boys, always seems to hang back and doesn't seem as "boyish" as she always is. I feel particularly sorry for the snobs or society "chicks" of my grade. Everybody knows the type. They will probably never hear the gospel and if they do would never accept it. I once thought it was "fun" to wear miniskirts (I had a really good figure then, but no longer worry about that shit) and look good for boys and men generally. I rationalized, "Why not? It's fun and they like it." I read all the literature on women's liberation and still wore skirts. But then I heard about the momentous decision by the judge who said that principals could no longer tell girls what to wear, and I went up to my principal; he said he couldn't stop me, but he thought slacks "were in bad taste." Anyway, since that, I've worn dresses or skirts about five times—one time it was to the Passover Seder. Since I began wearing pants I have discovered two things: (1) I feel more equal with boys, and (2) I no longer have to worry as to how my legs are placed and all that bullshit as I had to when I wore skirts. I no longer feel myself fighting other girls for the attention of boys, and am generally much more at ease with the world.

In seventh and eighth grade you have the trimester along with the regular report card. The trimester consists of three subjects—Music, Art, and Home Ec "for girls" and Shop "for boys." I began thinking about a groovy idea—taking Shop instead of Home Ec. So I talked it over with my mother (whom I consider far more liberal than my father) who sent a note off to the junior high girls' guidance counselor. She said I couldn't, but she didn't really tell me why. Then my mother sent a letter off to my principal, repeating that I wished to take Shop and could he please voice his opinion on that. Three weeks later his reply came back. I thought this was a deliberate delay tactic on his part. He is a very clever conservative always having this fantasy that he's on the students' side, which of course is bullshit. Anyway, in his letter he cited several reasons why I couldn't take Shop: 1) it was traditional that a girl took Home Ec, 2) there wouldn't be enough room in Shop for one more pupil, 3) the teacher in Shop would be overworked. He knew that we would go over him to the school supervisor, Dr. Larson, so he sent Larson a copy of his letter. I obtained an appointment with Dr. Larson five days before Home Ec was supposed to start. I explained to him my reasons why I didn't want to take Home Ec. I said I thought that the school system is the mold for people in this society and that in giving a course in Home Ec just for girls and Shop just for boys they were trying to mold girls into being "homemakers" and boys into what molds people thought define "masculinity." I was very impressed by the interview because Dr. Larson, outside of one understanding teacher, was the only school official who took me seriously and listened to me while discussing school affairs. Well, Dr. Larson passed on the request to the district superintendent, Dr. Russo. Larson sent me Xerox copies of the letter to Russo and Russo's letter to an official up at Albany, so I could trust him. Word was passed along to me that nobody in Albany wanted to touch the issue, and they finally sent down an edict that I could do what I wanted to.

While this was going on Home Ec and Shop had already started and I was given a Study Hall during the period that Home Ec/Shop was in. I requested this since I am a pacifist and do not believe in confrontation politics. I wasn't trigger-happy for a confrontation like many SDSers are. (I don't mean to offend any SDS people reading this. Some of my best friends are in SDS.)

The first day I started Shop I was very apprehensive about how the boys were going to react to me being in the class. I have two very good friends in that class (including Dr. Larson's son Mark), and they congratulated me on my success. One of the boys is very condescending toward me, always speaking in the patronizing, gentle voice that really makes me angry. "Connie, let me help you," they say. "Well! I just want to tell you—fuck you, damn it, and go home and stop farting out all that chickenshit, man, just quit it!" I say furiously, but silently. But Shop is fun if the "teacher" isn't paying attention because you can goof all you want to. One thing I realized when I walked into the room the first day was that I could *never* cut, because my absence would be too noticeable.

The whole scene at a suburban school I realize is different than a city school in many ways, of which the maybe most important is that Edgemont is very isolated from other schools and the things you hear about other schools are from either the *New York Times* (who believes them?) and the lower-county paper, the *Reporter Dispatch,* based in White Plains (truthfully called the Distorter Repatch). And you can guess from their nickname what they print. The whole middle-class values, including the meek, passive, "feminine" girl and the strong, overpowering, "masculine" boy are very evident here as in any suburb but especially here since Westchester is such a wealthy suburb-county. The whole bit with the school dances where the boys ask the girls helps brainwash girls and boys into thinking that girls' places in the social caste of a social life and school and elsewhere are lower than boys. As a girl, I often find myself tongue-tied when trying to argue points with older boys, but can talk with boys my age successfully.

I am sure some people when reading this will say, "But surely there's a contradiction in Connie being a pacifist and trying to break down the old definition of femininity as passivity!" I became a pacifist simply because I do not believe that wars solve anything but only create new ones such as new hates, refugees, etc. That is also why I think that Joan Baez is correct in saying all the New Left has is anger and that anger doesn't solve anything just as war doesn't. (I assume I am misquoting her out of context and putting things in her mouth that she never said.) My belief as a vegetarian has grown out of my belief as a pacifist and a lover of life.

ON DE-SEGREGATING STUYVESANT HIGH by Alice de Rivera

Before I went to John Jay High School I hadn't realized how bad the conditions were for students. One of the things that changed my outlook was being involved with the hostilities of the New York City teacher strikes in the fall of 1968. Students were trying to open the school and the teachers were preventing them. I was disillusioned by the low-quality, high-pay teaching we received afterwards, and soon became involved with expressing my discontent.

It was then I found that students had no rights. We had no freedom of the press: many controversial articles were removed from the newspapers by the teacher-editors. We were not allowed to distribute leaflets or newspapers inside our school building, so that press communication was taken away from us. We also had no freedom of speech. Many teachers would put us down in class for our political ideas and then would not let us answer their charges. If we tried to talk with other students during a free period about political issues, we were told to stop. The school was a prison —we were required by state law to be there, but when we were there we had no rights. We had to carry ID cards and passes. We could be suspended; we were considered guilty before proven innocent.

It was this treatment which made me as a student want to change the schools. When I talked to students from other public high schools in the city, I found they had been oppressed within the schools in much the same way.

I have been writing about the student's plight in general because it was my first encounter with oppression. It is such a familiar experience to me now, that I think I can try to define it. Oppression, to me, is when people are not allowed to be themselves. I encountered this condition a second time when I realized *woman's* plight in the high schools. And for the second time I tried to help change the schools so that I and other girls would not be hurt.

The first time it really occurred to me that I was oppressed as a woman was when I began to think of what I was going to be when I was older. I realized I had no real plans for the future—college, maybe, and after that was a dark space in my mind. In talking and listening to other girls, I found that they had either the same blank spot in their minds or were planning on marriage. If not that, they figured on taking a job of some sort *until* they got married.

The boys that I knew all had at least some slight idea in their minds of what career or job they were preparing for. Some prepared for careers in science and math by going to a specialized school. Others prepared for their later jobs as mechanics, electricians, and other tradesmen in vocational schools. Some just did their thing in a regular, zoned high school.

It seemed to me that I should fill the blank spot in my mind as the boys were able to do, and I decided to study science (biology, in particular) much more intensively. It was then that I encountered one of the many blocks which stand in the woman student's way: discrimination against women in the specialized science and math high schools in the city.

Many years before women in New York State had won their right to vote (1917), a school was established for those high-school students who wished to specialize in science and math. Naturally it was not co-ed, for women were not regarded legally or psychologically as people. This school, Stuyvesant High School, was erected in 1903. In 1956, thirty-nine years after New York women earned the right to vote, the school was renovated; yet no provision was made for girls to enter.

There are only two other high schools in New York which specialize in science and math: Brooklyn Technical, a school geared towards engineering, and Bronx High School of Science. Brooklyn Tech moved from the warehouse, where its male-only classes were started, into a modern building in 1933. It was renovated in 1960, yet still no provision was made for girls.

This left only Bronx Science. Bronx High School of Science is the only school where girls can study science and math intensively—it is co-ed. It became so in 1946, the year it moved into a new building. However, although it admits girls, it still discriminates against them; it admits only one girl to every two boys.

Out of these three schools I could try out for only one. This one, Bronx Science, is one and one-half hours travel time from my home. It presents very stiff competition because of the discriminatory policy which allows only a certain number of girls to enter, and also because all the girls who would otherwise be trying out for Stuyvesant or Brooklyn Tech have Bronx Science as their only alternative. I became disgusted with this, not only for my sake, but for all the girls who hadn't become scientists or engineers because they were a little less than brilliant or had been put down by nobody having challenged those little blank spots in their minds. After talking about it with my parents and friends, I decided to open up Stuyvesant and challenge the Board of Education's traditional policy.

I took my idea to Ramona Ripston, co-director of the National Emergency Civil Liberties Committee, and she accepted it warmly. Pretty soon I became involved in trying to get an application for the entrance exam to Stuyvesant filled out and sent. It was turned down and we—NECLC, my parents, and I—went to court against the principal of Stuyvesant and the Board of Ed.

The day on which we went to court was the day before the entrance exam was scheduled to be given. The Board of Ed granted me the privilege of taking the test for Bronx Science (which is the same as the one given for Stuyvesant), and the judge recognized that the results of this test would be used in another court hearing to resolve whether on not I would be admitted. Five days after the other students had received their results, we found out that I had passed for entrance into both Stuyvesant and Bronx Science.

We went to court again a couple of months later, in April. Our Judge, Jawn A. Sandafer, seemed receptive to our case, but he reserved his decision. Later we were told that he wished an open hearing for May 13. This was a great break for us because if what the judge needed was public support, we had many important people who were willing to argue in my favor. However, on April 30 the New York City Board of Education voted to admit me to Stuyvesant High School in the Fall. The superintendent had wanted to continue the court fight.

This seemed a victory to us at first, but in actuality it would have been better if we could have continued the case and received a court order. We hoped to establish that public funds could not be used to support institutions of learning which discriminate against women. Such a ruling would have been the key to opening up the other sexually segregated high schools in New York City.

There are a great many battles yet to be fought. Aside from being discouraged to study for a career, women are discouraged from preparing for jobs involving anything *but* secretarial work, beauty care, nursing, cooking, and the fashion industry. During my fight over Stuyvesant, I investigated the whole high-school scene, and found that out of the twenty-seven vocational high schools in the city, only *seven* are co-ed. The boys' vocational schools teach trades in electronics, plumbing, carpentry, foods, printing (another example of Board of Ed traditional policy—there is hardly any work for a hand-typesetter today), etc. The girls are taught to be beauticians, secretaries, or health aides. This means that if a girl is seeking entrance to a vocational school, she is pressured to feel that certain jobs are masculine and others feminine. She is forced to conform to the Board of Education's image of her sex. At the seven co-ed vocational schools, boys can learn clerical work, food preparation, and beauty care along with the girls. But the courses that would normally be found in a boys' school are not open to girls. There are only two schools where a girl can prepare for a "masculine" job. Charles Evans Hughes High School in Manhattan is coed for teaching technical electronics. Newtown High School offers an academic pre-engineering course of study for boys and girls. However, this school is zoned for the Borough of Queens only.

In conclusion, there are three types of schools, twenty-nine in number, that the Board of Ed has copped out on. These schools are composed of the specialized science and math school Brooklyn Tech, twenty vocational schools which teach students their trade according to what sex they are, and the eight traditionally non-co-ed academic schools.

These eight academic schools are zoned schools which admit only boys or only girls. The argument against these schools is that "separate but equal" is not equal (as established with regard to race in the Brown Deci-

sion). The psychological result of the school which is segregated by sex—
only because of tradition—is to impress upon girls that they are only
"flighty females" who would bother the boys' study habits (as a consequence of girls not being interested in anything but the male sex). This
insinuates immaturity on the part of girls—and certainly produces it in
both sexes. A boy who has never worked with a girl in the classroom is
bound to think of her as his intellectual inferior, and will not treat her as if
she had any capacity for understanding things other than child care and
homemaking. Both sexes learn to deal with each other as non-people. It
really messes up the growth of a person's mind.

Out of the sixty-two high schools in New York City, twenty-nine are now
sexually segregated. I believe that it is up to the girls to put pressure on

are children

Are children people? Quite simply, that is the controversy which is now rag-
ing between public school authorities on the one hand and increasing numbers
of students on the other. Certain guarantees of political freedom exist without
question for all Americans. Prominent among these are the rights to free
speech, assembly and expression, and the right to fair and just procedures in
all government dealings—what lawyers call "due process of law."

But there are several classes of Americans who, solely because of their special status, are denied their rights. In the army, for example, people—merely
as a consequence of their special status as soldiers—normally have their First
Amendment rights seriously curtailed and their rights to due process thoroughly compromised. The rationale for such denials is that soldiers are not
like ordinary people and that the usual standards of liberty must fall for the
sake of military discipline.

The schools—the only other compulsory institution in America besides the
military—similarly deny that the Bill of Rights applies to them. In public
schools, people—merely as a consequence of their special status as children—
normally have their First Amendment rights of speech, assembly and expression almost totally abrogated, and their rights to due process limited or ignored. The rationale for such denials is that children are not people and that
the usual standards of liberty must fall for the sake of school discipline.

the Board of Education to change this situation. I myself cannot live with oppression.

All girls have been brought up by this society never being able to be themselves—the school system has reinforced this. My desire at this time is to change the educational situation to benefit *all* the students. But I'm afraid changes *could* be made that benefited male students, leaving the status of females pretty much as it is. Female students share the general oppressive conditions forced upon everyone by the System's schools, plus a special psychological discrimination shown to women by the schools, the teachers, *and* their fellow students. So, since I don't want *my* issues to get swallowed up in the supposed "larger" issues, I'm going to make women's liberation the center of my fight.

IRA GLASSER

But if, as U.S. Supreme Court Justice Abe Fortas said in the *Gault* decision, "neither the 14th Amendment nor the Bill of Rights is for adults only," then a major civil liberties problem exists in our public schools. Indeed, the number of complaints from students and their parents about violations of students' civil liberties by school authorities is growing at an alarming rate. Not a day passes at NYCLU's offices without the receipt of at least 3–5 complaints. These complaints fall roughly into three categories: 1) Repression of Individual Expression (mainly long hair and dress styles) ; 2) Denial of Due Process; and 3) Harassment and Suppression of Political Activity.

The long hair and dress style cases have included some of the most bizarre and arbitrary standards imaginable; denials of due process have involved things like summary suspensions, punitive transfers to other schools, hearings without benefit of counsel, police interrogations of young children on school property, and illegal searches and seizures. Harassment of political activity has taken many forms, including suspension for circulating leaflets or petitions, repression of student clubs organized for political purposes, prohibition of armbands or other political insignia and reprisals for participation in protest demonstrations. . . . the central questions remain invariant: does the Bill of Rights apply to the schools? Are children people?

HOT time in a COLD town

NEW YORK CIVIL LIBERTIES UNION

In early January [1968], an extraordinary movement of arctic air kept New York City at near-zero temperatures for more than a week.

In an effort to ward off the unusual cold, many parents sent their daughters to school wearing slacks instead of miniskirts. It seemed like a reasonable thing to do. But the principals of the New York City High Schools, ever alert to the seeds of sedition, thought otherwise: between January 10 and January 12, NYCLU received more than 500 complaints from girls who had been suspended or prevented from attending classes in at least seven New York City High Schools—Evander Childs, Seward Park, George Washington, Theodore Roosevelt, Martin Van Buren, Forest Hills and John Bowne. Their crime? They wore slacks, aided and abetted by their parents. Clearly, this was mass action that could not be taken lightly. As one principal said, "If we let them wear slacks, that will lead to bikinis, which would leave the navel exposed." Obviously, the revolution of rising expectations had hit the New York City public schools.

As the NYCLU telephone switchboard began to clog, legislative director Neil Fabricant whipped into action. First he exhausted both himself and his administrative remedies by sending a telegram to four of the principals involved, reminding them that in the *Dalrymple* case, March 14, 1966, New York State Commissioner of Education Allen had reinstated a girl suspended from school for wearing slacks. "The Board of Education," said Allen, "does not have the power to compel students, at the peril of expulsion from school, to wear a uniform or particular kind of clothing."

In broad language, Commissioner Allen made it quite clear that the only bases on which student appearance could be regulated were: (1) that the appearance of the student could be shown to be educationally distracting; or (2) that the item of clothing was in some way dangerous. The Commissioner went on to give concrete examples and then ruled that slacks specifically can not be regulated under these criteria, nor can long hair, in and of itself be considered disruptive.

Informed of the Commissioner's ruling, the principals chose to ignore it, which was hardly surprising. During the past few months, complaints by students and their parents about arbitrary impositions of personal taste by school principals have been received by NYCLU at the rate of several each day. We usually handle such complaints by telephoning the principal involved. In almost all cases, the response we get is rude, arrogant and proudly defiant of anyone—including Commissioner Allen—who has the temerity to suggest that the law should apply to high school principals.

The following facts seem clear: (1) The law concerning dress codes in public schools is unambiguously settled by Commissioner Allen's rulings.

(2) Many principals are openly flouting the law and in the process depriving students of both their civil liberties and—perhaps more relevantly—their right to education.

(3) In no case that has come to our attention has there been a showing of either distraction or danger; indeed, virtually all the rulings have verged on the absurd. In several schools, turtlenecks have been banned. In at least one school, turtlenecks have been banned for boys but not for girls. A Queens high school principal has banned blue jeans but allowed all other colors. And in Brooklyn, one principal has established a means test in his school: boys may not wear blue jeans and girls may not wear slacks unless they can establish that they are too poor to own "appropriate" clothing. In none of these instances is there even a shred of legitimate purpose in such regulations.

(4) NYCLU has been unable to find an effective remedy for this situation. Principals continue to behave

outrageously and illegally and higher authorities seem reluctant to compel them to obey the law. Commissioner Allen has declined to issue a general policy statement on the ground that his position in *Dalrymple* is well-known. And ignored. The Suprintendent of Schools in New York City has on several occasions failed even to acknowledge NYCLU complaints.

(5) If no effective relief is forthcoming from within the school system, NYCLU intends to institute civil damage suits against individual principals. It may be the only way.

There are some civil libertarians who feel that too much effort is expended by the Civil Liberties Union on long hair and dress code cases, that these infringements are relatively minimal, if not trivial, and that it does not become serious civil libertarians to get so heated up over a marginal and perhaps frivolous issue.

Yet the insane fact remains: hundreds of students all over the state—and indeed all over the country—are being harassed, obstructed from receiving education, and quite seriously punished by the loss of grades, diplomas and college recommendations for refusing to conform on a minor, nonessential matter of personal taste that is wholly unrelated to legitimate educational purposes. These cases are not trivial because the punitive effects on students are not trivial. It is the

principals, and not the students or their defenders who are behaving with monumental childishness and colossal irresponsibility.

But there is another reason why the complaints involving long hair and dress regulations are important. School authorities regulate hair styles and dress for the same reason the army does: to create an atmosphere in which obedience and discipline will flourish. Individual expression, to the extent that it fractures the context of conformity, is a threat to authority, which in the end is antithetical to freedom. Personal appearance is one of the most obvious manifestations of social control or the lack of it. The army knows that full well, and it appears that school principals know it too. As one New York City principal recently said, "If I allow long hair and slacks and turtlenecks, discipline will break down. And you can't have a school without discipline."

Thus the long hair and dress code cases emerge as a symptom of a much larger problem: the suppression of substantial civil liberties in the schools. For it is now clear . . . that violations of First Amendment and due process rights are widespread in the schools. And it just may be that dress codes are the mechanism used to create the context which makes such violations more likely.

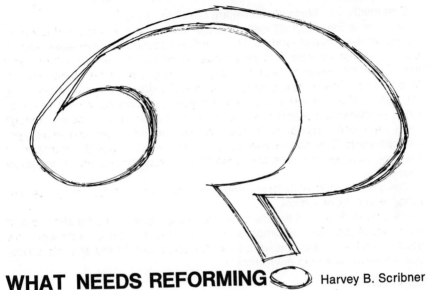

WHAT NEEDS REFORMING

Harvey B. Scribner

As educational and social institutions, the schools of big-city America are in serious trouble.

The educational problem is exemplified most readily by the record of academic failure that is built every day by large numbers of urban youth—a chronic trouble historically. The social dimension of the trouble is seen most easily by the increasing demand for police and civilian guards to maintain order in many city schools. Thus do the schools not only display their educational troubles, but also reflect serious social illness; and thus do the problems of the society help to dramatize, by the stationing of guards in the schools, the inherently compulsory nature of schooling.

Some of the troubles of the schools will be resolved only when the social ills of the nation are cured. But many other troubles—of an educational nature—will remain until the schools begin to reshape themselves in a number of fundamental ways.

Basic change in the style and content of the schools—in the way education is defined, measured and packaged—is imperative. On that, there is relatively little disagreement.

The disagreement is over the kind of change. Does school disruption, for example, demand more security guards—or better and more varied educational programs and improved counseling services, as well as schools (and a society) that more clearly practice all the rules of democracy? There is, moreover, uncertainty over how much basic change is possible.

In short, the question that confronts urban public education is not *whether* to change, but *what* to change, and how to secure a wide enough consensus to accomplish any reforms at all without irreparably damaging the fragile concept of public education in the process.

Essentially, two kinds of reform are possible.

The first is the kind that was sought with a burst of energy and good intention in the nineteen-sixties. Then, with a substantially increased spending power, the schools reformed large elements of the curriculum, most notably in mathematics and the physical sciences; established and intensified all kinds of new programs for special groups of youngsters, from the poor to the creative and the handicapped; purchased more and newer kinds of classroom equipment; constructed hundreds of modern (though often traditional) school buildings, and assembled larger and more specialized staffs. The nature and scope of the effort raises the question of whether, as a result, education came to be overprofessionalized and overspecialized.

The second kind of reform—and the kind most needed today—is less tangible and more radical.

It would strike not at the trappings on the periphery of education, but at the heart of the learning process. It would seek to deal directly with how youngsters learn, and thus with how (for good and ill) the schools devise and revise the learning environment.

STEREOTYPES CHALLENGED

The language would include options, alternatives, flexibility, diversity, individuality, choice and institutional self-renewal. The goal would be to destroy stereotypes on which many (perhaps most) schools presently tend to operate; that learning and education are the exclusive domain of the schools; that knowledge is dispensed exclusively by the teacher; that learning is confined to the age span of five to eighteen, the hours of 9 to 3, five days of the week and ten months of the year; that Fact is logically divisible into permanent academic compartments; that education consists of the taking of courses and the accumulation of credits; and that schools, planned and managed by adults, are rightfully empowered to determine the student's path to becoming educated.

Reform in the nineteen-seventies ought to be directed at the structures and the systems of education. If the kind of reform undertaken in the nineteen-sixties proved anything, it proved that for all the spending and all the effort, and despite the successes that were achieved, the basic character of the schools was changed very little.

LABELS UNIMPORTANT

At the elementary level, we need first to identify those specific though broadly defined provisions that are essential to learning, and then to construct programs including those provisions. It is not the label of the program—the British infant school, the open classroom, Montessori, the "traditional" school—that is critical. It is whether the program—whatever its label—is conducive to learning and human growth.

We need to decide whether we believe it is imperative to inculcate individual responsibility and a sense of dignity and self-respect; whether we want teachers to *teach at* youngsters, or to enable them to learn; whether we believe learning is a matter of discovery or indoctrination; whether we believe schools should foster personal diversity, or homogeneity; whether we believe learning is a part of growing up, or a separate experience and thus properly institutionalized in the school; whether we will tolerate and compensate for differences in learning rates and learning styles; and whether we will seek to capitalize on the proven fact that students of all ages learn a great deal from each other, both in and beyond the classroom.

There is nothing "wrong" with traditional classrooms except that there are too many of them—or, to put it another way, too few alternatives to them.

MORE OPTIONS NEEDED

The traditional style of teaching can be as effective as any other kind, and it is—for many kids. But there are other ways of teaching, too, and given the diversity of students in this country, particularly in the cities, there is good reason to provide a variety of kinds of classrooms, and to let the parents, with counsel and advice from the school, pick and choose among them.

At the secondary school level, reform ought to be directed at the educational bill of fare. More options, more alternatives should be the goal. Since students are individuals, there is every reason to provide individualized programs of learning, especially in the high schools where students have some sense of personal interest and a moderately developed style of learning.

If a student learns best by working, let him work. If he learns well independently, set him free with a program planned in cooperation with his school. If he would benefit by a year away from school, let him, with his parents' permission, travel or work; and on his reentry into the classroom, let his experience be given appropriate academic credit.

Are we in the business of granting diplomas on the basis of years in school or acquired knowledge? The answer is all too obvious, and that precisely is the reason that the system of granting credit needs drastic and immediate revision, as does the pattern of programs on which the credit system rests.

There are critics who say the schools are oppressive, inflexible and monopolistic. And there are many parents in many communities, especially in the heart of the cities, who say the schools are bureaucratic and unresponsive. The criticism is too widespread and too deeply felt to be ignored and brushed aside.

"LIFE-FORCE" AT WORK

The level of dissatisfaction with the schools of the cities is too high, and probably growing. The schools, as a result, are in pain. But pain, at least, is evidence of life.

As Gloria Channon, a New York City teacher, has said, turmoil and dissatisfaction and disruption are not all destructive and all dangerous. For they represent, she said, "the life-force which is exploding from our dry, long-buried, long-dormant seed, the life-force that threatens us with salvation."

The point is that the articulation of dissatisfaction is the prerequisite to change, and that the discontented society is usually the society that possesses the capacity for self-criticism and the will to progress.

In the cities, the salvation of public education demands rapid changes in organizational structure, school policy, course content, the style of teaching and learning, and the systematic pattern of programs that schooling presently comprises.

It demands acceptance of the basic concepts that education antedates and transcends the school, that school effectiveness is in part a product of school responsiveness, that diversity of program is a legitimate institutional goal, and that the overriding priority in all matters of educational policy is the welfare of the learner.

If the schools of the cities are to be radically altered in structure and style in the seventies, it will be the result of collaborative efforts among classroom teachers and policy-makers, school people and laymen, politicians, community groups, critics and students.

DECENTRALIZATION

City schools are often thought of as "a different kind of animal." But the most important characteristic about urban education may well be its similarity to public education in other settings. Curriculum, methods, materials, behavioral norms and the generally fuzzy, genteel and ill-defined goals of urban education are those which are traditional and prevalent throughout the entire country.

As a result of this similarity, I would maintain, we can learn from the massive failure of big city school systems much about what is wrong with schools any- and (almost) everywhere else. That is, the city schools are a glass magnifying the flaws of

At least in the schools of the cities, I see little possibility of imposing programs of reform, however progressive, from the top by administrative fiat.

Nor do I see much chance of widespread change at the grassroots level of the classroom, until teachers sense that they have the freedom to change without fear of subtle (or not-so-subtle) punishment. No matter how determined and skilled the classroom teacher, unless the atmosphere in the schools encourages change and tolerates the associated risks, the influence of inhibition is likely to prevail.

I suspect that collaboration for change will tend to be more pragmatic than ideological, and that it will develop issue by issue. New kinds of teacher training will have its advocates; new kinds of programs will have others; new systems of school governance will have still others.

But in the schools of the cities, it seems likely that group effort will be required. For the stakes of fundamental reform and the political nature of the populous city virtually ensure that teachers, policy-makers, parents and citizen groups can no longer go it alone with the expectation of producing change that will directly touch life in the classroom.

AND URBAN SCHOOLS

Mark R. Shedd

general educational practice to such a degree that they cannot be glossed over.

I believe there are two fundamental reasons why this is so:

1 / The sheer mass of urban systems has created bureaucracies which convert instructional tradition, educational clichés and general peda-gogic inertia into a stifling philosophical and procedural rigidity.

2 / The pupils of urban systems, particularly low-income pupils (white and Negro), are unable or unwilling to conform to our commonplace and usually complacent notions of what children and/or schools should be. The results cast in bold relief the ir-

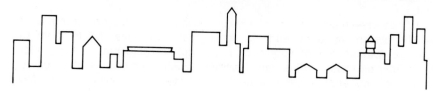

relevance of so much of the school experience to the basic concerns and needs of children and young people.

Thus, while this article will devote itself to a brief discussion of certain educational problems in an urban context, it would perhaps be well to bear in mind what a study of urban education can tell us about schools in general.

LACK OF RESPONSIVENESS

The most fundamental crisis in urban education today, as I see it, is a failure to produce organizations capable of adapting the program of a given school to the needs of a given child.

Urban bureaucracies have tended generally to codify and enforce systemic values which divert attention from the presumed focus of education—the classroom. Symbolically, children and teachers rarely appear on the tables of organization. Centrally dictated curriculum and personnel assignments; central office monopoly on status positions; centrally formulated rules and procedures, which gain the force of moral dicta; these are the identifying marks of large school systems.

Uniformity becomes an implicit goal; guidelines become mental corrals; individual cases are handled by general precepts; caution and acquiescence are the keys to survival and promotion; communication is supplanted by directive; interaction is confused with convention and stability is equated with stolidity. And so on. The net effect is that those at the bottom of the bureaucratic pyramid—principals and teachers—become clerks. And children, who bear the total weight of the structure, are not so much educated as processed. Ironically, as one principal put it, "We'd have a great school system if it weren't for the kids."

But there are rumblings around the country that neither students (particularly at the college level) nor parents (particularly in the ghettos) nor teachers (with increasingly militant organizations) are given to tolerating the lack of responsiveness and the general insularity of big city systems. Their combined pressures, perhaps more than any other factors, may force needed changes.

NEED FOR DECENTRALIZATION

One inevitable conclusion is that the bureaucracies of big city schools must either transform themselves internally or be dismantled by assault from the outside. This means decentralization; decentralization is an attempt to disperse the *emphasis* as well as the functions and powers from the central office to the individual schools and classrooms in order to transform the experience of school for the thousands of youngsters who now reject it.

The details of decentralization will vary from situation to situation, but there are a number of common problems. These include distinguishing between decentralizing certain personnel, operations and powers, and deciding at what level each should be decentralized. Critical to these decisions is whether or not to loosen central control over budget making and control.

One might, for instance, limit central office control of funds merely to granting an allotment based on the number of pupils in each school, thus leaving the allocation of expenditures to the principal of each school. This implies a larger decision: whether to decentralize all of the critical functions and powers of a school system or simply the less essential clerical operations which clutter a central office. The implementation of a decentralization plan obviously must proceed cautiously in order to avoid the negative side effects of individual school autonomy: anarchy, on the one hand, and a proliferation of autocracies on the other—without returning to a stifling central control policy.

But above and beyond, and prior to, each of these delicate and complex matters, there is a more fundamental philosophical question. Is decentralization merely viewed as a way of increasing efficiency by reducing central overload, or is it seen as a way to transform radically both the system and the *process* of education which it determines? Both are undoubtedly necessary, but forced with a choice, I would opt for the latter.

The structural inability of school systems to achieve meaningful metamorphoses perhaps explains why so many attempts to upgrade urban schools have been frustrated. I refer to the apparent failure to make a dent in the problem of "cultural deprivation" by saturating schools with cultural enrichment programs, reduced pupil-teacher ratios, team teaching arrangements, and the whole array of compensatory education programs which were so dismally reviewed by the U.S. Civil Rights Commission study of *Racial Isolation in the Public Schools*. To oversimplify, I suspect the failures of such approaches result from feeding them into—or tacking them onto—a dysfunctional system which overwhelms, swallows or pollutes them.

The same quagmire, I suspect, lies in wait for various schemes for improving instruction (team teaching, programmed learning, computer-assisted instruction); for integrating schools (educational parks, Princeton plans, massive busing); and for teacher education (microteaching; closed circuit training laboratories; on the job, in-service training); unless there are fundamental changes in the operational values and procedures of educational systems, these innovations will wither on the vine. It is not

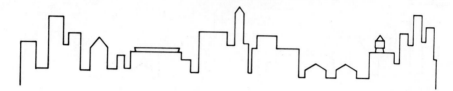

that these schemes lack inherent merit. Rather, they will only flourish and achieve their potential in a proper context.

The trick, then, is to *remake* and revitalize through decentralization the quantitatively massive and qualitatively sluggish school systems; the ultimate question is what ends would such decentralization serve? These two aspects are inextricably related.

The first step, as I see it, in making a big, urban system more responsive to the needs of individual children, teachers and schools is to create a climate in which beneficial changes can flourish.

A CLIMATE FOR CHANGE

Such a climate includes an honest respect for the individual needs and concerns of all the participants of the educational process: administrators, teachers, parents and, most of all, children. General directives must be replaced with individual attention. Responsibility and accountability for individual participation in the activities of the school must be placed at the local level. Teachers and children should be given freedom from inhibiting, bureaucratic requirements in order to explore, to experiment and to develop.

While the primary responsibility for setting such a tone lies with the words and deeds of the superintendent of schools, a similar responsibil-

ity rests with all of the organizations whose influence affects educational decision making. Teachers' organizations or unions, community groups, and the state department of education must continue to combat the impersonal "objectivity" and procedural rigidity of the school bureaucracy.

A second step in decentralizing the big city schools involves changing the available career patterns and reward systems. In the past, salary, prestige and power have been dependent upon satisfactory (i.e., non-controversial) progress up the bureaucratic ladder. If new arrangements of teachers into teaching and curriculum development teams were to make leadership and the rewards of leadership more accessible at the classroom level, then the creative talent of teachers would not be channeled into the conformist behavior previously rewarded by promotion to administrative positions. The gambler, the innovator, the boat-rocker must be recognized and rewarded at the classroom level.

A third requirement for a more responsive urban educational system is greater use of the community's resources. By this, I do not mean merely more field trips. City schools should bring the children and the talent and resources of the metropolitan area into greater and more meaningful contact with each other. Social studies, for example, might best be taught and learned in the courts, the

legislatures, or even on the streets with community action groups. Humanities courses should involve real artists, musicians and writers, just as vocational courses should involve the community's plumbers, salesmen and industrialists. High school students might well spend part of their day working in the community developing relationships with adults and the world of work. The involvement of the community in planning, operating and evaluating the schools would do much to eliminate the isolation, complacency and irrelevance of urban education.

I cannot discuss community involvement without mentioning the need for more cooperation between public and non-public schools and between urban and suburban school districts. The problems of school construction, technological systems, comprehensive education and racial integration will go unsolved until all of the schools in the city and its suburbs realize their mutual need for each other. Arguments showing the gains in economic efficiency will not alone transcend the provincial smugness of the various school systems. Perhaps a moral appeal to the common values and humane concerns of the metropolitan community will. Equality of educational opportunity certainly cannot be limited by arbitrary political boundaries.

A fourth step in making the schools more responsive involves making people more responsive to each other. Schools can play a significant role in establishing the attitudes and behaviors which determine our relationships with our fellow human beings. If teachers genuinely care about children, and if parents genuinely care about the experiences their children have in the schools, then education cannot help but be more responsive and more meaningful. Children can learn a great deal about warmth and sincerity in human relationships from adults who care. This "step" in decentralization is nothing less than an appeal for a deeper commitment by people to the welfare of their fellow man.

Decentralization provides a mechanism by which persons with deep commitment may become concerned and actively involved. In conclusion, decentralization, in all of the areas outlined above, essentially amounts to making all of the participants in the educational process (teachers, principals, children and administrators) more responsible for what they do and thereby making the whole system more responsive to the needs of the community's children. These then are the "how" and "why" of decentralizing educational systems, urban or otherwise. The alternatives to the multi-level involvement of decentralization seem to be isolation, irrelevance and alienation: no school system has the luxury of choice.

someone's doing

something right

You, Dear Reader—
You are Amazing Grace.
You are a Precious Jewel.

Only you and I can help the sun rise
each coming morning. If we don't, it
may drench itself out in sorrow.

You—special, miraculous, unrepeat-
able, fragile, fearful, tender, lost,
sparkling ruby emerald jewel, rain-
bow splendor person. It's up to you.

Would it embarrass you very much if
I were to tell you . . . that I love
you?

JOAN BAEZ

A Little Bit of Chaos

by **BEATRICE** and **RONALD GROSS**

"British Infant School," "Leicestershire Method," "Integrated Day," "The Open Classroom"—these names are heard increasingly among theorists and practitioners of early childhood education. The terms all refer to a new approach to teaching that discards the familiar elementary classroom setup and the traditional, stylized roles of teacher and pupil, for a far freer, highly individualized, child-centered learning experience that may hold the key to a radical reformation of primary education.

This approach—for which the Open Classroom seems the most useful label—is based on a body of new theory and research on how children do and don't learn, but its attractiveness for educators is even more directly attributable to the fact that it is highly effective under a variety of circumstances for children between the ages of five and twelve. It has spread widely throughout the British school system since World War II, and in the past five

years it has been introduced in a variety of American schools, ranging from rural Vermont and North Dakota to inner-city classrooms in Philadelphia, Washington, Boston, and New York.

This year the Office of Economic Opportunity sponsored twelve Open Classroom training centers in nine cities as part of Follow Through, its program for continuing the social and intellectual growth of "deprived" children graduating from Head Start programs. The Open Classroom movement has also won the support of the Ford Foundation, which is funding several efforts to encourage its dissemination in public schools.

There are four operating principles of the Open Classroom. First, the room itself is decentralized: an open, flexible space divided into functional areas, rather than one fixed, homogeneous unit. Second, the children are free for much of the time to explore this room, individually or in groups, and to choose their own activities. Third, the environment is rich in learning resources, including plenty of concrete materials, as well as books and other media. Fourth, the teacher and her aides work most of the time with individual children or two or

three, hardly ever presenting the same material to the class as a whole.

The teachers begin with the assumption that the children want to learn and will learn in their fashion; learning is rooted in firsthand experience so that teaching becomes the encouragement and enhancement of each child's own thrust toward mastery and understanding. Respect for and trust in the child are perhaps the most basic principles underlying the Open Classroom.

From the application of these principles derive the most notable characteristics of learning in such a classroom: a general atmosphere of excitement; virtually complete flexibility in the curriculum; interpenetration of the various subjects and skills; emphasis on learning rather than teaching; focus on each child's thinking and problem-solving processes, and on his ability to communicate with others; and freedom and responsibility for the children.

From the moment you walk in the door of such a classroom, the difference from the conventional procedures is striking. In most classrooms rows of desks or tables and chairs face the front of the room, where the teacher is simultaneously presenting material and controlling the class; the children are either quietly engaged by what the teacher is doing, surreptitiously communicating, daydreaming, or fooling. Even in classrooms using innovative materials, such as the Individually Prescribed Instruction, in which each student works on a math sheet prescribed for his particular level of achievement, the basic pattern is one in which all the children do the same thing at the same time, sitting at their desks with the teacher watching from up front.

But in an Open Classroom, there is none of this. There is no up front, and one doesn't know where to look to find the teacher or her desk. She is usually to be found working intensively with one or two children, or, if things are going as they should, often standing unobtrusively aside but observing each child's activities with great diligence. There are no desks and few chairs—fewer than the number of children. And the children are everywhere: sprawled on the floor, in groups in the corners, alone on chairs or pillows, out in the hall, or outside in the playground if it's good weather.

"The children are working on fractions." This kind of description of what's going on in a class, which comes so easily in a conventional situation, can never be applied to an Open Classroom. Each child uses the room differently, according to his own interests, concerns, and feelings on a particular day.

How does the day proceed? As they arrive, the students check the Chore Chart to see what their housekeeping responsibility is for the day. They take turns doing such chores as bringing up the milk, watering the plants, cleaning the animal cage, mixing new paints, sharpening pencils, taking attendance.

Many Open Classroom teachers call a general meeting after the children arrive, focusing on some interesting experiment several children did the day before, something brought from home, an unusual item in the newspaper, or a sentence she has written on the board to be corrected by the class. The children squat on their haunches or sit cross-legged in whatever area most comfortably holds the whole group.

After the meeting, children choose the areas in which they would like to begin their day. Some prefer to start quietly reading, curled up in the overstuffed chairs. Some like to get their assigned work out of the way first, but others may not have a choice if the teacher has noticed, for instance, that they have been neglecting math or need work in punctuation, and she tells them that they should start the day working with her. Soon the room is full of action, used as it will be for the remainder of the day, unless some special visitor or specialist focuses the group's attention for a special activity.

The layout of the room supports the program. An aerial view of a typical second-grade class in the middle of a morning would show that the room is divided into six sections, defined by open bookshelves that hold appropriate equipment, all of which is easily accessible to the children.

The child is free to choose, but whatever choice he makes he will be confronted with a wealth of opportunities for exploration and discovery. In the math section is everything he can use to measure and figure, including the Cuisenaire rods, balance scales, rulers and a stop watch, workbooks, and counting games such as Sorry and Pokerino. Similar riches await him in the language arts section, where he can read, make a tape recording or type, write, and play word-games and puzzles; or in the arts area with its paints, clay, dyes, and sand.

Other corners are devoted to science, music, and blocks.

The child's freedom, autonomy, and independence—as well as his responsibility—are epitomized by the largest and most elaborate of the many charts and pictures around the room. It is the "Activity Chart," and it lists by word and appropriate picture all the possible activities in the room: from reading, typing, playground, painting, right through to visiting and gerbils. Next to each are several hooks, on which the child hangs his name tag to indicate what he's doing. A simple device, but it says much about the respect for the child and the relationship between the child, the teacher, and the room. The equivalent in the conventional classroom is the notorious Delaney Book, still widely used, which represents each student by a little card tucked in a slot corresponding to his desk position, fixing the child in a constrained position, with the teacher clearly in charge.

In the Open Classroom, each child's day is distinctive and different from every other day. To give him a sense of his progress, each child may keep a diary, which is also used to communicate to the teacher. Some typical entries indicate the flow of activity, and the frustrations and concerns of the children:

Today I read *Horton the Elephant.* I began the green series in SRA. Ollie helped me with the words in the *Horton* book. I helped John and Sara make a staircase with the Cuisenaire rods.

I played in the Block Corner most of the day. We were making a suspension bridge. We talked a lot about our water tower and how it got flooded by Jimmy and what we should charge for a toll. I'll do my math tomorrow. Okay?

We had a turtle race today. Mrs. White taught me how to break words down. I can read words, but I can't break them down. We timed the turtles with the stopwatch. They tried to climb over the side of the box.

We're making a book of fables like "How the Snake Lost His Legs"; "How the Elephant Got His Trunk"; "How José Got to Be a Genius"; "How I Got to Be Invisible."

The variety of the activities mentioned in the diaries suggests the highlights of each child's day, but many educators and most parents find it difficult to define clearly what is being learned at any one moment and are usually resistant to the idea that a relaxed and unpressured atmosphere can stimulate serious work.

The evidence that this approach does work and the reasons why were first presented to a wide public in *Children and Their Primary Schools,* a 1967 report of Great Britain's Central Advisory Council for Education. Popularly known as the Plowden Report, after Lady Bridget Plowden, chairman of the council, these fat volumes were handsomely responsive to the council's mandate to "consider primary education in all its aspects." The Plowden Report is one of those classic official documents that only the British seem capable of producing: generous-spirited, concrete, progressive, and written with charm and spirit.

The report is comprehensive in scope: some half-million words covering topics as diverse as the rate of growth in height for boys and girls, religious instruction, salaries, school building costs, sex education, the handicapped, and team teaching. But the aspect of it that has had the most impact on American educators is its portrayal and analysis of the new mode of teaching.

The Plowden Report does not just discuss the theory and marshal the evidence from various fields and disciplines. It goes the further step of showing that it can be *done,* that in fact it already *is* being done. And it is being done not just in the small private schools that have harbored such education for decades, but in the mainstream of Britain's state-supported, mass education system.

In surveying the state of British primary schooling, the Plowden Report discovered that one-third of the primary schools had already dispensed with a fixed curriculum, a teacher-dominated unified classroom, and narrowly focused one-way teaching measured by tests, and replaced them with Open Classroom techniques and practices.

To make its preference for this approach perfectly clear, the Plowden Report gives negative criteria as well as positive ones. In the schools that were found to be damaging children, administrative and teaching practices hadn't changed significantly in the past decade, creative work in the arts was considered a frill, much classroom time was spent in the teacher's teaching in ways that generated few questions from the children (and those narrowly circumscribed by the teacher), and there were too many exercises and rules, resulting in frequent punishments and many tests.

Against this paradigm of educational stultification, the report poses the ideal: emphasis on each child's interests and style, lots of gabble among the kids, an abundance of fascinating concrete materials, and a teacher who stimulates and sometimes steps back.

All of this came to the attention of American educators through a series of articles by Joseph Featherstone in *New Republic* in the autumn of 1967. Featherstone was the perfect publicist for the Plowden Report. His down-to-earth style and modesty matched the report's manner perfectly. By speaking in a low voice, Featherstone raised a storm of interest and triggered a hegira of American educators to England. Lillian Weber, who is now the Open Classroom expert for New York City's schools, and who was virtually alone in the schools in England in 1965, could hardly elbow her way past the study teams from twenty American cities when she returned in 1969.

The theoretical basis of the Open Classroom is found in the work of the Swiss child psychologist Jean Piaget. His work began to influence many other experimental psychologists in the 1950s when his studies were published, but not until recently has his work been interpreted and popularized in the mass media.

Piaget is best known for his finding that intelligence—adaptive thinking and action—develops in sequence and is related to age. However, the ages at which children can understand different concepts vary from child to child, depending on his native endowment and on the quality of the physical and social environments in which he is reared.

But Piaget's books—*The Origins of Intelligence in Children, The Psychology of Intelligence,* and *The Construction of Reality*—based on his research on how children learn, also proved that it is a waste of time to tell a child things that the child cannot experience through his senses. The child must be able to try things out to see what happens, manipulate objects and symbols, pose questions and seek their answers, reconcile what he finds at one time with what he finds at another, and test his findings against the perceptions of others his age. Activity essential to intellectual development includes social collaboration, group effort, and communication among children. Only after a good deal of experience is the child ready to move on to abstract conceptualizations. Piaget is critical of classrooms where the teacher is the dominant figure, where books and the teacher's talking are basic instructional media, and where large group instruction is the rule, and oral or written tests are used to validate the whole process. Clearly from his findings, traditional teaching techniques are ineffectual. But for children who must depend on the school environment as the richest they are to encounter, it can be downright damaging; denied a chance to grow, their minds may actually atrophy.

Can the Open Classroom approach transform American primary education as it is doing in England? To Lillian Weber, this is the basic question. As assistant professor of early childhood education at City College, she feels there is a ground swell of interest.

"When I started placing student teachers, after coming back from England, there wasn't one classroom in New York City that I could put a teacher into where she had the slightest chance of being able to apply the theories of how children learn that she was studying at the college." Now, as the result of three years of intensive effort, there are thirty-seven, mostly on the Upper West Side and in Harlem, and Mrs. Weber is swamped with requests for help in introducing these theories in more schools.

Considerable progress has also been made in Philadelphia, where the reform school administration of Mark Shedd got behind this approach as one element of its attempt to "turn on the system." Under the guidance of Lore Rasmussen, eighteen teachers are using the Open Classroom approach in five schools, and twenty more are trying it on their own.

On the national level, the Educational Development Center, a nonprofit curriculum-development agency in Newton, Mass., sponsors workshops, provides advisory and consultant services, and develops materials under grants from the Ford Foundation and the federal government's Follow Through program. To spearhead the movement in this country, EDC has brought over experienced educators, such as Rosemary Williams, who directed the Westfield Infant School, portrayed so vividly by Joseph Featherstone. Through these activities, EDC advises teachers in more than 100 classrooms in eight states.

Three questions are asked most

often by educators and parents first exposed to Open Classrooms in operation. What problems loom largest? Do the children do as well on standardized tests? And what about cost? Do the additional training and the wealth of materials add greatly to the cost of schooling?

The problem cited most frequently is the fad psychology of educational reform. The trajectory was documented by Anthony Oettinger in *Run, Computer, Run.* An innovation comes roaring in on a wave of rhetoric, there is a bustle to get on the band wagon, things seem to be burgeoning, and then suddenly disenchantment occurs when reality falls short of the glowing press releases.

"The biggest threat is that the approach will catch on and spread like wildfire," insists Ann Cook, who has served widely as a consultant on Open Classroom projects. "Then it would fall into the hands of faddists who are unwilling to give it sufficient time to evolve and mature. Developing the necessary talent to make this work is time-consuming, and Americans are an impatient people."

For this reason, advocates of the approach want to win their battle classroom by classroom, rather than by convincing educational administrators to install the new approach through ukase. "Careful work on a small scale," Featherstone has written, "is the way to start reform worth having. . . . The proper locus of a revolution in the primary schools . . . is a teacher in a classroom full of children."

Another common problem is the tendency to confuse the self-conscious freedom of the Open Classroom with mere "chaos" and disregard of the children. Conventional educators observing an Open Classroom for the first time are often so fixated on the children's informality and spontaneity that they fail to note the diligent planning and individual diagnoses by the teachers and the intellectual and sensuous richness of the prepared environment. These latter qualities, however, are hard-won, and to "open" the classrooms without having developed these strengths is to invite mere mindlessness and frustration.

How do the children score on standardized tests? That question is regularly asked by parents and teachers, as if it gets to the heart of the matter with hard-nosed exactness. But Open Classroom theorists refuse to accept the assumption behind the question. They insist that our new understanding of how children learn and grow makes the present standardized tests obsolete.

"In England there is never any pressure to test in Infant Schools," explains Rosemary Williams, "but since there is pressure here, someone must come up with realistic tests. We've got Princeton's Educational Testing Service at work on tests that will measure original thinking, independency, and creativity—the kind of thing our program is out to develop."

The available evidence indicates that, even measured by the present tests, Open Classroom children progress normally in reading and arithmetic scores. But an increased *desire* to read and write is also evident, and children score higher, on the average, in math comprehension. This is startling, since traditional classrooms focus principally on reading and arithmetic the first

More on Infant Schools

Additional information about the British Infant Schools can be obtained from the following sources: Educational Development Center, 55 Chapel Street, Newton, Massachusetts. EDC has a large number of free pamphlets available, including *Plan for Continuing Growth* by David Armington, which deals with the application of Infant School techniques in Follow Through programs; *Leicestershire Revisited* by William Hull; excerpts from the Plowden Report; and *Reading in Informal Classrooms* by Rosemary Williams.

Institute for Development of Educational Activities (I/D/E/A), Post Office Box 446, Melbourne, Florida 32901. I/D/E/A has published a $1 pamphlet, *The British Infant School,* which summarizes the findings of a group of American, British, and Israeli educators that visited a series of Open Classroom schools in England to look for ideas and practices which could be transplanted in the United States. In addition, I/D/E/A also will rent a seventeen-minute film on British Infant Schools at $10 for three days. Prints may be purchased for $120. Reprints of Joseph Featherstone's articles are available through the *New Republic,* 1244 19th St., N.W., Washington, D.C. 20036.

---

two years, while Open Classrooms accord them equal status with such activities as painting and block building.

The question of cost also arises in many people's minds when they see the richness of materials and equipment in the classroom. And indeed there are considerable start-up expenses. David Armington of EDC estimates that to fill an Open Classroom with the most elaborate equipment available in a situation where money is no object costs $1,100 to $1,200, making an initial investment of $36 per child the first year. However, roughly half the equipment is highly durable and does not have to be replaced in subsequent years, and operating costs can be reduced by using parents and older children as aides. For educational value received, its advocates argue, the Open Classroom is a bargain—but, like good buys, it can often be least afforded by those who need it.

In the present climate of American education, the Open Classroom approach sometimes seems like a flower too fragile to survive. The demands on the schools today are harsh and often narrow. Many black parents demand measurable reading achievement and other test scores to assure that they are no longer being given short shrift. At the same time, white parents are often concerned that the schools continue to give their children an advantage in status over someone else's children.

In such a climate, the Open Classroom seems precariously based on a kind of trust little evident in education today. Teachers must trust children's imagination, feelings, curiosity, and natural desire to explore and understand their world. They also must learn to trust themselves—to be willing to gamble that they can retain the children's interest and respect once they relinquish the external means of control: testing, threats, demerits, petty rules, and rituals. School administrators, in turn, must trust teachers enough to permit them to run a classroom that is not rigidly organized and controlled but, rather, is bustling, messy, flexible, and impulsive. Parents must trust school people to do well by their children, without the assurance provided by a classroom atmosphere recognizable from their own childhoods and validated, however emptily, by standardized tests.

Much recent experience suggests that the basis for trust such as this may not exist in American education at present. But perhaps the existence of classrooms where learning based on such trust is taking place will itself help create the beginnings of a new climate.

THE OPEN CLASSROOM

Humanizing the Coldness of Public Places

ARTHUR J. TOBIER

At 9:30 A.M. teacher aides and student teachers begin to line the small, L-shaped section of the corridor with tables and chairs. Out of a storage room they bring out boxes full of materials and spread the contents on the tables. There are scales, Cuisenaire rods, water vessels, musical instruments, a dozen different kinds of math puzzles, counting devices, hexagons, trapezoids, animals, clay, all manner of measuring devices. Singly, and in pairs, threes, and fours, children filter into the corridor from five classrooms, the doors of which are open and inside of which teachers are conducting lessons. Outside, the corridor has become another kind of place. Some children move directly to activities, having learned the corridor's offerings. Others, sometimes with a friend in tow, shop around before settling down to one thing. And others, perhaps first or second graders, after staying awhile, move through the corridor into one of the classrooms, perhaps a kindergarten or prekindergarten, to listen to a story or play a piano, or to play with animals or with the workbench. At one table a four year old girl is manipulating a game about people, identifying relationships. Behind, a six year old has spread herself on a piece of newsprint on the floor while a student teacher traces her form in crayon, which she will then measure in blocks and hang on the wall. Other children are pacing off distances, measuring with string. At another table a five year old boy, who until the previous week had been disruptive, doing nothing in the corridor but running back and forth, has just put together, with an effort of intense concentration, a puzzle consisting of triangular and rectangular shapes. Encouraged to show his teacher what he's done ("Show her, Paul, she doesn't know you can do this"), he brings her into the corridor. Lillian Weber, who set up the corridor, comes by and suggests that the boy record his feat. A second grader is called over to write what he describes. Another second grader who has just entered the corridor stops Mrs. Weber and announces she is about to write a story about the educator. Mrs. Weber stands absolutely still as the girl counts the 114 stripes on her dress. In a minute, both stories are completed, passed around, read and re-read, and posted on a bulletin board already 12 deep in stories and records of activity. A few feet away a group of four has been working steadily for an hour weighing shoes and discussing relationships with the corridor teacher, a young graduate student hired for the job. Two kindergarten boys come by, full of themselves and of being on their own, puffing hard from running. A visitor holds one boy, tells him how fast his heart is beating, and gets him to listen to his friend's heart beat. Now the movement in the corridor is fluid. There is a lot of doing and a lot of telling.

Questions are investigated in many ways. Nothing that is said or done is left unexamined. Children return to their classes, others come out, work continues in all the rooms. A child pauses at the entrance of one room before going in to show her teacher a paper flower she has just made. Inside the room, run along formal lines, there is a striking absence of restlessness. Children are hard at work despite the sounds and movement from the corridor. In sharp contrast, a second grade class next door operates informally in small clusters of children. A teacher comes to the doorway of her room, watches the activity in the corridor for a time, and returns to her work. By 11 A.M. the corridor begins to clear. Materials, tables, and chairs have been returned to their storeroom. Left on the corridor walls are the paper cutouts of children's figures. It is only then, when the corridor is empty, that a visitor notices how dark it is inside the school.

Two years ago [1967], Lillian Weber, assistant professor of early childhood education at City College, came back to this country from an 18-month work and study trip in England firm in her conviction that public schools in New York City had a long way to go to be supportive of the way children learn.

At the time, public discussion here about early childhood education centered on Head Start. Did it or didn't it work to eliminate the difficulties that children, euphemistically called "educationally disadvantaged," had with formal schooling.

Most of the experts felt Head Start's approach to schooling—sometimes tutorial; sometimes bits and pieces inherited from the nursery school tradition—closed some kind of gap, or at least ameliorated a difference in motivation, between the middle class children who traditionally made it in school and the welfare class children who didn't. But the statistical gains disappeared, it was found, when the children entered into the conventional process of public school life.

Reflecting on the regression, the educationists decided the problem derived from a basic lack of continuity between Head Start and public school experience. Teaching styles differed, they argued, expectations differed, the degree of intellectual enrichment differed. A program of "follow through" was proposed to extend Head Start's notions of compensatory education to a second year of schooling, a bridge in other words, and last fall the U.S. Office of Education began a two-year field test of some dozen follow-through models in "ghetto" schools throughout the country.

Mrs. Weber saw the roots of the problem elsewhere. In England, she had steeped herself in infant school techniques and traditions. Working eight hour days, five days a week for the better part of her stay there, she made intensive observations in 56 schools, mostly in London, Birmingham, and Bristol, and mostly in working class areas; she talked to hundreds of government officials, headmistresses, teachers, parents; she made voluminous notes; and she made a movie about the infant school.

The English infant school experience—fashioned over a 50-year period, not overnight as some publicists for change would have it—provided for the kind of continuity the Americans sought, Mrs. Weber felt. By this, she meant "a rich environment, allowing for self-directed activities, the integrating of all kinds of experiencing with skill learning, an allowing of movement to the environment, a use of overflow (corridor or hall) areas in an in-and-out way, and open door classrooms."

In some English schools, she said, this approach became "an integrated day, where reading and other skills are going on with some small group at all times of day, and other self-directed activities are going on with other children, at all times of day. The teacher moves to individuals or forms small groups. Mixed age grouping allows for beginning learning at all points, allows for back and forthness of a child's learning, allows for continuation in the older child's experience of the rich concreteness we accept for the younger. The teacher's isolation is gone with the open door classroom. The teacher is freed, in this structure, of the constant need to control and tell. The child is freed to reinforce his learning from the richness of the environment."

Believing in the integral relationship of structure to its roots, Mrs. Weber did not expect to translate English structure to the American scene. But even the use of the ideas in the context of our own setting, she felt, would meet stumbling blocks—a chief one being the typical public school building. The design of the city's school buildings, no less than its public housing, has never paid but the most minimal attention to the way people in those buildings live their lives. The schools have tended to be collections of isolated rooms in outsized buildings that eschew intimacy, and that lend themselves to nothing so well as to the isolated experience, the grade-oriented, prescribed curriculum, and the block class structure, conventions which a substantial body of research and practice argues are anathema to the way children go about learning.

In such a setting, Mrs. Weber said, overflow space is difficult to arrange; corridors are restricted to passing through by virtue of the fire law; and without overflow space, movement to multiple activities, the provision of a really rich environment, the concentration needed for small group teaching in the midst of multiple activities, are all difficult to arrange. Control, in such a setting, becomes the school's primary concern. How could one make schools give up some of their excess control to implement children's ways of learning?

Mrs. Weber started to shape an answer to that question in the spring of 1967. City College had assigned her as consultant to P.S. 123 (District 6), one of four schools in Harlem affiliated with the college's teacher education department, and where she had helped formulate the prekindergarten program before going to England. Once again, there was this mammoth school; teachers working in isolation, teachers with distrust for one another because of the burden of children who didn't learn but who were passed along from the previous year; and children, their goodwill being exhausted by the failure toward which they ineluctably moved. And there were the system's future teachers, unprepared for the reality of a school classroom. How honest was it, Mrs. Weber asked herself after awhile, to evaluate student teachers on what they could not do when the objective circumstances of the school made it impossible for them to do otherwise?

Gradually, with the learning atmosphere of the infant school as reference point, the idea took root, Mrs. Weber said, that by cutting off a small section of the school it might be feasible to operate it as a unit with a mixed grouping of classes, and use the corridor as the connecting link and overflow space. She floated the idea to her faculty heads and the district office, won their support, and on the strength of this got the principal of P.S. 123 to let her test her notions. For his part, the principal arranged to have a prekindergarten, two kindergartens, a first grade and a second grade in the five rooms that opened off a first floor corridor. The teachers consented to a minimal participation in the project. At the same time, Mrs. Weber submitted a proposal to Washington outlining her model and requesting financial support. In the fall, she began to sit in on classes to observe.

The teachers met her with reserve. She was, after all, an outsider whose purposes they still didn't know. Neither were they unhappy with the way they worked. Aware of this, Mrs. Weber bided her time, never discussed theory, never tried to alter their teaching style. She focused on designing a structure for the corridor, and imperceptibly, she engaged them in the process of planning, emphasizing detail. The corridor was to serve as a model adjacent to the classroom which they could observe and get to like and draw from or not as they chose. Since Mrs. Weber was committed to not directly altering their teaching style, the significance of the corridor, as she saw it, was that it allowed the teachers constant access to a model without forcing it on them. She was sure they would see the children learning in different ways and at least become interested.

She had them figure out the kinds of materials they'd want, and how they'd rearrange their schedules to have time to use the materials. She had them think about a special kind of material they might want that would reflect something they each particularly wanted to do in class and were willing to share with the other teachers. (A teacher chose animals, another a phonograph, dancing, a third picked a workbench, and one chose an oven, all of which Mrs. Weber purchased for them out of a $1,000 grant she had obtained from a small foundation.) Most difficult, because of the varying scheduling of teacher prep periods, she asked them to arrange a common free time to use all of the enrichments. In each case, however, the teachers found workable solutions.

The corridor would operate along informal lines, no matter how the teachers organized classes in their rooms. Each teacher would release as many as five children at a time to visit the corridor or any of the other four rooms and in turn take in as many as three from outside. The planning sessions, delayed by the teacher strike, lasted through the fall semester. On March 6 the open corridor came into being, one hour three days a week.

The teachers met regularly with Mrs Weber. They made adjustments, and exchanged insights, particularly about movement, since that was the essential innovation as far as they were concerned. "Perhaps the older children have annoyed us," Mrs. Weber suggested at one meeting, "but almost all of them have not really annoyed us except in the fact of their passing through. They have been interested in seeing what is going on. And I think the system of saying, 'Well, would you like to look for a minute,' has become a good one." "They are really there," said a teacher, "because they're a little lost and because they have seen something that interests them. For a short time, involving them and including them gives them reason to have some sort of contact with you, and it ends up being a much more positive thing than hurrying them up and running them off with an angry growl in your voice."

At first the teachers decided where the children were to go and how long they stayed, but as the children learned more about what was available, free choice prevailed—even to the point where the teachers became less concerned with "giving" children "full experiences," letting them take their time to explore instead.

By the end of the term, the open corridor had clearly made an impact. Movement between classes had begun to continue even after the corridor period had ended, and had begun to extend beyond the children in the five classes on the corridor. Student teachers had learned to "make do" and adapt to things quickly and without fuss and bother. In the corridor children had become active and creative and in the classroom both the need for control and discipline had diminished sharply. The style of the corridor—informality and exchange—had even started to filter into the classrooms of a few teachers.

But the filtering process for other teachers worked very slowly. Mrs. Weber, in a term-end review, judged that the project hadn't developed a deep enough relationship with teachers. The necessary involvement of the teachers in the problems of further development of the project didn't happen, and so they had only limited identification with the project. The developmental process, particularly at the beginning, needed more time.

Similarly, she felt the project had failed to develop enough real understanding of its goals among parents and in getting parents to help with small adjustments. But just as teachers—despite Mrs. Weber's concern—elected to continue the project, parent *support* was obtained. "I think the parents' and the schools' identification with the project grew during the term as the parents saw this total commitment to coping and small adjustments. But it grew even more markedly in the last month. Projects usually end with the end of the college term. The commitment to the project seemed proved to the parents by the continuance of project personnel to the very last day of the term. Small things like the project party for one of the departing teachers, including many of the school administrators, helped break through the isolation typical of many college projects. Certainly, during the last packing-away week, it was clear that the parents had warm feelings toward us. As they came to say goodbye and as we sought them out to say goodbye, we spoke together as part of a common enterprise that would start again next year—with or without funding."

One other event of note occurred during the spring term. Parents and teachers from P.S. 84 in the Joan of Arc complex (District 5) came up to Harlem to observe the open corridor in P.S. 123 and, impressed, successfully lobbied their district office to invite in Mrs. Weber. The invitation, and the financial support, came from the district's eight-school Balanced Class Project, under Jack Isaacs' direction.

Thus, at the start of this school year (without funding: the open corridor is a unitary plan and the USOE asserted it was funding only those projects "doing" a grade at a time), the open corridor expanded to nine classrooms: the original five at P.S. 123 (in a low income, racially separate area) and four more (two kindergartens and two first grades) at P.S. 84 (in a low-to-high income, racially integrated area), with the extra dimensions in the latter of having teachers eager to reorganize, not only the corridor, but their classrooms.

. . .

Over the past school year, Mrs. Weber has refined the open corridor at P.S. 123, expanded into a daily morning period, roughly from 9:30 to 11, and made it by all accounts into a powerful medium of learning. Movement has become more fluid for the children; it has become almost second nature for them to bring their classroom teachers into the corridor to look at and comment on their work. Children who lacked the confidence to recognize and develop respect for their own achievements now acknowledge them freely, according to teachers. When a child discovers how to solve a math puzzle he automatically looks for someone to explain and read what he's done. The same holds for drawing, writing, weighing, measuring, and other activities. Most of the children observed in the corridor do not appear anxious about getting approval. On the contrary, most of them display self-acceptance as learners. "From a child's standpoint," a clinical psychologist, who observed the corridor period recently, said, "the Weber model (a term Mrs. Weber adjures against) gives a child the chance to explain and record what he's doing and lets him be responsible for feedback to the teacher. He not only decides what to do, he lets everyone know what he's doing. In a traditional classroom you're not held accountable for the activities you're engaged in."

Besides the project's growing impact on children it has become, in effect, a continuous teaching model, affecting not only the student teachers (City College early childhood students in Mrs. Weber's seminar as well as other seminars are expected to show their ability to set up multiple activity situations in classes), but the teachers in the classrooms—some in the extreme. One second grade teacher, thoroughly traditional at the start of the project, has reorganized her class on informal lines. The relationship of all the teachers to the project has deepened, particularly in the way teachers have opened themselves to learning about their children's capabilities from their experiences in the corridor.

Downtown, at P.S. 84, after nearly nine months of planning, adjustments, and adapting to the loss of the corridor, the principle of moving to the environment, of access and overflow, is still intact. In fact, but unofficially, the movement extends to one fifth grade and one sixth grade class whose two teachers restructured their classes along informal school lines even prior to Mrs. Weber's coming to the school. (In their classes, the prescribed curriculum is covered, but with a richer variety of materials than normally obtains in traditional classes, and there is much more trust in the free choices of children and their ability to become deeply involved in their work, as well as trust in children to help each other.) Their example, as well as Mrs. Weber's model, has generated interest in the teaching style among other teachers.

Not all of the four project classes can claim the same accomplishment, but the best is exemplary, Mrs. Weber feels. On a recent visit to a first grade class an observer made note of the following: Children worked in about four separate small groups, while others worked by themselves. There was a math lesson going on directed by the teacher. A visiting parent was reading to three girls. An aide sat among a gathering of five children showing them how to knit. A fifth grader who had dropped by for a visit was showing two of the first graders how to clean a rabbit cage. Children were building boats, shaping clay, painting. A reader came up to the teacher to ask a question, listened for a minute at the math table and decided to stay and participate. When the teacher excused herself to talk to a visitor, one of the children took over the task of leading the group in a game involving mathematical relationships. A high level of enthusiasm continued throughout the day. Children, on their own, left their groups and helped themselves to various pre-reading games set up in large envelopes along the blackboard ledge. These included games that required putting together parts of sentences or words to make complete sentences or words, as well as lotto games. Other children worked from similar setups on opposite walls for number and measurement activities, science, and perceptual discrimination practice. Most of the material had been designed and constructed by the teacher. None of the children or the adults working in the room seemed in the least bit put out by the level of noise. Voices adjusted to the immediate group. The teacher was in continual movement, stopping sometimes five minutes, sometimes fifteen minutes, to work with a group or a child. In the course of a week, she explained, she would check on the progress of all the children at least once to insure the ground she wanted covered was indeed being covered.

Where the internal reorganization has occurred, as at P.S. 84, and children are doing so many different things, the need to develop new ways of recording to match the new life of the classroom is very great. It is one of the things on which Mrs. Weber has spent a lot of time with teachers.

*Obviously, the teacher needs to know what it is that the child has done. . . .
These very enterprising teachers of the first grade have already gone ahead
in many ways. They have set up checklists in areas, name sign-up sheets
when you are in an area. There's still much to work out. Thinking in terms
of the need for the child's management of this, of the teacher knowing
where he is, one idea is the use of masonite disks with names on them that
a child could hang up to record attendance and that he would take with him
if he leaves for the corridor.*

*In the basic areas of number and of language, the teacher has to think
through which experiences does she want to know whether the child has
had, whether the child has lived through and accomplished. Suggestions on
recording came from patterns taken from the Nuffield junior mathematics
books, of certain major areas of progress and certain needed areas of
progress with a page per month on each child. The Nuffield material also
supplied a large chart illustrating the interrelationship of all aspects of both
language and abstract conception or mathematical conception in all the
aspects of the program, in the uses of sand, of clay, of water, of art materials, of housekeeping corner, of block building and in the more obvious
handling of the concrete mathematical materials and in the more obvious
language area.*

*Unless the teacher is clear about this interrelationship of all aspects of
experience, she will not be stressing and picking up and focusing and responding to the emergence of the linguistic and the numerical conception
in all aspects of the child's experience. The general aims for the child can
be expressed as having the experiences and developing the skills that he feels
are worth knowing and that he discovers that he can know and with the aid
of an environment that's worth knowing and that he discovers is connected.
In the most generalized way, long range aims for number, for language, for
science, have been worked out and will be used as a chart in front of the
teacher at all times.*

This longer range planning and new life in the classroom does not fit well
with the old administrative requirement of weekly lesson plans still demanded
of teachers, so Mrs. Weber has helped teachers meet it but on these new terms.

*The weekly plan should be a very simple one that does not overburden the
teacher or prevent her from relating to her long-range aims. Stories, songs,
and dramatization are considered as reinforcement for large areas of
number, language, natural and social science, art and music. In the weekly
plan, there would be a focus that the teacher would relate to along with all
the other things in the extended environment that had already been made
available to the child and to which he can return for repeated experiences.
She would focus with small groups on this, exploring possibilities in a multi-
level way, and at the end of the week would say what had been done, what
hadn't been done, and therefore plan her next week in this way. Two
rexographed sheets would be given to the teacher each week; one to hand*

in to the office to fulfill administrative requirements, the other to have in her room to relate to her long range aims which, after all, are the meat of all the incidental learning that goes on in addition to any focus that she may have.

Any idea that there would not be planning is obviously a fallacious idea and a simplistic notion of what such a program is about. On the contrary, only the deepest thinking through and thinking into the possibilities of an experience will make the teacher available to help.

It is this thoroughness, this deep thinking through, finally, observers say, that distinguishes the open corridor/open classroom project. Mrs. Weber sees no simpler approach to the process of learning. The necessity for continuing or rearousing a child's inquiring attitudes toward what can be asked of the world, she says, must be conceived of, and considered, as a whole. She doesn't think answers can be given to a child in a few pieces of information. "Outer reality is a whole," she has written, quoting the English educator, Nathan Isaacs, "and the child's frame of reference is a whole—but constantly being revised. This revision is essential to what we mean by the very process of learning, the process that results from the fact that "actions" produce "effects" but not necessarily ones that are expected . . . Often there are discrepancies and these impel the accommodations that become necessary as the previous frame of reference falls short. Unexpected experiences, discrepancies, can be fostered, in this way helping learning. Obviously the reinterpretations, necessary accommodations of discrepancies and distortions in the previous frame of reference, can be most direct if the reordering is what the child finds to reorder—his own problems."

Next year, the project will expand still further. A few classes will be added at P.S. 123. At P.S. 84, a new ruling is still being sought on the use of the corridor but meanwhile, and in the way developed this year, 13 teachers representing all grades are interested in joining the effort. In addition, a second school in District 5 has been talking with Mrs. Weber about her bringing the project there. Finally, with an eye out for future growth, Mrs. Weber has been trying to interest an educational laboratory in devising a prototype for a corridor module that could be folded back against the wall.

In both schools, Mrs. Weber reports, "parents approve the project, feel learning is taking place. At P.S. 84, they are eager to help with the getting of materials and they are also needed to help establish at least some semblance of bilingualism. They are needed to help in all kinds of things that would be difficult without their assistance, from the care of animals, to the establishment of window planters, to the areas of sewing, to knitting, to all kinds of supervision of a rich program."

Earlier this spring, the New York State Urban Education Department funded the project in P.S. 123, but only through June. P.S. 84's project will continue to be funded by the Balanced Class Project. The Center for Urban Education's Program Reference Service will publish a detailed report of the project in the fall.

Anything Goes

**Youths Do Almost Anything
That Interests Them, Go
Off in Every Direction**

DO MATH, GRAMMAR
SINK IN?

By Richard Martin

MINTO, N.D.—The fifth-grade classroom in this tiny, windswept farm community worries the principal, horrifies other teachers, infuriates the janitors and stuns parents.

It's a scene of near chaos. Desks are scattered. Melon-crate bookcases overflow with wood scraps, encyclopedias, games, puzzles and magazines. A rabbit, a hamster and two white rats are caged amid the clutter. There's an aquarium, too, and chicken eggs are hatching in a homemade incubator. Giggles punctuate the constant hum of conversation, and most of the 20 pupils seem to be in motion most of the time. Some sprawl on the floor reading, writing and painting. At one point, two boys are playing chess. Two others, who have crawled inside a crude cardboard hut, are working math exercises.

A lot of people say this is no way to run a classroom. But growing numbers of educators are just as strongly convinced that it is an ideal setting for developing the initiative, creativity and critical thought processes individuals need to cope with the increasing complexity of life in a fast changing society. Schools should be set up to bring out the most in each child, whatever his talents and regardless of his intelligence, not just to maintain order and stuff heads with facts, these educators contend.

Mr. Silberman's Views

In his new book, "Crisis in the Classroom," which is based on a three-year $300,000 study commissioned by the Carnegie Corp. of New York, Charles E. Silberman urges a remodeling of elementary school classrooms along less rigid lines as part of a vast reordering of U.S. education aimed at producing "a more humane society." The author, a Fortune editor and former Columbia University professor, says North Dakota's informal classrooms "are in many ways more exciting, and certainly more innovative, than anything one can find in the Scarsdales, Winnetkas, Shaker Heights and Palo Altos of the United States."

The informal classroom isn't a North Dakota phenomenon, by any means. Such classrooms are widespread in England and have cropped up in scores of U.S. cities in recent years. At least one other state, Vermont, is considering introducing "in-

"formal" classrooms on a statewide scale. In contrast to the usual snail's pace of educational change, the concept has swept across this frozen farm state like a January blizzard.

In many ways, North Dakota is ideally suited to its unaccustomed role as a test model for educational innovation. "If we can't do it here, it can't be done anywhere," says Kenneth Underwood, Fargo's superintendent of schools. "Our classes are relatively small, and, compared to much of the rest of the country, we just don't have any financial or social problems here. There's no racial strife, and we don't have to negotiate with unions for every minute of our teachers' time."

Move Aside, Teacher

Thus, schools scattered throughout the state are creating informal classrooms like Minto's, shoving desks, lesson plans and even teachers out of the way to give youngsters plenty of room to satisfy their natural curiosity and eagerness to learn.

The driving force behind the drive to bring informal classrooms to the state comes from a radically different kind of teachers' college, the New School of Behavioral Studies in Education. A small experimental unit of the University of North Dakota in Grand Forks, the New School has scrapped conventional college methods of teacher training and has knocked down the traditional barriers between teachers college campuses and the public school classrooms.

The New School opened two and a half years ago to a barrage of criticism. Its plans to promote educational changes were opposed by many faculty members of the university's big, 87-year-old college of education. The New School was attacked by members of the state's John Birch Society, and some state and local school administrators were hostile to its goals.

But since then the opposition has faded fast.

This year 34 of the state's 375 school districts are participating in the program, up from 13 in the 1968–69 school year. Currently about 10% of the 74,000 children in North Dakota's 593 elementary schools are attending informal classrooms, which cost no more to set up and operate than normal classrooms. "It's quite a thing for this to take off as fast as it has when you consider how many programs of a demonstration nature never succeed in moving off dead center," says Kiaran Dooley, director of state and Federal programs for the State Department of Public Instruction in Bismarck.

Fans and Skeptics

So far, the New School has sent 150 new teachers out into classrooms and has "retrained" another 210 experienced ones. It tries to send its graduates into schools in groups of two or three so that they can give each other help and moral support. Making a changeover from a traditional to an informal classroom is usually a complicated, painful process, and the difficulty is often increased by the skepticism, and occasional hostility, of some principals and veteran teachers.

Vernon J. Schreiner, Minto's elementary school principal, is one of the skeptics. "The fifth-graders are enjoying school all right, but I'm not sure how much they're learning," he says. "I don't think math and grammar are getting enough emphasis. And I wonder how they'll adjust to a traditional sixth-grade classroom next year."

In Grand Forks, Doris Onstad, who got a master's degree at the New School and transformed her first-grade classroom last year after 15 years of traditional teaching, recalls: "I was so excited and so eager, and the other teachers just laughed at me. It hurt." Peggy Wambolt, a sixth-grade teacher in Fargo with six years' experience, says: "The other teachers still look at me sideways sometimes, but I think that more and more I'm being accepted. They come and visit now. They still say my room's a mess, but with 28 different things going on it has to be."

Mrs. Wambolt, in her second year of informal teaching, is usually in her classroom from 8:30 A.M. to 6 or 7 P.M. "I just can't keep ahead of these kids. I can never seem to have enough work ready for them," she says. In Grand Forks, Roger Graham, with nine years' experience teaching fifth-graders and sixth-graders, says the informal class "is much more demanding of my time and effort. I go home

just shot. But there's a much more rewarding, very personal relationship between teacher and students than I ever had before."

Keeping a classroom from sliding over the thin line between freedom and chaos adds to the strains on a teacher for at least the first year of informal teaching. "Few kids learn to read by happenstance, and you have to be sure they do learn," says Neil Hensrud, one of three New School faculty members who spend much time visiting classrooms in the state to encourage and advise. "Some framework must exist for kids to work within. The teacher can't just turn the classroom over to them."

The idea is to provide lots of options that will get children actively involved in learning but that will let them set their own priorities. Instead of being a prime source of frustrating defeats, "classrooms need to be places where children can test their ideas, find their strengths and share what they learn with others, so they can feel they are worthwhile persons," says Sharon Melancon, who teaches a combined class of third- and fourth-graders in Fargo.

"Children basically want to learn and are interested in finding out about the world because it is just so very interesting," says Mrs. Melancon, who is in her second year of informal teaching after eight years in conventional schools. "Common sense tells us that a certain portion of the day needs to be spent by young children mastering the basic skills in math, reading and writing. But these activities can be made more interesting by tying them in with the interests of the child."

"Too Concerned With Gimmicks"

For example, a story about children who built a clubhouse prompted her class to try building one, too. Her pupils drew plans, using their own measurements, arithmetic and geometry. They listened to tape recorded lessons on handling tools. A group then went to a lumberyard and got some old wood, and the class built a small playhouse on the schoolground. They wrote stories, poems, songs and letters telling of their experiences. Small groups studied such related topics as termites, Indian homes, the homebuilding industry, skyscrapers, trees and the evolution of tools.

Some parents, nevertheless, worry that their children are having too much fun in informal classrooms to be learning as much as they should. Hank Yagelowich, a chemist in Grand Forks, frets that his son "is getting shortchanged" in his informal first-grade class. "It's fine if you can combine educational value and fun, but there's some stuff that you just have to grind out," he believes. "Educators today are too concerned with gimmicks."

No two informal classrooms are alike, but most share a number of common characteristics. There is emphasis on ingenuity and improvisation. Mimeographed math exercises sometimes contain no instructions; figuring out what to do is part of the exercise. First-grade reading materials often consist mostly of story books and stories the children themselves have made up and dictated to an adult.

Frogs, fish, snakes, birds and animals are standard equipment. Cast-off sofas and battered easy chairs are common, along with rugs, pillows and cushions to make the floors more comfortable. There are gasoline engines, electric motors and an incredible variety of puzzles and games to take apart and manipulate.

A favorite piece of equipment is a $3.25 microscope made of a chunk of wood, two knobs, a piece of mirror and a cheap plastic lens. It can be dropped without harm "and the kids love them," says Leonard Marks, who teaches science at the New School. "They're always bringing stuff in to look at and by playing with one of these they can learn a lot more about how lenses work than they could from an expensive microscope that has to be put away and locked up most of the time."

Involving the Parents

Mr. Marks shows teachers how to make cheap, durable cardboard rocking chairs, tables, playhouses, study carrels and other furniture and how to build a variety of classroom equipment, including games and puzzles, for only 10% to 20% of the cost of buying similar commercial products.

"Listening stations" equipped with tape recorders, phonographs and many sets of earphones, are usually present, too. Principals say the extra cost of projectors is offset by savings on workbooks and texts, since teachers want only two or three copies of a textbook, instead of one for every pupil.

One unusual aspect of an informal classroom is the presence of parents —reading to children and listening to them read, telling about their own travels and interesting experiences and helping out with a multitude of more mundane chores. Parents also chaperone groups of two to four youngsters on field trips for research projects they are pursuing on their own. Teams of Fargo sixth-graders, for example, recently visited a medical center for a study of arthritis, called on a bank for research on the history of money and interviewed a snowmobile maker about possible harmful effects of his product on the local ecology and wildlife.

"Parents today are involved in the schools less than they used to be and less than they want to be; too many teachers haven't wanted them around," says Vito Perrone, director of the New School. He crisscrossed the state talking to 10,000 parents in homes and schools in the New School's first year of operation, and he credits their involvement in the program with much of its growth.

"Once they see what we're doing, parents tend to become very supportive," he says. "But many have been supportive from the beginning. All the time principals and superintendents were telling me that parents would never accept the changes we wanted to make that first year the parents were telling me they sounded great."

Measures of Success

Parents in towns throughout the state have held evening workshops where New School faculty members talk about the program's methods and goals, field questions and let parents play with the puzzles and equipment their children use in class. One workshop last month drew 100 parents to the school in Milnor, which has a population of only 658.

Mr. Perrone frequently attends such gatherings. "Most college deans would rather make a speech to a state convention or a civic club, but Perrone will drive across the state at the drop of a hat to talk to parents," says Sheldon Schmidt, a New School professor. "He's very persuasive," adds Mr. Schmidt. "I saw him operate on a state official once. He ended up with a grant and the guy's support and at the outset of the meeting the official was determined not to give him either."

Some skeptics are being converted. "I can see some distinct benefits to an informal classroom, even though I can't swallow the whole package," says Mr. Schreiner, the skeptical Minto principal. "Just having them here has put a certain amount of pressure on the rest of us to change, to individualize our other classrooms more." George W. Starcher, president of the University of North Dakota, says the program "has really shaken up education in this state, and the thing that delights me is seeing these old superintendents changing their ways and seeing other colleges and school administrators beginning to imitate New School programs."

There are other measures of success, too. Tentative findings of tests aimed at comparing learning gains in both informal and traditional classes "indicate that what we're doing does help the kids," Charles Nielson, a New School testing specialist, says cautiously. "We're certain that at the very least kids aren't doing any worse," he adds.

"My kids are learning every bit as much, that's for sure, and there's no comparison in their attitudes toward school now," agrees Emma Jo Kunnanz, who has two youngsters in informal classes in Bismarck.

"This Is No Mecca"

Informal classrooms all over the state, including those on the four Indian reservations, report attendance rising sharply, discipline problems disappearing and some children making strong gains in reading, math and science.

These successes are drawing school superintendents, principals and teachers from all over the U.S. and Canada to the New School and the state's informal classrooms. "Most efforts to change the behavior of teachers have failed utterly," says Warren D. Strandberg, a New School faculty member. "So people are coming from everywhere to see great and wonderful things and worship at the font of change," he adds wryly. "But this is no Mecca. We're just some very average people trying to do some very difficult things."

a school
designed for kids

JAMES CASS

Most schools are designed for adults, for the comfort and convenience of faculty and administration. The Beloit-Turner Middle School in Wisconsin, by contrast, was clearly conceived as a place for kids—or, more accurately, it was artfully designed to house a program based on the special nature and needs of early adolescents.

The visitor's first impression of the school is one of openness—of wide-open, visually attractive space. His second impression is one of almost constant movement, relatively quiet, purposeful, and relaxed, but unceasing. Only later in the day does he realize that he has heard no bells ringing to signal the end of class periods, and that classes of various sizes have met for differing lengths of time, and then have dissolved and reformed with a minimum of disturbance.

The heart of the school consists of three large classrooms—or pods, as they are called—each serving as a homeroom for 125 to 150 students, and as a classroom for varying numbers of students throughout the day. These pods

The most important characteristic for teachers at our school is that they like kids. It's nice if they know a little English or math or science, but that's not half as important as how they feel about kids.

Herbert Jackson, Principal, Beloit-Turner Middle School

> **Doors lock a kid's mind. The moment he walks into a classroom he has about eighteen by thirty feet, and that's it. He's shafted. He can't move. If we're going to give kids the right to think and explore, and discover, they have to be in a building where they have freedom to move, freedom to think. Movement and thinking go hand in hand.**
>
> **Herbert Jackson**

are arranged in a U-shape around a central core of administrative and special service offices, and a large, open instructional materials center. The remainder of this central core consists of an ingeniously tiered cafeteria/commons, which connects the two side pods at the open end of the U, and doubles as a classroom for either large or small groups, as well as a "socializing center" for students. Divisions between the various open areas are marked only by the different colors of carpeting that covers virtually all the floors in the school—including the cafeteria. Adjacent areas house the auditorium, gymnasium, and facilities for music, art, home economics, and industrial arts.

Designed by architect Jack Reif of John J. Flad & Associates (Madison, Wisconsin), the school incorporates elements of open design that are by no means new, but are employed with a sensitivity that not only makes it possible for an unusual educational program to function, but actively supplements and enhances it.

The program itself is based on the assumption that sixth-, seventh-, and eighth-graders have special interests, needs, and objectives—and that the school should work with these special qualities rather than against them. Conceived by Professor Rolland Callaway of the University of Wisconsin, Milwaukee, the program specifically assumes that these early adolescents need an active, social school environment, because they are deeply involved in questioning who they are and in exploring the nature of their relationship to everyone and everything. Consequently, this is not the age at which a child is ready to confine his study to the separate, highly organized disciplines. Rather, his study should draw upon the disciplines, and he should begin to develop varied academic skills, but the emphasis should be placed on the exploration of social issues and problems, with particular attention to the development of individual interests, values, and attitudes.

To keep the program as flexible as possible, the day is divided into three large blocks of broad objectives. One half of the day is allotted to "Developing Social Sensitivity and Understanding" (which draws on the social studies, English, and foreign languages), one quarter of the day to the "Physical Environment" (which focuses on science and math), and the remainder of the day to "Developing Creative Interests and Abilities" (which offers students freedom to develop their own interests in art, music, home economics, and industrial arts). Each large group of students works with a team of teachers, teaching assistants, student teachers, and interns, as well as with specialists. The instructional program itself is not predetermined, but

> The typical school is organized on the assumption that if one child talks to another he is either out of order or he's cheating. At Beloit-Turner, however, the school building is designed to encourage social activities and relationships. For example, the cafeteria is used by the children for a variety of purposes. Besides eating lunch and socializing here, they may come at any time of the day to work in small groups or merely to take a "Coke break" from their studies.
>
> Dr. Rolland Callaway, Professor of Education, University of Wisconsin-Milwaukee

is "relegated to on-the-spot, day-by-day, week-by-week planning of the teaching team and the students." The part of the day devoted to the creative arts leaves the student free to choose his own area of interest—and to change it at will.

The school was opened just last September [1969], and all facilities were not completed until early December, but both the school and it program appear to enjoy substantial community support. Although located in a typical Midwestern rural-suburban area that is far from affluent, no federal, state, or foundation funds were involved. It was purely a community effort that has, perhaps, been characterized best by former board of education president William D. Behling, executive director of the Beloit *Daily News*. "The Turner Middle School," Mr. Behling says, "is the remarkably successful result of an uninhibited effort by an improbable group of people who sought only to find a better way of meeting the educational needs of the early adolescent."

It is far too early to assess the ultimate success of the school, but teachers and students are enthusiastic. The teachers, to be sure, are rather more restrained in their adjustments—not least, perhaps, because they find it less easy to adjust to the openness and the constant movement, and because their responsibility for developing an effective instructional program is so much greater than it would be in a traditional school. Yet nearly all are firmly committed to the concept of the school and seem to have reservations primarily about whether they have discovered how best to employ their professional skills in the unfamiliar environment.

But the children have no doubts. "It's the freedom that's so great," they say, "you can do what you want." And they add: "Yes, we learn just as much as we did last year—we learn more. Sure, we still have to study science and math, but it's different." The ways in which it differs may vary for individuals, but they have a common theme that echoes Professor Callaway's assertion that, when we enforce rules of quiet conformity on students, we "foist behavior patterns on youngsters in our schools which we, as adults, would not live with."

"The teachers don't push you into learning," a diminutive sixth-grader explains, "they let you come in by yourself and do it the way you want. We learn more because we want to—and it's so great because after you've done your work nobody cares if you visit with your friends." Three eighth-grade girls, alternately studying and talking in a little corner formed by movable tables with low tack-board backs, agree with their sixth-grade colleague. "It's better when you get the latest gossip while you study," they say. And one adds: "You only really learn when you want to." A seventh-grader is entranced by the freedom allowed him to go play chess when he has finished his math lesson. And others clearly share his pleasure—two or three chess games are in progress at almost any time of the day, a dozen during the noon hour.

But Danny, a bright, articulate eighth-grader who has been a serious discipline problem in the past, sums it up: "You can't help but learn more, there are so many things to do—and in the afternoon [during the time allotted to creative interests] you can do anything you want." However, Danny's friend, who has a similar history, has had more difficulty in adjusting to freedom—and provides the counterpoint. "Last year when you did something you weren't supposed to do, and got away with it, you had a feeling of accomplishment. This year nobody cares. Take gum. They say go ahead and chew gum in class—so I lost my taste for it. Nobody chews gum any more—maybe two or three guys in the whole school."

It will take much more time to get a final reading on the Beloit-Turner Middle School. The program is still evolving, and its eventual success will depend in large measure on the skill and the dedication of the teachers who implement it. But perhaps the best interim assessment has already been made by the students themselves. As a result of their demand, the school is open seven days a week. It's the most interesting place in town.

Should a student or a group of students become inspired to engage in role-playing or the construction of a model or set, he is allowed to proceed to the Creative Interests and Abilities area to take advantage of his momentary inspiration. The same holds true if a student feels that he wishes to listen to music, or paint a picture, or work out an experiment in the Physical Environment area. Although it is absolutely necessary to have some sort of schedule structure, whenever possible, it is ignored.

Carl Strassburg, Superintendent, Beloit-Turner Joint School District No. 1.

A VISIT TO THE "SCHOOL WITHOUT WALLS"

James D. Greenberg
and Robert E. Roush

America has never had an educational system worthy of itself. Why is the American high school so out of touch with American life? It is because the boundaries of education are no longer correctly drawn.

Our schools imagine that students learn best in a special building separated from the larger community. Teachers and administrators are included in the group of educators; parents, employers, businessmen, ministers are excluded. The year-around Parkway Program sets up new boundaries and provides a new framework in which the energy of all of us can be used in learning, not in maintaining an obsolete, inefficient system.

There is no schoolhouse, there is no separate building; school is not a place but an activity, a process. We are indeed a school without walls. Where do the students learn? In the city. Where in the city? Anywhere and everywhere.

John Bremer, *The Parkway Program,* Philadelphia. The Philadelphia Public Schools, 1970, pp. 3–4.

The preceding quotes are excerpted from a booklet written by John Bremer, director of Philadelphia's Parkway Program, whose ideas of how students learn and how schools should relate to the environment have been implemented in what is perhaps this country's most interesting new "high school." Parkway's humanistic philosophy of how students learn is one of the program's most outstanding characteristics, but the actual use of the city as the classroom is probably its greatest departure from the traditional high school and its most unique contribution to educational practice.

An Overview of the Program

The Benjamin Franklin Parkway is the downtown area of the city in which some of Philadelphia's great institutions and museums are located—a logical place for learning. Thus the name "Parkway Program" evolved. The program began early in 1969 with 140 students and this year [1970] the school has 500 students, 30 faculty members, and 30 university interns. Admission is made on a random basis, the only requisite being that the heterogeneous elements of the city's population be equally represented. The only criterion for admission is the expressed interest of the prospective student and his or her parents.

Three basic units, called communities, comprise the organization of the school. The three communities—Alpha, Beta, and Gamma—each have about 150 students who are divided into 10 groups of 15 called "tutorial groups." One full-time faculty member and one university intern are assigned to each tutorial group, which functions as the unit in which personal encouragement, support, and counseling are given and is the unit responsible for the acquisition of basic skills in language and mathematics.

Each student may choose to participate in a management group whose function is to provide the services necessary for the Parkway's successful day-to-day operation. This allows the students to be involved in a meaningful way in determining the nature of their program. The Town Meeting, which occurs once each week, offers an opportunity for the whole community to discuss and resolve common problems.

The academic curriculum (the requirements for graduation are the same as those of any other high school in Philadelphia) consists of institutional offerings, basic skills offerings, and elective offerings. Institutional offerings are those courses offered, generally at the request of the student, by participating Parkway institutions, of which there are nearly 200. Basic skills offerings are math and language arts courses taught by the Parkway staff. Elective offerings are classes in the humanities, physical sciences, and social studies taught by the Parkway staff. Conventional grading patterns are not used; courses are only offered on a credit, no-credit basis. In addition to the academic curriculum, each student is encouraged to conduct a special problems course in an area of his own interest and to participate in work problems of the Parkway institutions as an extra nongraded component. . . .

Exciting Alternative

The sign proclaiming "Parkway Program" emerged from the bleak background of Philadelphia's Market Street as a welcome promise of relief from the cold drizzly February morning. We entered the door following the inevitable arrow and nodded automatically to the few young people who sat on the inside steps smoking and conversing. Then a thought, spontaneous and irrepressible, registered itself on my dampened brain: "Why aren't these kids in school?" Just as quickly, however, I realized that they were in school—in the very different type of alternative school we had come to see, one likely to provide many more unconventional and unexpected scenes in the time ahead.

At the top of the stairs was a single large room filled with people, some at desks or telephones, others in transit, some talking, others listening, some standing, others sitting, some in groups, others alone. The whole scene oozed with activity and life and while there was no apparent order to it all, a sense of purpose seemed evident. I assumed that some of the players in this intriguing scene were teachers and that others were students, but it was difficult to tell which was which and impossible to define the nature of the activities in progress. Consequently, in our later talk with John Bremer I asked if he would identify the kinds of things that were going on about us. His response—quick and unqualified—was to the effect that he had no idea what the activities consisted of, that it was furthermore not his business to know, and that the participants had defined the content, value, and details of their pursuits and were probably doing whatever it was they therefore felt it important to do.

For me this was a key moment; Bremer's forthright reaction showed that it was at once futile and wrong to try to define this particular experience in terms of my traditional conception of "school" and that this program must be viewed on its own terms. One of those terms—indeed, a philosophical undergirding that is pervasive and essential to the program—is the emphasis-goal of the student's becoming self-reliant, self-defining, and self-directed; a responsible individual and worthwhile member of a dynamic social group. It then seemed clear to me that Parkway had gone beyond mere verbalization of this ideal and had implemented an honest follow-through which properly allowed students the liberty of self-determination and the freedom to act it out. Since the honesty of the commitment required that students not be saved from "bad" consequences nor artificially steered toward "good" ones, Bremer fairly had no business knowing everybody else's business and made the point unflinchingly.

In the brief time we had to visit all three communities of Parkway, I gleaned what seemed to be a consistent positive attitude toward the openness and self-responsibility aspects of the program's operation. At a time when "humanizing the school" has become a universal but unrealized goal, Parkway may be well on the way toward achieving humanization. There is tolerance, friendliness, respect, and common purpose—all on a true people-to-people basis. Teachers, students, and administrators are on a first-name basis with each other and are free to dress ivy, mod, "freaky," or whatever. But beyond breaking down superficial barriers to self-expression and to truly personal relationships is the deep, conscious seeking for a reality atmosphere that will allow people to become and be themselves, to know and accept each other for what they are, and to define their destinies in light of option-loaded but value-equal alternatives.

The kids were great. The teachers and administrators were great. And everybody thought the Parkway Program was great. Almost to a man, the people I talked to embraced with jealous fervor the new educational alternative in which they were involved. The schools from which they came were retrospectively viewed with varying degrees of disenchantment, disgust, and despair. Some students came from poor ghetto schools, others from the finest academic high schools; but all came seeking an alternative to the inadequate and/or repressive experience they felt had been offered before. Most of them expressed satisfaction at having found a good thing. There was a real chance to learn for yourself here and learn what you wanted: no grades to create destructive competitiveness and external reward emphases; no rigid requirements to restrict horizons and close off inquiry; no strict authority figure wielding "discipline" to punish self-expression and limit personal freedom. The result: interest in learning, heightened awareness, and a sense of responsibility for one's actions. Most of all, there was a general rapport that was extremely satisfying and a rare sense of mutual respect. I had no reason to doubt the claims that a significant degree of racial harmony had developed in this integrated (60 percent black, 40 percent white) population and that it was likely to continue.

Of course I didn't believe everything could be so rosy, and the existence of problems was readily admitted. Among other things, many students shared with the staff the recognition that transition from a traditional school context to this new, free environment caused difficulties. Lots of students wasted time and not everyone found everything to his liking. Conflicts persisted about how to manage certain issues, what to do about graffiti on the walls, and other decoration options. But I agreed with many who felt that the process of resolving these problems was integral to the overall learning experience and that the chance to make mistakes, to fritter away time, and to suffer consequences of self-made decisions was ultimately a positive opportunity for meaningful development.

The humanistic orientation of the Parkway Program was not the only unique, nor the most celebrated, aspect to be encountered. It was rather the "school without walls" concept and the use of the city as the classroom that had mainly attracted national attention. John Bremer's philosophy on this point was hard for me to disagree with: If we set ourselves the job of helping kids to grow up and live in the world, we are doing them a disservice by blocking off that very world with the four walls of a monolithic school building. Consequently, Bremer acted to break down the walls and get the students out in the city—to use it, learn about it, live in it. Not only were the variety and type of resources multiplied manyfold by expanding into the city, but the quality of the experiences was enhanced. I also couldn't help but think of a connection which was impressed on me in some meetings of the U.S.O.E. [United States Office of Education] task force on environmental/ecological education. That is, we have to get teachers and students to become more aware of the environment and to study it. Well, what could be more on target in an urban setting than a school which had its whole being integrated with the very environment encompassing it?

Students went to art classes in museums, economics seminars in banks, auto mechanics "classes" in service stations, and leathermaking classes in little leather shops. I visited a leather shop activity down in a section of emerging off-beat boutiques and stores displaying handcrafted wares. It was a real leather shop, with hides hanging all around. The proprietor looked like an artist (stereotype A) and clearly produced like an artisan. He was working on a project and so was the young girl with the leather punch. It turned out she was from Parkway and this was one of her classes. It just all seemed to fall into place: a great environment for learning the subject and for learning about the small business and practical problems of artisans, all the tools and resources right at hand, a teacher who was superbly qualified and proficient in his field. She loved the class and loved the Parkway Program for providing the experience. He dug the teaching bit without having to be tied down like a regular teacher. It struck me hard that there must be many people in the world who share that desire to teach or help others in some way but don't get an opportunity to do it. What a waste!

So Parkway was a great experience. Kids got to share in planning their whole curriculum and were free to choose courses to their liking. They weren't restricted by buildings and could express themselves by helping to "create" the spaces that they did have. They didn't get failing grades, but they got much personal evaluation and the chance to evaluate their program in turn. The kids like it, the teachers like it, the director likes it, and all are eager to work to overcome any problems and improve the situation they have begun. The participants are volunteers and they almost all stay once they have come. Most of all, this is just an *alternative* and is billed as nothing more. No panacea or "answer" for public education, Parkway offers an option within an otherwise fairly monopolistic system. It is not good for everybody. But it is a needed alternative for Philadelphia and a viably transportable concept to form the base of similar programs in many other cities. Last summer there were 10,000 applications for only 500 places—they've got a good thing going and it's a seller's market.

· · · · *Vive la différence!*

PORTLAND'S UNCONVENTIONAL ADAMS HIGH

John Guernsey

When school lets out for the summer in a month or so [1970], the John Adams High School in Portland, Ore., will be one school year old. Its brief life has been a volcano of controversy because of its almost complete departure from the conventional approach to high school education.

"Adams High does not teach respect for authority, discipline, basic scholarship, or orderly use of time. The school teaches gross egotism, extreme self-centeredness, myopic self-delusion, and general anarchy," says one Portland resident.

"We're learning to live with other races and other people here at Adams," says a student. "And all the math, English, Chaucer, and history teaching in the past didn't teach our parents how to do that."

"My daughter's education is being neglected at Adams, and I am having her transferred to another high school," says a parent who meant it. His daughter now attends a different high school.

"I'm all for Adams," says another parent. "My daughter went to another high school for two years, but this is the first time she has taken the initiative to do studies and projects on her own."

Robert Schwartz, the 32-year-old, mercury-minded principal, describes Adams as "a school where students want to go, and want to learn because they are curious and interested—not because an attempt is made to force them to learn." He has stayed in the saddle during the bucking first months of the operation, and is now convinced that "the school will gain momentum and support as it goes."

What's so different about Adams that has inspired such diametrically opposed opinion?

For one thing, it's the school's curriculum itself, which is split into general education problem-solving courses and an electives program. The general education part works like this:

All students spend about half of each school day, either the morning or the afternoon, on different teams that study ways to cope with such problems as air and water pollution, unemployment and welfare, reducing student unrest, improving student-adult understanding, keeping the automobile from destroying the metropolitan area, reducing the crime rate, and lessening race-related friction in the school and community.

There is no breakdown by grades or ability in these problem-solving sessions: All study teams are mixtures of juniors, sophomores, and freshmen (the school will not have a senior class until 1970–71).

Teachers attempt to encourage older students to help the younger ones, the faster ones to help the slower ones, and each student works on the part of a problem that is compatible with his ability. The problem-solving tactic also avoids the compartmentalization of subjects: The students do not study English for 40 minutes, or social studies, math, science, or history as specific courses; they deal with all these basic subjects as parts of a study of a given real problem during the general education program.

As an example of the value of the general education approach, Schwartz refers to an incident that occurred just as Adams opened last fall. Several Portland high schools began the year with serious race-related student problems, resulting in numerous assaults and police action. The most severe disturbances were at Adams, where the philosophy is to bring together students from all backgrounds, representing many ranges of abilities, and where the student body is 22 percent black.

General education study teams jumped right into the action and undertook to develop solutions to Adams' racial problems. In fact, race relations occupied the whole general education program for the first couple of weeks of school. A race relations committee held assemblies where students could talk matters out, and black and white student leaders began to take command of the situation. Since then, although assaults and confrontations haven't ceased altogether, there has not been another major racial flare-up at the school.

Schwartz explains the problem-solving education approach: "Students need to learn what will help them function effectively in society, regardless of what type of work or what further education they plan to go into after high school."

The courses at Adams were put together almost entirely by the teachers, with help from about 100 students, during the summer of 1969. Schwartz would have liked to have had even more of the school's 1,300 students take part in curriculum planning.

The teachers kept several questions in mind while putting together the courses. What should students know and be able to do after leaving high school? What parts of the individual disciplines can contribute the most to the overall general studies courses?

"The program is tied to something inside the kid that interests him," says Schwartz. "Then it must be tied to something on the outside that is real." By real, Schwartz and his teachers mean the problems of today, race, pollution, crime, and so forth—not material that deals with national problems of 100 or 200 years ago, although they insist they do not ignore historical perspective.

"The important thing is that students should learn the techniques of problem solving and how to adjust to change. These abilities should prove useful throughout the rest of their lives," Schwartz adds.

It is noon now, and half the students have completed their problem-solving sessions. During the afternoon they will attend specific classes but they take what electives they please or they can do independent study, meet with student-faculty committees, or even goof off a part of the time. Each student is scheduled for some electives at which attendance is expected.

Of the elective courses, some require a full school year and others are mini-courses that last about six weeks. The mini-courses meet just about every imaginable interest: computer application and technology, astrology, coed badminton, and even such special studies as "From Bach to Bartok." Schwartz explains the large number of elective courses and the free time in which students can study what they wish: "Give kids a chance to try some of the things they're interested in. They must have the chance to be curious, to explore adult roles, and have meaningful choices."

Schwartz also points out that the academic and college bound students can use the elective periods for taking in-depth and continuous studies in math, English, physical and social sciences, history, and other college requirement courses.

Adams is well tuned to the fact that of each 10 students who begin as freshmen in high school, only about two will go on to complete college. Consequently, the $5.8 million high school has strong and wide ranging job-related programs in which a good percentage of Adams students are enrolled.

Schwartz and his staff hope eventually to encourage business, industry, and the professions to participate in the school's training program and to sponsor students in half-day on-the-job training apprenticeships. They also hope to invite business and industrial representatives as guest lecturers and assistant teachers, and they plan to arrange for some vocational-technical classes at outside plants during the evenings.

For 60 students who don't really seem to be turned on by the academic or vocational program at Adams, there is a mobile school where they spend most of their general education time. A big bus, accommodating about 30 youths each morning and afternoon, roams the metropolitan area on scheduled visits to industrial plants, art museums, city and county operations, conservation projects, airports, and the like. In an attempt to add relevancy, Adams uses the community itself as a basis for these youngsters' education. On returning to Adams, the students write, tell stories, or make movies concerning their outings, and teachers try to motivate them toward more concrete learning experiences.

Some parents, especially those whose youngsters are headed for college, are uneasy about the school's relatively lax requirements that specific courses be completed in order to qualify for graduation. However, college officials have assured them that their children will not be denied college admission because of that. Grades are optional at Adams. At the beginning of each course students can, with their parents' approval, choose to receive either a regular letter grade or a pass-fail notice.

Another of Adams' major educational tenets is that students learn better and teachers teach better when the students and teachers have a close understanding of one another via more personal contact and less formal relationships.

To combat the impersonality of largeness, Adams operates as four smaller high schools in one—at least for the general education program and for administrative purposes such as counseling and disciplining. Each smaller school—known as a house—has about 300 students, mixed as to class (freshmen, sophomores, juniors), race, and social and economic background. Two teams of teachers work with the students in each house, and the same teachers stay with the same students as much as possible for more than one academic year.

Counselors are part of each house team and work with the students and other teachers all day long. In this manner the counselors get to know the students better and can do more to help them with their problems. They also help teachers improve their counseling abilities.

One of the most innovative changes at Adams is in the area of school policy-making. While the ultimate responsibility for the operation of the school rests with the principal, Adams is experimenting with a mechanism to permit majority rule voting by students and faculty members on some issues. With the aim of teaching students how

democracy works so they will be better qualified citizens when they reach voting age, the Adams operation duplicates, in some respects, the functioning of the U.S. Government.

"The whole issue of decision-making in conventional high schools is wrong," says Schwartz. "The students and faculty members want more voice, so we're experimenting with the delegation of authority."

At Adams there is a school legislature made up of a student-elected student senate and a faculty-elected faculty senate. Joint committees representing these bodies meet jointly on such issues as curriculum and grading, or on policies that most directly affect students and teachers.

In other cases the senates function separately. If the issues involve student conduct, dress codes, and so forth, the policies are made and enforced by the student senate. If they involve working conditions and other areas of primary interest to teachers, they are dealt with by the faculty senate.

Schwartz and other administrators make up the executive branch of the school government. Changes or new policies developed and approved by the senates, jointly or separately, require the principal's signature before they can become school policies. Although the principal has veto power over bills sent to him, the legislative bodies have been empowered to override the principal's veto by a two-thirds vote. The override policy, however, is currently under reconsideration.

Adams also plans to set up a judicial branch which will probably be some sort of appeals body made up of students, faculty members, and administrators. However, Schwartz and his staff have found that there are many legal implications involved that require careful study. "A school is not a court," said Jerry Fletcher, coordinator of research and evaluation at Adams. "We have to be very careful in setting up quasi-judicial procedures."

In addition to introducing changes that could make education more interesting and relevant to students and teachers, Adams includes numerous clinical programs to influence teacher preparation, teacher enthusiasm for teaching, and community involvement. Schwartz and his staff feel that the clinical approach is one of the most important aspects of the experimental school. They challenge the long-standing education concept that college and university campuses are the best places for training teachers and performing educational research.

"The truth is that a university is just not a very relevant setting for training teachers and doing much educational research," says Schwartz. "As it is now, a college student training to be a teacher does not get into a regular school classroom until very late in his training—the last part of the senior year. He gets far too much of his material from theory and hearsay from a professor." So Adams has worked out an arrangement with officials of Reed College, Lewis and Clark College, and Oregon State University that permits junior year teacher trainees to receive college credit for working in Adams classrooms. Nearly all of Adams' 80-member faculty is made up of experienced teachers, but the school also has a great many trainees—nearly 100 of them this year. They are teamed off with regular teachers so that the inexperienced learn from the experienced in actual classroom situations.

Some of the teachers at Adams also hold assistant professorships at the colleges with which the high school cooperates. Schwartz views this as a very necessary advancement in education. "There must be closer educational ties between the four-year campuses and the grade schools and high schools," he stresses.

In one training program that Adams carries out in cooperation with Oregon State University, eight interns, most of them black, are being trained for teaching in inner-city schools. The interns either have no college degrees or majored in something other than education. They are learning on the job at Adams, getting a full year of actual classroom experience and taking training for college credit from the Adams teachers who double as professors. Schwartz hopes that the experiment, sponsored under the Education Professions Development Act, will result in more blacks with teaching potential being able to enter the teaching field.

Schwartz believes the on-the-job training for both blacks and whites without college training in the field of education can have two major impacts:

1. Elementary schools and high schools throughout the nation want more black teachers than they can find, because not enough blacks have college backgrounds—especially in the field of education. On-the-job training like that provided in the Adams-OSU program could qualify many more in a hurry.

2. Preparing teachers without an overload of educational theory courses could modify long-standing teacher credential requirements which deny schools the use of many persons who are experts in their fields and who would like to teach but will not take the methods courses necessary to qualify.

Adams also hopes to add to the significance of educational research, since the school has its own researchers and evaluators right there on the job as part of the teaching teams. "Research is much more meaningful and reliable when conducted in and around actual classrooms," Schwartz emphasizes.

This 21st century high school is the creature of Schwartz and six other secondary school teachers who, in 1967, were in their final year of study at the Harvard Graduate School of Education. They set out to develop a model for a school program that would make possible the achievement of many of the educational objectives that were commonly voiced by educational and social analysis but had not been established in practice or adequately tested.

The Harvard graduate students envisioned, in short, a clinical high school—one where instruction of students, curriculum development, preservice and inservice training, and research could all go on simultaneously. A high school, they believed, might be made to function somewhat like a teaching-hospital does in medicine.

"We realized that our individual voices would be drowned out, but if we had our own high school and worked as a team, we could make the changes we believe are necessary," says Schwartz.

The seven graduate students developed a detailed plan of how they believed a high school should operate. Then they sent a proposal to half a dozen metropolitan school districts and kept their fingers crossed that they would get a taker. They got several but were most impressed by the enthusiastic reply from Portland school officials and school board members.

Now, after eight months, is the school living up to the expectations of Schwartz and his codesigners?

"It's hard to say," the innovative principal is frank to admit. "The battle was simply for survival when the school first opened. Then the problems with questioning parents occupied much of our time. It has moved so fast, so far, that we haven't had much time for measuring and analysis. I believe we are through the roughest part now, and

can get on with better teaching, learning, and measuring."

There's no question that parent opposition to the school has simmered down. Adams now has four parent advisory groups, one for each student house, totaling more than 160 persons. These groups usually meet at least once every two weeks, and some of the members are parents who continue to look askance at the school.

"And that's the way we want it," Schwartz says. "We don't want the parent groups made up totally of parents who are there to tell us what a great job we are doing. We have learned a lot—and continue to learn—from what the critical parents have to say. What we want most is to have them all involved with the school."

Adams won't claim that it has solved all attendance problems or convinced 1,300 students there to love school. But many of the students obviously do like Adams, and their enthusiasm has been instrumental in quieting down a large number of questioning parents. As one parent put it: "I still don't understand the damned place, but it's the first time my kid has actually been excited about going to school. So how can I knock it?"

Some students feel they are

learning more at Adams. Others like the school because they have more voice in what they will study or a chance to be on their own. Then there are some who really don't know why they like it more than other high schools. "We just feel better here," they'll say. But most will tell you, "We're getting more out of school here because our teachers are more than teachers—they help you with all kinds of problems."

Since Adams teachers have less time scheduled in classes than teachers at other Portland schools, they have more time for other contacts with students. "A very positive point," says Patricia Wertheimer, coordinator of social services at the school, "is that the teachers have a genuine interest in their kids. How many other schools do you know where teachers visit a student's home or phone if the student is absent too many times?"

A visit to the school at 3 p.m. verifies this. People aren't stampeding one another to check out and leave for the day. Many students and teachers stay until five, six, or seven because they're working on something—or with somebody—they're interested in.

THE RISE OF THE "FREE SCHOOL"

Bonnie Barrett Stretch

For the past seven years, critics have been telling parents and teachers what is wrong with the public schools. Such writers as John Holt, Herbert Kohl, Jonathan Kozol, George Dennison, and Paul Goodman have described the authoritarianism that structures many classrooms, the stress on grades and discipline at the expense of learning, and the suppression of the natural curiosity and instincts of the young. Many parents and teachers have begun to see for themselves the boredom, fear, and grievous lack of learning that too often accompany schooling—not only for the poor and the black, but for suburban white youngsters as well—and they have begun to ask what can be done about it.

The revolt is no longer against outdated curriculums or ineffective teaching methods—the concerns of the late Fifties and early Sixties. The revolt today is against the institution itself, against the implicit assumption that learning must be imposed on children by adults, that learning is not something one does by and for oneself, but something designated by a teacher. Schools operating on this assumption tend to hold children in a prolonged state of dependency, to keep them from discovering their own capacities for learning, and to encourage a sense of impotence and lack of worth. The search is for alternatives to this kind of institution.

In the past four years, increasing numbers of parents and teachers have struck out on their own to develop a new kind of school that will allow a new kind of education, that will create independent, courageous people able to face and deal with the shifting complexities of the modern world. The new schools, or free schools, or community schools—they go by all these names—have sprung up by the hundreds across the country. Through a continuous exchange of school brochures and newsletters, and through various conferences, the founders of these schools have developed a degree of self-awareness, a sense of community that has come to be called "the new schools movement."

The new schools charge little or no tuition, are frequently held together by spit and string, and run mainly on the energy and excitement of people who have set out to do their own thing. Their variety seems limitless. No two are alike. They range from inner-city black to suburban and rural white. Some seem to be pastoral escapes from the grit of modern conflict, while others are deliberate experiments in integrated multicultural, multilingual education. They turn up anywhere—in city storefronts, old barns, former barracks, abandoned church buildings, and parents' or teachers' homes. They have crazy names like Someday School, Viewpoint Non-School, A Peck of Gold, The New Community, or New Directions—names that for all their diversity reflect the two things most of these schools have in common: the idea of freedom for youngsters and a humane education.

As the Community School of Santa Barbara (California) states in its brochure: "The idea is that freedom is a supreme good; that people, including young people, have a right to freedom, and that people who are free will in general be more open, more humane, more intelligent than people who are directed, manipulated, ordered about. . . ."

The Santa Barbara Community School is located in a converted barracks on a hill above the town. The

. . . a new kind of school that will allow a new kind of education, that will create independent, courageous people able to face and deal with the shifting complexities of the modern world.

fifty or so children (ages three to fourteen) almost invariably come from wealthy, white, fairly progressive families who want to give their children "the nicest education possible," as one teacher put it. Inside the building are a large meeting room; some smaller rooms for seminars, discussions, and tutorials; a wood and metal shop; classrooms for the younger children; and a small library. Classes for the younger children are based on the Leicestershire model. Rooms are organized by activity centers—a math corner here, a reading corner there. Parents' money has helped provide a remarkable amount of creative learning materials. Children are free to move from one thing to another as their interest shifts, and children of all ages frequently work and play together. For the older kids, the method is largely tutorial: one, two, or three youngsters working with a teacher. Although there is a "core curriculum" of literature, science, and social studies, the classes follow the interests and preferences of the students.

Outside and behind the building is enough space for a large playground, a pile of wood and lumber, a large pile of scrap metal including bicycle and car parts, and an old car, whose motor the older children are dismantling as a lesson in mechanics or physics (depending on whom you talk to). Children of all ages use the wood and metal to carve or weld into sculpture, as well as to fix bikes and build toys. "It's important for kids to learn about tools," explained a teacher. "Most kids don't know how things work. You really have to see a six-year-old in goggles with a welding torch to appreciate what it means."

The parents like the school, although they sometimes worry about how much the children are learning. By "learning" they mean the three Rs, social studies, etc. Parent pressure has led the Community School to place more emphasis on traditional subject matter than many free schools do. Teachers, on the other hand, are more concerned about another kind of learning. They would like to help these white middle-class youngsters develop a better sense of the world, to expose them to styles of life and work besides those of their families. There are frequent trips to ranches, factories, local businesses, and other schools. But these experiences, being interludes, remain essentially artificial to children. What are real are the comforts and concerns that inform their daily lives and that are shared with their friends.

In contrast to this isolation is the Children's Community Workshop School in New York City. Situated in an economically and racially integrated neighborhood, the school makes a conscious effort to keep its enrollment one-third white, one-third black, and one-third Puerto Rican. Because it is intended specifically as an alternative to the public schools, the Community Workshop charges no tuition. It is supported primarily by foundation grants and private donations, but the scramble for money is a continuous one that taxes a great deal of the energy of the school's director, Anita Moses.

Like the Santa Barbara Community School, the Community Workshop bases its structure on the Leicestershire method. And, again like Santa Barbara, it does not hold strictly to the method. There is a great deal of emphasis on the children's own interests, and new directions and materials are being tried all the time. A visitor to the school may find one group of children at a table struggling to build arches out of sugar cubes; another two or three children may be working with an erector set, others with tape recorders and a typewriter. In the midst of all this independent activity may be found one teacher helping one child learn to write his name.

Except for the use of Leicestershire techniques, there is little similarity between the Children's Community Workshop and the school in Santa Barbara. The heterogeneity of the student body makes the educational and human problems far more complex. Where achievement levels and cultural backgrounds vary widely, there is a great deal of accommodation necessary on the part of teachers and parents. At the same time, there can be no question that the children are learning more than the traditional three Rs.

Both the Community Workshop and the Santa Barbara Community School, however, have more structure than many free schools. The tendency in these schools is not to stress conventional intellectual training, to offer it if and when the children want it, and in general to let the youngsters discover and pursue their own interests. The new schools agree fully with Piaget's statement that "play is the serious business of childhood," and a child may as easily spend whole days in the sandbox as in the reading center. The lack of structure, however, leads to a lot of noise and running around, and all this activity may seem like chaos to a visitor. Often that's exactly what it is. It is a difficult skill to attune oneself to individual children, and to build on their individual needs and concerns, and few teachers have mastered it.

Often, too, older youngsters, suddenly released from the constraints of public school, will run wild for the first few weeks, or even months, of freedom. But gradually, as they work the pent-up energy out of their system, and as they learn that the adults really will allow this freedom, they begin to discover their own real interests and to turn their energy to constructive tasks.

"The longer they've been in public school, and the worse their experience there is, the longer it takes for them to settle down, but eventually they all do," says Bill Kenney, who has taught at Pinel School in Martinez, California, for ten years. Pinel is an essentially Summerhillian school where classes in subjects such as reading and arithmetic are offered, but the children are not compelled to attend. Based on his experience at Pinel, Mr. Kenney believes that in a school that is solidly middle-class it can be expected that any happy, healthy child will eventually learn to read, write, and do basic arithmetic, whether or not he is formally taught. The experience of other middle-class free schools tends to corroborate this assumption.

The appeal of this philosophy is enormous, judging from the number of students and teachers applying to the new schools—all these schools report more applicants than they can handle—and from the constant flow of visitors who come to watch, ask questions, and sometimes get in the way. A few schools have had to set up specific visiting days in an effort to stem the tide. Three major conferences on "alternatives in education" took place this spring [1970]— in Cuernavaca, Mexico; in Santa Barbara, California; and in Toronto, Canada—and people flocked to them by the hundreds to talk to such "heroes" as John Holt and George Dennison, and to talk to one another and learn who's doing what and how. Representatives from foundations, universities, and the U.S. Office of Education also came, eager to know whether the critics' ideas can be given life.

Through the conferences and through correspondence and exchanges of school newsletters, a self-awareness is developing among the new schools, a sense of themselves as part of a growing movement. Much of this increased consciousness is due to the work of the New Schools Exchange, an information clearinghouse that grew out of a conference of 200 schools a year ago. During its first year, the exchange set up a directory of new schools, put teachers and kids in touch with schools, and schools in touch with teachers, kids, materials—and even, occasionally, money. In that year, too, 800 new names were added to the exchange list, and the exchange helped many through the labor pains of birth by offering nuts-and-bolts information about how to incorporate a school, and ways to get through the bureaucratic maze of building, fire, and health regulations.

But the mortality rate among these new schools is high. Harvey Haber of the Exchange estimates about eighteen months is the average life span. This includes those that endure for years and those that barely get off the ground. Money is universally the biggest hassle and the reason most commonly cited for failure. Even those schools that endure are seriously hampered by the constant struggle for fiscal survival that too often must take precedence over education. Most schools are started by people who are not rich, and charge little or no tuition, in an effort to act as an alternative for the common man (the rich have always had alternatives). Teachers work for pennies, when they are paid at all. "How do I survive?" one teacher laughed a bit anxiously. "I found a nice landlord who doesn't bug me about the rent. I dip into my savings, and get my parents and friends to invite me to dinner—often. Then, there are food stamps, of course. Mostly we rely on each other for moral support and help over the really rough places."

This kind of dedication, however, is too much to ask of anyone for any length of time. Working with children in an open classroom with few guidelines makes tremendous demands on teachers, Anita Moses of the Children's Community Workshop points out. Furthermore, teachers must often give their time for planning, for parent conferences, or for Saturday workshops with new teaching techniques and materials. There are intrinsic rewards for this, of course, but extrinsic rewards are also necessary, Mrs. Moses stresses, and those rewards should be in terms of salary.

There are other hurdles besides money—red tape, harassment by various state and city bureaucracies, and hostility from the community at large. In Salt Lake City, for example, a citizens committee tried to close a new Summerhill school on the grounds that the school was immoral and the teachers were Communists.

But perhaps the most fundamental factor for survival is the degree of commitment on the part of the teachers and parents. For brochures, newsletters, and other public pronouncements, it is possible to articulate the concept of freedom and its importance to the emotional and intellectual development of the child. But basically the appeal is to a gut-level longing for love, joy, and human community, and often the schools are run on this romantic basis. "If you stop putting pressure on the kids, the tendency is to stop putting pressure on the staff, too," one teacher observed. Schools that fail within a few months of opening tend to be those begun by people merely interested in trying out a new idea. When the idea turns out to be more complex, and its implementation more difficult than anticipated, the original good feeling evaporates and a deeper determination is required.

Parents and teachers who have worked out their ideas together, who have similar goals, who know what they want for their children and why, have a better chance of keeping their school alive. Nonetheless, almost every school follows a similar pattern. If they make it over the physical hurdles of getting money, finding a building, and meeting bureaucratic regulations, they run into the spiritual struggle. Usually, somewhere in the first three to six months, according to Harvey Haber, comes the first great spiritual crisis: "structure" vs. "nonstructure." Having experimented with the idea of freedom, and having discovered its inherent difficulties, many parents and teachers become impatient and anxious. Are the children learning anything, they wonder, and does it matter? Frequently there is a slowdown in the acquisition of traditional academic skills. Children, it turns out, would rather play than learn to spell, and the blossoming forth of innate genius in a warm, benevolent atmosphere fails to occur. Anxious adults begin to argue for more structure to the school day, more direction for the kids, more em-phasis on the familiar three Rs. Others insist upon maintaining the freedom, and upon learning to work with children on a new freer basis that really tests its limitations and possibilities.

As Robert Greenway, whose sons were enrolled in the Redwood Association Free School in Sonoma County, California, wrote:

It seems to me that this anxiety that gets aroused about "what's happening to our kids" is understandable and inevitable. In a public school, we turn our children over to the wardens; there is no illusion about the possibility of influence to torture us. . . . But a truly cooperative venture arouses every possible hope about involvement in the growth of our children —and probably every latent frustration about what we think *didn't* happen to us as well. . . . I suggest that, unless we find a way of dealing with the real anxieties and concerns that this type of enterprise arouses, then we'll fail before we've hardly started (I'm responding to my own growing sense of frustration and anxiety, and to the sign of sudden and/or premature withdrawals from the school, and to the growing hue and cry for "more organization").

The Santa Fe (New Mexico) Community School went through this crisis in the middle of its second year, a bit later than most. Parents were willing to go along with the school as long as the teachers seemed confident about what was happening with the children. But when one teacher began to articulate the fears many parents had tried to suppress, the situation came to a head. There was a period of trying to impose

135

more order on the kids, and the kids rebelled and refused to take it. Some staff members were fired, and parents demanded more teachers with bachelor's and master's degrees, but found they could not get them for a salary of $200 a month. There were endless pedagogical debates, and finally some of the parents simply took their kids back to the public school. "Unfortunately, those who left were the ones with the most money," sighed one teacher. "We're poorer now, but the people here are here because they're dedicated."

After the crisis, the school was reorganized. Previously ordered by age clusters, it is now divided into activity centers, and children of all ages move freely from one center to another. On a bright Southwestern day a visitor may find a couple of boys sitting in front of the building, slumped against a sun-warmed wall, eating apples and reading comic books. Inside, in the large front room, a group of children may be painting pictures or working with leather or looms. In a quiet, smaller room, someone else is having a guitar lesson. A room toward the back of the building is reserved as the math center; a couple of teachers are math enthusiasts, and many of the older children pick up from them their own excitement for the subject.

In the playground behind the building is an Indian kiva built by students and teachers learning about the culture of local Indian tribes. The Southwest is a multicultural area, and the Community School has tried to draw on all these cultures. There are Indian and Spanish children enrolled, as well as white, and each is encouraged to respect and learn from the cultures of the others.

But despite its efforts to reach into the Indian and Spanish communities, the Santa Fe Community School remains essentially a white middle-class school. The Chicanos and Indians, mainly poor or working-class, tend to shy away from such experiments, partly because their cultures are traditionally conservative with highly structured roles for adults and children, and partly because the poor cannot afford to take a chance on the future of their young. Middle-class whites can always slip back into the mainstream if they choose. But for the poor, neither the acquisition of such intellectual tools as reading and writing nor a place in the economy is guaranteed.

These fundamental differences show up clearly in the community schools operated by and for black people. Black people on the whole bring their children to these schools, not merely because they believe in freedom for self-expression or letting the child develop his own interests, but because their children are not learning in the public schools, are turning sullen and rebellious by the age of eight, and are dropping out of school in droves. The ideology in many of these schools is not pedagogical, but what one school calls "blackology"—the need to educate the children in basic skills and in pride of race. In the black schools there is much more emphasis on basic intellectual training and much more participation on the part of parents. By and large, parents are the founders of these schools; they are the main source of inspiration and energy. They have the final say in selecting both teachers and curriculum, and their chief criterion is: Are the children learning?

As in the white schools, classrooms for the younger children are frequently patterned after the Leicestershire model. But the approach is deliberately eclectic, providing closer guidance and more structured activities for youngsters who need it. The academic progress of the children is carefully observed and quietly but firmly encouraged. "We want teachers who will try a thousand different ways to teach our children," said one mother.

Equally important is a teacher's attitude toward race. Although some schools would like to have all-black faculties—and in a number of cities, parents are in training to become teachers and teacher aides—they must still hire mainly whites. "When I interview a teacher," said Luther Seabrook, principal of the Highland Park Free School in Boston, "I always ask, can you think of a community person as an equal in the classroom?" Many teachers cannot, either because of racial bias, or because of notions about professionalism. Even after a teacher is hired, the going is still rough where feelings run high on the part of blacks and whites, but there is a determination to confront these problems directly through open discussion and group sessions.

The same approach applies to daily work in the classroom. Teachers and aides are encouraged to talk openly about their successes and problems in weekly planning sessions, to admit mistakes, and to try out new ideas. Such sessions are frequently the keystone of the teaching process in these schools. They are the times when teachers can get together and evaluate what has been happening in the classroom, how the children have responded to it, and how the teachers have responded to the children. "It's a tremendous place to grow," one teacher remarked. "You're not tied to a curriculum or structure, and you're not afraid to make mistakes. Everyone here is in the same boat. We get support from each other and develop our own ways of handling things."

There is little doubt that the youngsters prefer the community schools to traditional schools. The humane and personal atmosphere in the small, open classrooms makes a fundamental difference. The children work together writing stories or figuring math problems, working with Cuisenaire rods or an elementary science kit. They are proud of their work and show it eagerly to visitors. There is virtually no truancy, and many youngsters hate to stay home even on weekends, according to their mothers.

But perhaps the greatest achievement of these schools is with the parents. They develop a new faith, not only in their children but in themselves. "Now I know," said a New York City mother, "that, even though I didn't finish high school, it is possible for me to understand what they are teaching my child." In changing their children's lives, these parents have discovered the power to change their own lives, as well. Parents who are not already working as aides and coordinators in the classrooms drop by their schools often to see how Johnny is doing. At the East Harlem Block Schools in New York, stuffed chairs and couches and hot coffee put parents at ease, while teachers talk with them as equals and draw them into the education of their children.

Nonetheless, black schools share many of the problems with the community that white schools have. People are suspicious of new ways of teaching, even though their children obviously are failing under the old

ways. Parents who enroll their children out of desperation still grow anxious when they see the amount of freedom allowed. In integrated schools, like Santa Fe or the Children's Community Workshop, there is the added problem of race and class, as middle-class parents learn that all the children are not necessarily going to adopt middle-class values and life-styles, that cultural differences are valid and must be accepted.

Some schools are fed up with "parent education"; it takes too much time away from the children. A number of schools already are taking only children whose parents are in sympathy with their aims, parents who won't panic if the child doesn't learn to read until he is eight or nine.

But as a school grows more homogeneous, it faces the danger of becoming an isolated shelter against the reality of the outside world. Instead of educating kids to be strong and open enough to deal with a complex world, the schools may become elitist cloisters that segregate a few people even further from the crowd.

Once again the free schools must ask themselves what they are all about. If one assumes (as many free schools do) that any healthy, happy youngster will eventually learn to read and write, then what is the purpose of school? Is it enough simply to provide one's children with a school environment more humane than the public schools, and then stay out of nature's way?

At a California high school in the Sausalito hills, teachers and students think that that in itself is quite a lot. After going through a typical cycle of kids getting high on freedom and doing nothing for six months, getting bored, and finally facing the big questions—What am I doing? Where am I going?—students and teachers think they have learned a lot about themselves and each other. But as the youngsters return to studying and start to seek answers to those questions, they find the teachers have little to offer besides a sympathetic ear. Some kids return to the public school feeling better for their experience with freedom. (Feeling, too, perhaps, that it didn't work, that they really do need all the rules and discipline their parents and teachers demanded.) Gradually, those who remain have forced the teachers back to the traditional textbooks as the chief source of knowledge.

The humane atmosphere remains, but missing is a curriculum that truly nurtures the independence of thought and spirit so often talked of and so rarely seen. It takes extraordinary ingenuity to build on students' needs and interests. A few brilliant teachers, such as Herbert Kohl, can turn kids on, meet them where they are, and take them further—can, for example, take a discussion of drugs and dreams and guide it through the realms of mythology, philosophy, and Jungian psychology. But what do you do if you're not a Herb Kohl? According to Anita Moses, you "work damn hard." There are other things, too: You can hire a master teacher familiar with the wide range of curriculum materials available. Little by little you can change the classroom, or the school itself, to make it do the things you want it to do. And little by little, through working with the children and hashing out problems with help from the rest of the staff, you begin to know what it is you want to do and how you can do it.

But even this does not answer the deeper questions—questions that are

implicit in every free school, but that few have faced. Is it only a new curriculum or new ways of teaching that we need? Or do we need to change our ideas about children, about childhood itself, about how children learn, what they learn, what they need to learn, from whom or from what kinds of experience? It is clear that our ideas about teaching are inadequate, but is it possible that they are simply false? For example, children can often learn to read and write without any formal instruction. This is not a miracle; it is a response of an intelligent young being to a literate milieu. It is also clear that children learn many cognitive as well as social abilities from their peers or from children but a few years older than themselves. What, then, is the role of the adult in the learning of the child?

In simpler times, children learned from adults continually, through constant contact and interchange, and through their place close to the heart of the community. Today, the society has lost this organic unity. We live in times when children often see their fathers only on weekends. We live in a world that separates work from play, school from the "real" world, childhood from personhood. The young are isolated from participation in the community. They seem to have no integral place in the culture. Too often schools have become artificial environments created by adults for children. How is it possible to forsake these roles?

Young people are trying. Many will no longer accept without question authority based solely on tradition or age. They are seeking alternatives to The Way Things Are. But the venture into unfamiliar territory generates enormous anxieties. The young are painfully aware of their own inexperience; they lack faith in themselves. But who can help them in their conflicts both within themselves and with the outside world? Surely, this is a function of education. But in today's world there are few adults who can do this for themselves, far less for their children. For who can respond with assurance to the anxieties of young people over sex, drugs, and the general peril in which we live? Who knows how to deal with others when the traditional roles are gone?

And yet it should be possible for adults to relate to young people in some constructive way. It must be possible because the young, in their alienation and confusion, and the culture, in its schizoid suffering, demand it. In the words of Peter Marin, former director of the Pacific High School, a free school in California:

Somebody must step past the children, must move into his own psyche or two steps past his own limits into the absolute landscape of fear and potential these children inhabit. . . . I mean: we cannot *follow* the children any longer, we have to step ahead of them. Somebody has to mark a trail.

Is that what the free schools are all about? Few of them have asked these questions. Few will ever want to. But the questions are implicit in the movement. The free schools offer alternatives—alternatives that may be shaped to meet new needs and aims. At least, they offer a first step. At least, the possibility is there.

Finding Out About Free Schools

The sources of information about free schools are many and varied, but tap one and it will lead to many others. Here are a few to start with:

NEW SCHOOLS EXCHANGE (*2840 Hidden Valley Lane, Santa Barbara, California 93103*)—the best single source of information on free schools: where they are, how to start one, problems to anticipate, and almost anything else you need to know.

. . . .

THE BIG ROCK CANDY MOUNTAIN (*Portola Institute, Inc., 1115 Merrill Street, Menlo Park, California 94025*)—a new publication similar to the popular Whole Earth Catalogue, but devoted to "resources for ecstatic education." The catalogue reviews schools, teaching methods, toys and games, publications, teaching laboratories, films, tapes, records, and highlights new approaches that "make the student himself the content of his learning," are nonmanipulative, and encourage exploration and creativity ($4 per copy; $8 per year subscription—two issues plus four supplements).

. . . .

THE FREE LEARNER—a remarkably complete survey of experimental schools in the San Francisco Bay area, compiled by Constance Woulf (*4615 Canyon Road, El Sobrante, California 94803*), available at $2 a copy.

. . . .

NEW SCHOOLS MANUAL—a mimeographed booklet put out by New Directions Community School (*445 Tenth Street, Richmond, California 94801*) that provides some useful clues for meeting bureaucratic rules and regulations.

DIRECTORY OF FREE SCHOOLS—a list of free schools across the country, published by Alternatives Foundation (*1526 Gravenstein Highway, Sebastopol, California 97452*). The pamphlet includes an essay on "How to Start a Free School," by Frank Lindenfeld, founder of several California free schools.

. . . .

A BIBLIOGRAPHY FOR THE FREE SCHOOL MOVEMENT—a wide-ranging list of books on children and education, published by the Summerhill Society (*339 Lafayette Street, New York, N.Y. 10012*). Available for 50 cents.

"We have created a school

CAMBRIDGE, MASSACHUSETTS

The Cambridge Free School doesn't cost anything to go to. Some of our friends let us know that they think we're suicidal. Nothing upsets people so much, we've discovered, as our slight disrespect for money. The Free School is also free in terms of the spirit. This, people tend to assume about us.

John and Renee Davis founded the Free School and named it. They keep it free because the tuition system, even at its most benign, categorizes people on the basis of their ability to pay. Heavy. (The best way to know about that is to be the victim of a large scholarship at a small private school. Or live in the suburbs.) The Free School in Cambridge is the revolution not because of a radical curriculum but because it's a place to make a stand. You say, "Thank you for your moral views. How do you pay the rent?"

Here's how. Teachers are not paid or paid very little. Next year they will still be paid very little again but at least a little more. We make money with bake sales and rummage sales. We sell fruit on the Common and flowers in the Square. We silk screen posters and put out canisters for change in stores. We get some large donations. We're at the point now of starting an educational consulting service but one with some differences: if the client likes our ideas about classrooms and teacher training, we'll build the classroom with the teachers that are going to be using it and we'll stay around until people feel comfortable with our innovations and our reasons for innovating.

We're making nursery school furniture from waste materials. Our stools and high chairs are hand crafted and elegant. When we have more money, we will buy the equipment with which to make them more quickly.

An interesting point about our struggle for independence is that it forces us to deal with the system, i.e., buying and selling, but in ways that are personal, direct and reasonably satisfying. Presumably that's an aspect of the revolution.

The school itself is based on the Leicestershire model, an import from England, stressing a rich and expressive environment within which young children can learn what they want, when they want. We have a lot of grown-ups who are keen on things and a lot of keen things. There are 26 children in the school, ages 3–6, most of them in their second year. Together they form a strong, supportive group, a community. Together we work for survival. Nothing we do is obscured from adults or children. For now this covers what we mean by "growing up."

Our location is in the middle of black, white, student, working Cambridge. But we're really a system ready to root wherever there's a private or public school. If you would like to help us or if you would like us to help you, get in touch. You know, "A free school in a rich city is the revolution."

where . . . "

EAST HILL FARM

R.D. ANDOVER, CHESTER, VERMONT

East Hill is a small, proprietary, coeducational school community founded in 1957.

From its beginnings as a summer farm fourteen years ago, East Hill had to develop a good life for children and young people within a very simple context. From our first day, we had little income beyond the out-of-doors; yet we discovered quickly both how simple and how precious that income was. The farmstead became our endowment, as well as goad to our imaginations, source of our materials, and realistic frame for our practical daily concerns. We learned we could have a good deal of physical and emotional freedom within the ritual of daily farm life, but we also found that freedom was exactly as long as the time between milkings. We learned also how to create dance and plays, make music and strive for solid good work with our hands and tools.

Working together over the years, we have built our houses and workshops. In daily meeting, we have worked out reasonable ways to explore alternatives as well as goals. On our 385 acres, we are now producing—without sprays, fumigants or commercial fertilizers—all our own milk, eggs, poultry and meat; also a good share of our fruits and vegetables in season. In the early fall, we preserve a substantial amount of food for the winter.

We see our job here as essentially three-fold: learning how to stay healthy in body, mind and emotions; learning how to earn a living; learning how to think through and meet a problematical planetary future. We are obviously not a utopian retreat, a vocational school or a tutoring school for college. Clearly we are our total life together as something more than school.

Where it is necessary, formal study is short, active and quick. Learning groups are small—never more than six students. Each study area is taken up in the season, manner and mode most natural and appropriate to it. Students move at their own speed. Periods of concentration in a study are followed by periods of hibernation or change in emphasis. No formal grades are given, and all work is jointly evaluated by students and teachers. Pass-fail grades in each subject are forwarded to the colleges when required.

Concern with the landscape immediately around us—learning how to read tree successions, hogs, ponds, old fields and cellar bones; concern with the changing daily weather; living through at least two full farm years—winter and summer; study of the rise and decline of towns and old river industries; several field trips and cruises aboard our yacht; all this begins to increase our fluency in understanding the natural and social world within which man has lived. Our spring trip from mid-March to mid-April takes us 4,000 miles through the folded Appalachians, down to southwest Georgia. We live in several communities which we have been studying for four years. Teaching in our school for little children and counselling on the Farm in the summer all helps us understand who we are, what we can and must do.

LEAPschool

540 E. 13th St.
N.Y.C. 10009
temp. phone OR38800

January 15, 1971

LEAPschool is a changing almost three year old,
lower east side, Puerto Rican, white and black as-
pirer to community made up of about a hundred people
15 to 60 from the surrounding ghetto and the far
away suburbs none of whom pay tuition but all of
whom work and hustle to get the foundation, corpora-
tion and individual money, muscle and materials
necessary to build and support a completely renovated
A&P in the lower east side ghetto and a not so completely renovated 125 acre resort hotel in the Cats-
kill Mountains of New York which someday will be a
self-supporting community but which now is a security
blanket for the Young Lord, Panther, college bound,
Weathermen and suburban types and kin, some of whom
live together but all of whom collide with each other
in group raps, systems meetings, information sessions
covering such things as trigonometry, ghetto law,
anthropology, community political education, botany,
street medicine, American History, American Revolution (the first one), Third World Class, psychology,
Eastern religion, Western religion, creative writing,
animal behavior, freak history and other things that
come up and in from time to time central to which are
the group raps which can be called by anyone for any

reason and where people seem to find out the most
in both violent and non-violent ways depending on how
few or little words people use to cover themselves
with victim bag or other self-inflicted bullshit none
of which is ok with anybody which is also true for
the use of hard drugs and other tricks of fucking
one's self up and preventing them from becoming change
agents which if you are, around LEAPschool, is highly
desirable but if you are not and are into something
personal is ok too only since students are part of
every aspect of the school's life and victims are
worth less than changers there is a hierarchy based
on this worth that doesn't get in the way of people
getting their own things like college boards and
diplomas if people want them or the ability to survive otherwise or involve oneself with revolutionary
action if that seems to be the way, while realizing
it is not the game you play but where you're at in
playing that counts.

where
do we go
from

Gee, You're so Beautiful That It's Starting to Rain

Oh, Marcia,
I want your long blonde beauty
to be taught in high school,
so kids will learn that God
lives like music in the skin
and sounds like a sunshine harpsi-
* chord.*
I want high school report cards to
* look like this:*

Playing with Gentle Glass Things
* A*

Computer Magic
* A*

Writing Letters to Those You Love
* A*

Finding out about Fish
* A*

Marcia's Long Blonde Beauty
* A+!*

RICHARD BRAUTIGAN

EDUCATION VOUCHERS

Christopher Jencks

OEO [Office of Economic Opportunity] announced in May [1970] that it hopes to fund an experiment which would provide parents with vouchers to cover the cost of educating their children at the school of their choice. This news has provoked considerable liberal opposition, including charges that the experiment is unconstitutional, that it is part of a Nixon plot to perpetuate segregation, and that it would "destroy the public school system." What, then, does OEO really have in mind?

If state and local cooperation is forthcoming, the first step will be the establishment of an Educational Voucher Agency (EVA) in some community. This EVA will resemble a traditional board of education in that it will be locally controlled and will receive federal, state, and local funds for financing the education of all local children. But it will differ from a traditional board in that it will not operate any schools of its own. That responsibility will remain with existing school boards, both public and private. The EVA will simply issue vouchers to all parents of elementary school children in its area. The parents will take these vouchers to a school in which they want to enroll their child. This may either be an existing public school, a new school opened by the public school board to attract families who would otherwise withdraw their children from the public system, an existing private school, or a new private school opened especially to cater to children with vouchers. If the school meets the basic eligibility requirements laid down by the EVA, it will be able to convert its vouchers into cash, which will cover both its operating expenses and the amortization of capital costs. Such a system would enable anyone starting a school to get public subsidies, so long as he followed the basic rules laid down by the EVA and could persuade enough parents to enroll their children in his school. It would also give low-income parents the same choice about where they sent their children that upper-income parents now have. This would include all the public and private schools participating in the system.

The effect of these changes on the quality of education would depend on how effectively the EVA regulated the newly created marketplace, and especially on the rules it laid down for determining which schools could

148

cash vouchers and which schools could not. Since the EVA would presumably be controlled by the same political forces that now dominate local school boards, some prophets anticipate that it would soon develop a regulatory system as complex and detailed as that now governing the public schools. If this happened, both publicly and privately managed voucher schools would soon be entangled in the usual bureaucratic and political jungle, in which everything is either required or forbidden. They would probably end up indistinguishable from existing public schools. Nothing would have changed, either for better or for worse.

This vision may, however, be unnecessarily gloomy. Today's public school has a captive clientele. As a result, it in turn becomes the captive of a political process designed to protect the interests of its clientele. The state, the local board, and the school administration establish regulations to ensure that no school will do anything to offend anyone of political consequence. By trying to please everyone, however, the schools often end up pleasing no one. The voucher system seeks to free schools from these managerial constraints by eliminating their monopolistic privileges. Under a voucher system, parents who do not like what a school is doing can simply send their children elsewhere. Schools which attract no applicants go out of business. But those which survive have a much greater claim to run their own affairs in their own way.

Most opponents of the voucher system worry more about the possibility that the EVA would establish too few regulations than about the possibility that it would establish too many. They particularly fear the development of a system in which schools would compete with one another in terms of social and/or academic exclusiveness, much as colleges now do. Left to their own devices, many schools would restrict admission to the brightest and most easily educated youngsters, leaving the more difficult children to somebody else. Many would also try to increase their operating budgets by charging supplemental tuition. This would have the not-always-accidental effect of limiting the number of low-income children in the more expensive schools.

An unregulated system of this kind would have all the drawbacks of other unregulated markets. It would produce even more racial and economic segregation than the existing neighborhood school system. It would also widen the expenditure gap between rich and poor children, giving the children of the middle-classes an even larger share of the nation's educational resources than they now get, while reducing the relative share going to the children of the poor.

Fortunately, OEO has shown no signs of funding a completely unregulated voucher system. Rather, OEO is contemplating an experiment in which extremely stringent controls are placed on participating schools' admissions policies, and also on their tuition charges. At the same time, it is hoping for an experiment which places minimal restraint on schools' staffing practices and programs.

In order to cash vouchers, a school would have to offer every applicant a roughly equal chance of admission. To ensure this, the school would have to declare each spring how many children it could take the following year. Parents would apply to schools each spring, and unless a school had more applicants than places, it would have to take everyone who had applied. If there were more applicants than places, the school would have to fill at least half its places by a lottery among applicants. It would also have to show that it had accepted at least as high a proportion of minority group students as had applied. Thus no school would be able to cream off the most easily educated children or dump all the problem children elsewhere.

The redemption value of a middle- or upper-income family's voucher would approximate what the local public schools are currently spending on upper-income children. Vouchers for children from low-income families would have a somewhat higher redemption value. This reflects the fact that schools with high concentrations of low-income children also tend to have more than their share of educational problems. It should also help discourage schools from trying to attract exclusively middle-class applicants. Participating schools would have to accept every child's voucher as full payment for his education, regardless of its value. Otherwise, parents who could afford to supplement their children's vouchers would inevitably have a better chance of getting their children into high cost schools than parents who could not supplement the voucher.

These regulations would not result in as much racial or economic integration as massive compulsory busing. But that is hardly a likely alternative. The real alternative is the continuation of the neighborhood school, whose racial and economic composition inevitably and deliberately reflects the racial and economic exclusiveness of the private housing market. Under a voucher system, no child could be excluded from any participating school simply because his family was not rich enough or white enough to buy a house near the school. Furthermore, the EVA would pay transportation costs, so that every family would have genuinely equal access to every participating school. Most families, both black and white, would doubtless continue to prefer schools near their homes. But at least no family would be legally or financially required to choose such a school if they thought it was educationally inadequate. Those black parents who wanted their children to attend integrated schools would be in an excellent position to ensure that they did so.

If all goes according to plan, the OEO experiment would be far more permissive with regard to schools' staffing and curricular policies than with regard to admissions. Schools would have to conform to existing state and local regulations governing private schools, but these are relatively lenient in most states. Experience suggests that while such leniency results in some abuses, the results over the long run seem to be better than the results of detailed legal and administrative regulations of the kind that shape the public schools. While these regulations often seem rational on their face (as in the case of teacher certification requirements), they generally create more problems than they solve. Teaching and learning are subtle processes, and they seem to resist all attempts at improvement by formal regulation. Rule books are seldom subtle enough to prevent the bad things that can happen in schools, and are seldom flexible enough to allow the best things.

So instead of telling schools whom to hire, what to teach, or how to teach it, the EVA will confine itself to collecting and disseminating information about what each school is doing. Every family will be given extensive information about every participating school. This should ensure that families are aware of all the choices open to them. It should also help discourage misleading advertising, or at least partially offset the effects of such advertising.

One common objection to a voucher system of this kind is that many parents are too ignorant to make intelligent choices among schools. Giving parents a choice will, according to this argument, simply set in motion an educational equivalent of Gresham's Law, in which hucksterism and mediocre schooling drive out high quality institutions. This argument seems especially plausible to those who envisage the entry of large numbers of profit-oriented firms into the educational marketplace. The argument is not, however, supported by much evidence. Existing private schools are sometimes mere diploma mills, but on the average their claims about themselves seem no more misleading, and the quality of the services they offer no lower, than in the public schools. And while some private schools are run for little but profit, this is the exception rather than the rule. There is no obvious reason to suppose that vouchers would change all this.

A second common objection to vouchers is that they would "destroy the public schools." Again, this seems farfetched. If you look at the educational choices made by wealthy parents who can already afford whatever schooling they want for their children, you find that many still prefer their local public schools if these are at all adequate. Furthermore, most of those who now leave the public system do so in order to attend high-cost, exclusive private schools. While some parents would doubtless continue to patronize such schools, they would receive no subsidy under the proposed OEO system.

Nonetheless, if you are willing to call every school "public" that is ultimately responsible to a public board of education, then there is little doubt that a voucher system would result in some shrinkage of the "public" sector and some growth of the "private" sector. If, on the other hand, you confine the label "public" to schools which are really equally open to everyone within commuting distance, you discover that the so-called public sector includes relatively few public schools. Instead, racially exclusive suburbs and economically exclusive neighborhoods serve to ration access to good "public" schools in precisely the same way that admissions committees and tuition charges ration access to good "private" schools. If you begin to look at the distinction between public and private schooling in these terms, emphasizing accessibility rather than control, you are likely to conclude that a voucher system, far from destroying the public sector, would greatly expand it, since it would force a large number of schools, public and private, to open their doors to outsiders.

A third objection to vouchers is that they would be available to children attending Catholic schools. This is not, of course, a necessary feature of a voucher system. An EVA could perfectly easily restrict participation to non-sectarian schools. Indeed, some state constitutions clearly require that this be done. The federal Constitution may also require such a restriction, but neither the language of the First Amendment nor the legal precedents is clear on this issue. The First Amendment's prohibition against an "establishment of religion" can be construed as barring payments to church schools, but the "free exercise of religion" clause can also be construed as requiring the state to treat church schools in precisely the same way as other private schools. The Supreme Court has never ruled on a case of this type (e.g. GI Bill payments to Catholic colleges or Medicare payments to Catholic hospitals). Until it does, the issue ought to be resolved on policy grounds. And since the available evidence indicates that Catholic schools have served their children no worse than public schools, and perhaps slightly better, there seems no compelling reason to deny them the same financial support as other schools.

The most common and most worrisome objection to a voucher system, in my view, is that its results depend on the EVA's willingness to regulate the marketplace vigorously. If vouchers were used on a large scale, state and local regulatory efforts might be uneven or even nonexistent. The regulations designed to prevent racial and economic segregation seem especially likely to get watered down at the state and local level, or else to remain unenforced. This argument applies, however, to *any* educational reform, and it also applies to the existing system. If you assume any given EVA will be controlled by overt or covert segregationists, you must also assume that this will be true of the local board of education. A board of education that wants to keep racist parents happy hardly needs vouchers to do so. It only needs to maintain the neighborhood school system. White parents who want their children to attend white schools will then find it quite simple to move to a white neighborhood where their children will be suitably segregated. Except perhaps in the South, neither the federal government, the state government, nor the judiciary is likely to prevent this traditional practice.

If, on the other hand, you assume a board which is anxious to eliminate segregation, either for legal, financial, or political reasons, you must also assume that the EVA would be subject to the same pressures. And if an EVA is anxious to eliminate segregation, it will have no difficulty devising regulations to achieve this end. Furthermore, the legal precedents to date suggest that the federal courts will be more stringent in applying the Fourteenth Amendment to voucher systems than to neighborhood school systems. The courts have repeatedly thrown out voucher systems designed to maintain segregation, whereas they have shown no such general willingness to ban the neighborhood school. Outside the South, then, those who believe in integration may actually have an easier time achieving this goal than they will with the existing public school system.

an essay on alternatives in education

EVERETT REIMER

WHAT SCHOOLS DO

Schools are supposed to educate. This is their ideology, their public purpose. They have gone unchallenged, until recently, partly because education is itself a term that means such different things to different people. Different schools do different things, of course, but increasingly, schools in all nations, of all kinds, at all levels, combine four distinct social functions: custodial care, social role selection, indoctrination, and education as usually defined in terms of the development of skills and knowledge. It is the combination of these functions that makes schooling so expensive. It is conflict among these functions that makes schools inefficient. It is also the combination of these functions that tends to make school a total institution, that has made it an international institution, and that makes it such an effective instrument of social control.

Custodial care is now such a universal aspect of schooling that it is hard to remember that this was not always the case. Children must, of course, be cared for, if they are really children, that is, and not just young members of the community taking part in its normal productive and social affairs. The latter is the situation for most youngsters all over the world, in the tribal, peasant, and urban dwellings of the poor. It is only mothers who have been freed from the drudgery of food production and preparation, and have time to take care of their children who, paradoxically, find it necessary to turn the care of their children over to others. Demand for child care appears only when the means are there to supply it. Supply also creates its corresponding demand. Schools provide child care for younger children that older children are prevented from supplying.

But child care costs money and although schools provide it relatively cheaply—about a dollar an hour per child in the United States—this is where most of the school budget goes. Since child care is the most tangible service schools provide and since parents are naturally concerned about the quality of such care, this function has a priority claim in school resources. Other functions must necessarily compete for what is left after prevailing local standards of safety, comfort, and convenience have been met.

As children get older, child care, again paradoxically, becomes more expensive and more pervasive. Actual hours spent in school increase, buildings are more luxurious, the ratio of paid adults to students increases, and the salaries of these adults also increase. The paradox lies in the fact that where there are no schools children contribute more to the community and cost less as they become older. High schools take more of the students' time than do primary schools, and cost more too, while most colleges and universities occupy the full time of the student, at an ever-increasing hourly cost to the community, as students progress up the academic ladder to higher degrees. The costs of higher education, especially, cover much more than mere custodial care but, at upper as well as lower levels, the time students spend in the enclave of school is an important cost factor. Space is another costly factor; the commodious college campus, ideally well insulated from the nonacademic environment, is obviously much more expensive than the neighborhood kindergarten.

Money costs, however, are the least of the costs of custodial care provided in schools. The really important consequence of packaging custody with the other functions of the school is the extension of childhood from age 12 to 25, and from the sons and daughters of the rich to the youth of the whole society.

So long as children remain full-time students they remain children, economically, politically, even legally. While no formal legal sanctions are available against students as such, students can always be deprived of their rights to schooling, and thus to employment in their chosen fields, with all that this deprivation implies.

The school schedule remains, also, one of the major supports for age restrictions on the right to vote, to work, to contract, and to enjoy other constitutional privileges and protections. The school itself, as custodian of ever larger numbers of people, for increasing proportions of their life span, for an ever growing number of hours and interests, is well on the way to joining armies, prisons, and insane asylums as one of society's total institutions.

A total institution is one that totally controls the lives of its clients. Schools have obviously not reached this point, as current student behavior vividly attests, but this behavior is also evidence of how far schools have gone in extending their scope to every aspect of student life. Evidence, especially from studies of prisons and asylums, indicates how overwhelmingly such institutions produce the very behavior they are designed to correct. In one experiment, almost all the members of a group of persons diagnosed as hopelessly insane, asylum inmates for over 20 years, were discharged as cured within a few months of being placed in a "normal" environment. In another experiment, a group of persons diagnosed as dangerously insane were allowed to institute self-government among themselves and managed without incident. The real cure for student unrest would be to stop making children out of people old enough to have children, support them, and fight for them. This would, of course, require other social changes in addition to the divorce of child care from education, but they are equally necessary changes if society is to survive.

A second function of schools, even more in conflict with their educational aims than custodial care, is the sorting of the young into the social slots they will occupy in adult life. A generally accepted aspect of this function occurs at the high school and college level, when students begin to opt for this or that profession or trade, entering special curricula of one to a dozen years in length for vocational preparation. The results of even this accepted aspect of job selection in school are wasteful and often disastrous. Part of the waste arises from the high proportion of dropouts, not only from professional and trade schools but from the professions and trades themselves, frequently after long and expensive investments have been made. Persons in large numbers find that medicine, teaching, or plumbing are not for them—something they could have found out much sooner and much cheaper with just a little direct experience. Even those who stay in the field of their choice do not escape extensive waste of time and money. According to most veteran specialists, the first several years in any vocation are spent forgetting what was learned about the vocation in school. Counseling and many other sincere and systematic efforts are made to minimize this kind of waste, but it is doubtful that, even at great additional cost, they do more than slow its acceleration. The ever greater separation of school from the rest of life widens a gap that no amount of effort can bridge.

But the major part of job selection

is not a matter of personal choice at all, but a matter of survival in the school system. The point at which he drops out determines whether a boy will be paid for his body, his hands, or his brains and also, of course, how much he will be paid. These factors in turn will largely determine where he can live, with whom he can associate, and the rest of his style of life. A hundred years ago, any profession could still be entered at the bottom. Today to do so is difficult even in countries that provide schools for only a tiny minority. In the United States it is difficult to become a carpenter without having graduated from high school. In New York City even a garbage collector needs a diploma.

While economic status is largely a function of the level at which a student drops out, power in the society depends more upon the sorting that occurs when high school graduates enter college. Admission to Harvard, as an undergraduate, practically guarantees access to the groups that control the major hierarchies of the United States. Berkeley is typical of the next level. State and local as well as national hierarchies are the products of the college lottery. Even international agencies are ruled by the graduates of a dozen world famous universities.

Power and wealth are not everything, of course, but in many parts of the world almost everything else depends upon them. Especially where the school system is dominant, respect, reputation, health, even affection of many kinds, can either be commanded or purchased—if they are not tendered as gifts to those who could order or buy them.

The school system has thus amazingly become, in less than a century, the major mechanism for distributing values of all kinds among all the peoples of the world, largely replacing the family, the church, and the institution of private property in this respect. In capitalist countries it might seem more accurate that schools validate rather than replace the value distribution functions of these older institutions. Family, religion, and property have such an important influence on access to and success in school that schooling alters only slowly and marginally the value distributions that it inherits. Jefferson put it well when he said, in arguing for public schools, that by this means we shall each year rake a score of geniuses from the ashes of the masses. The result of such a process, as the English aristocracy learned long before Jefferson, is to keep the elite alive while depriving the masses of their potential leaders.

Communist countries have, of course, abolished private property, have attempted to abolish organized religion, and, presumably, have weakened the role of the family. There are few data, unfortunately, to show how much redistribution of values has taken place in these countries but the general impression is that it is much less than had been expected. One of the strongest supports for this impression comes, precisely, from the great similarity of school systems in capitalist and communist countries. They perform the same functions and, as will be seen, share the same defining characteristics. There is not the slightest doubt that communist schools sort their students into jobs, vocational levels, pay differentials, power and privilege strata in just the same way as capitalist schools. The only question is whether the prizes go to the sons and daughters of the previously privileged in quite the same degree. Current events in communist countries strongly suggest that their leaders, especially in China, are greatly preoccupied with this question.

It is now clear why schools have grown so fast in space, students, functions, and social power. To the masses and their leaders they have held out unprecedented hope of social justice, of secular reward based on merit. To those concerned with conserving traditional social values they have been an unparalleled instrument, appearing to give what they did not, while convincing all that they got what they deserved. Only the great religions provide an analogy, with their promise of spiritual brotherhood always betrayed.

Betrayal of the hopes of schooling is implicit in the selection function that schools perform. Selection necessarily implies losers as well as winners, and, increasingly, selection is for life and for most of the good things of life. Add to this that school is a handicap race in which those who are slower and must cover a greater distance must also bear the increasing burden of repeated failure, while those who are quicker and with less distance to cover are continually spurred by success. Nevertheless, the finish line is the same for all and the first to get there win the prizes. All attempts to disguise the reality of this situation fail, partly because parents know the truth and, even more, because teachers and administrators are frequently compelled to tell the truth. Euphemisms about the transcendent importance of learning and about doing your best are, thus, self-defeating. It is no wonder, under these circumstances, that the slower children drop out and that the superior students work to win rather than to learn.

If schools continue for a few more generations to be the major means of social role selection, the result will be a meritocracy, in which merit is defined by the selection process that occurs in schools. Michael Young describes this outcome in his *Rise of the Meritocracy*. His picture of English society, 50 years from now, is a projection of Galbraith's New Industrial State with the technocrats in the saddle. The school system that selects these technocrats has become a super streaming system, constantly shuffling its students into the channels where their past performance suggests they belong. The slow students are not kidded in this system; they quickly learn where they stand and where they are going, but they are taught to like it. The quick also know where they are going and like it so well they end up trying to reestablish an hereditary aristocracy based on merit. This reverse English twist leads to a happy ending that takes humanity off the hook, but not until the author has made his—and repeated Dante's—point: any system in which men get just what they deserve is Hell.

Indoctrination is a bad word. Bad schools indoctrinate. Good ones teach basic values. All schools, however, teach the value of childhood, the value of competing for the life prizes offered in school, and the value of being taught what is good and what is true.

By the time they go to school, children have completed the most important and most difficult learning tasks of their lives. They have learned how to use their bodies, how to use language, and how to control their emotions. They have learned to depend upon themselves and have been rewarded for initiative in learning. In school these values are reversed. The what, when, where, and how of learning are decided by others, and children learn that it is good to depend upon others for their learning. They learn that what is worthwhile is what is taught and, conversely, that if it is important for them to learn something, someone must teach it to them.

In school children learn not only the values of the school but the acceptance of these values and, thus, to get along in the system. They learn the value of conformity and, while this learning is not confined to school, it is concentrated there. School is the first highly institutionalized environment most children encounter. For orphans and children who are sick or handicapped this is not the case, and the retarding effect of institutionalizing infants is impressively documented. Orphans learn so well not to interfere with institutional requirements that they seldom become capable of making a useful contribution to society. The argument for schools, of course, is that they strike the balance between conformity and initiative that the institutional roles of adult life require.

Other values are implicit in those aspects of curriculum that are alike in schools all over the world. These include the priorities given to dominant languages, both natural and technical. Examples of the first are the priority given to Spanish over Indian tongues in Latin America and to Russian over provincial languages in the Soviet Union. Examples of the second are the priority given mathematics over music and to physics over poetry. There are obviously good reasons for these priorities, but they are reasons derived from the world as it is, ignoring the claims of both the world of the past and the desirable world of the future. More than this, these decisions reflect not even all of the major aspects of today's world, but preponderantly the balance of political and economic power. Less people speak English than Chinese and far fewer speak physics than poetry. English and physics are simply more powerful.

Another value implicit in school is that of hierarchy. Schools both reflect dominant values and maintain a stratified world. They make it seem natural and inevitable that hierarchies are inherently correlated and cannot be independent of each other. Schools do not have to teach this doctrine. It is learned merely by going to school.

Finally, after performing their child care, social screening, and value teaching functions, schools also teach cognitive skills and both transmit and, at graduate levels, create knowledge. The first three functions are performed necessarily, because of the way schools are organized. Skill- and knowledge-teaching, though they are declared the principal purposes of schools, occur only insofar as resources remain after the built-in functions are performed. In urban ghetto schools of the United States, and in rural Brazilian schools attempting to operate on a budget of $50 per year per child, skill- and knowledge-teaching turn out to be impossible. In more fortunate situations, where they are possible, there are still major constraints on what can be taught and how. Exceptional teachers can, of course, teach and exceptional students can learn within the confines of the school. As school systems expand, claiming an increasing proportion of all educational resources, absorbing more students and teachers and more of the time of each, some true educational experiences are bound to occur in schools. They will, however, occur despite and not because of school. Paulo Freire and Paul Goodman, two current philosophers of education, proceeding from quite different premises, both provide carefully reasoned support for the preceding statement.

Paulo Freire is a Brazilian educator known for his success in teaching peasants to read and write effectively with a minimum investment of time and facilities. A gross oversimplification of his position is that people learn only in the process of becoming conscious of their true life situation, coming to see this situation clearly under circumstances that permit them to act effectively upon it. Schools could never provide their students with the action potential that this program requires. It is interesting that Dewey called for something like this action potential in his proposed experimental schools that never actually came into being.

Goodman's position in equally oversimplified form, is not so easily distinguished from Freire's. Goodman holds that people learn what they need to learn in the course of real-life encounters. Professions and trades are learned by practicing them. Scholars develop in communities of scholars. Schools can teach only alienated knowledge—knowledge divorced from both its origins and its applications and therefore dead knowledge.

The effect of transmitting dead knowledge, according to Freire, is to domesticate rather than to educate. Domestication is training in conformity and the development of either magical or mythical attitudes toward those aspects of life that contradict the pressures toward conformity. According to Goodman, the attempt to transmit dead knowledge either has no effect or leads to a sense that the world is absurd. Both men are probably right. The real world of the Brazilian peasant is perhaps too grim to be seen as absurd and must, therefore, be either repressed or enshrouded in magic. The New Yorker, on the other hand, may be protected enough to be able to view the grimness of his world through the semitransparent veil of absurdity.

Schools have an apparently better case in their claim to teach skills, especially language and mathematical skills. The most commonly heard defense of schools is, "Where would children learn to read?" Literacy has, in fact, always run well ahead of schooling. There are always more literate members of a society than persons who have gone to school and there are always children attending school who do not learn to read. In general, the children of literate parents learn to read even if they do not attend school, while the children of illiterate parents frequently fail to learn, even in school.

In universally schooled societies, of course, most children learn to read in school. Considering when children learn to read and when they begin to go to school, it could hardly be otherwise. Even in a fully schooled society, however, few children learn to read easily and well, although almost all learn to speak easily and well, a skill that is learned outside of school. Children who do learn to read well read a lot for their own pleasure, which suggests that good reading, like other skills, is the result of practice. Data on mathematics give even less support to school. Illiterates who participate in a money economy all learn to count, add, subtract, multiply, and divide while only a small percentage of people in a fully schooled society ever learn much more. Of those who have taken algebra or geometry in school, only a small percentage do

better than chance on an objective test.

There is a body of data collected by Jerome Bruner and his students showing that children who go to school learn concepts that are not learned by those who do not go to school. The same thing is true, however, of children who go to the city, as compared to those who do not. The effect of the city, that is, can duplicate the effect of the school, and vice versa, although school and city together are more potent than city alone. Clearly, however, there are other differences between city children who go to school and those who do not. Until a unique effect of schooling is demonstrated, with everything else controlled, Bruner's data show only that environments affect concept learning and, perhaps, that the more relevant the environment is to the concept the more effect it has.

Another claim is that schools teach structures, the grammar of language, the theories of mathematics, science, and the arts. Undoubtedly they do, but the real question is whether these things are learned in school more than they would be otherwise. Achievement tests give little support to schools. As in the case of mathematics, only a small minority of students do better than chance on the formal structure of any subject matter. Students who are interested in these matters learn them and those who are not do not. Whether interest in them is stimulated by schools remains very doubtful. Einstein, commenting upon a short period he had to spend in school, preparing for a degree examination, said that as a consequence he was, for several years afterward, unable to do any creative work.

This remark would seem to cast doubt upon the supposed merger of teaching and research in higher education. Research and teaching must, of course, go together but can they be combined in schools? There are several lines of evidence, based on different and perhaps conflicting points of view, that suggest a negative answer: the growth of research institutes, student protest that research is done at the expense of teaching, claims that research done to satisfy degree requirements is trivial. None of these objections hits the mark but they do suggest the real problem. Teaching, learning, and research are not, in fact, separate or separable activities, outside of schools. Only schools separate them and then, as with Humpty-Dumpty, are unable to put them together again. Learning can result only from research, and teaching can be no more than the guidance of research. The research, however, must be real, not academic. All this, of course, was said by Dewey, whose only error lay in believing that schools could be for real.

WHAT SCHOOLS ARE

It may seem academic to distinguish what schools do from what schools are, but the purpose of the distinction is very practical. Alternatives to schools cannot be formulated unless we can define school. Schools perform necessary social functions that, in some form and combination, will have to continue to be performed. Some people believe that schools can be reformed while others hold that no specialized alternatives to school are needed; that all the education men require can come as a by-product of their other activities. Neither position can be refuted or properly evaluated without a definition of school. The reasons for defining schools are heuristic—to know better what to do and what to avoid in planning alternatives. Consistency and precision are, therefore, less important in the definition than its usefulness in practice. We define schools as *institutions that require students at specific ages to spend most of their time attending teacher-supervised classrooms for the study of graded curricula*. All institutions that fit this definition completely are now called schools, as well as some institutions that lack one or more of these characteristics. The better this definition fits an institution the more nearly does the institution correspond to the stereotype of school. Alternatives in education can be most generally defined as moving away from this stereotype. Unless they move far enough and fast enough, however, to escape the "gravitational pull" of the school system they will be reabsorbed.

By specifying age norms schools institutionalize childhood. In schooled societies, childhood is now assumed to be a timeless and universal phenomenon. But children, in the modern sense, did not exist 300 years ago and still do not exist among the rural and urban poor who make up most of the population of the world. In his *Centuries of Childhood* (*L'enfant et la vie familiale sous l'ancien régime*) Philippe Ariès shows that, before the seventeenth century, children dressed as adults, worked with adults, were imprisoned, tortured, and hanged like adults, were exposed to sex, disease, and death, and in general were treated as developing adults. The subculture of childhood did not exist.

All cultures, of course, distinguish infants and sexually immature youth from adults. All cultures have initiation rites that signal entrance into full adult status. All cultures make some distinction between what adults and nonadults may do and have done to them. This is not to say, however, that all cultures have a subculture of childhood. In schooled societies children are not expected to work, except at their studies. Children are not responsible for any nuisance, damage, or crime they commit upon society. Children do not count, legally or politically. Children are supposed to play, enjoy themselves, and prepare themselves for adult life. They are supposed to go to school, and the school is supposed to be responsible for them, guide them, and temporarily at least, take the place of their parents. Childhood explains the priority that schools give to custodial care.

Childhood must also be viewed in contrast to modern, pre-retirement adult life. Childhood and the adult world of work have been drawing apart. While children have been increasingly indulged, pre-retirement adults—women as well as men—have been increasingly constrained by the world of machines and institutions. Childhood has become more child-centered, more indulgent, while adults have been increasingly required to accept reality. The argument for schools is that they provide a necessary bridge from childhood to adult life, that they gradually transform the indulged child into the responsible adult. Everything that schools are and do can be explained in these terms. Schools take the child from his own garden, by carefully graded steps, to a prototype of the world of work. They enroll the complete child and graduate the complete man.

As in the case of the school, childhood has probably served a useful purpose. The pre-childhood treatment of children was, and, is, undesirably brutal. Many of the protections childhood has brought to children are important and necessary—so much so that it is vital to extend them, not only to other children, but also to adults. This is impossible, however, if the indulgence of already indulged children is endlessly multiplied. Furthermore, while some protections and some indulgences are necessary and good, too many are bad, and we have reached and passed many thresholds in the institution of childhood at which benefits become liabilities. Many of these are obvious and need no argument. One that has already been noted is the extension of the age of childhood to include fully mature adults, so long as these adults remain in school. Much of the protest on the part of youth is related to this fact, as is the resentment of adults to this protest. The case for youth is obvious. Old enough to have children of their own and to fight for their country, they are granted leave only to do the latter and, at the same time, are denied the right to vote and to participate fully in the economic product. The adult case is also easy to understand. These children, they say, want to remain children and yet to enjoy the privileges of adults. In part, the adults are right. What they forget is that youth did not create the institution of childhood but were created by it.

Schools, as creators of social reality, do not stop with children. They also create school teachers. Before there were schools there were caretakers of children, gymnastic disciplinarians enforcing practice, and masters with disciples. None of these three assumed that learning resulted from teaching. Schools treat learning as if it were a product of teaching.

The role of the teacher in this process is a triple one, combining the functions of umpire, judge, and confessor. As umpire the teacher rules answers right or wrong, assigns grades, and decides upon promotion. As judge the teacher induces guilt in those who cheat, neglect their homework, or otherwise fail to live up to the moral norms of the school. As confessor the teacher hears excuses for failure to meet either academic or moral standards and counsels the student on choices to be made both inside the school and out. This description fails to sound strange only

because students are regarded as people without civil rights. Imagine combining the roles of policeman, judge, and attorney for the defense, or the roles of buyer, appraiser, and economic counselor, or the roles of referee, athletic commissioner, and coach. In a purely formal sense, the student in this situation is helpless, while the teacher is omnipotent. In fact, almost the reverse is true.

Teachers have the roles and powers described above; they also exercise them, but usually not effectively. This is partly because the system has broken down, but the breakdown is itself inherent in the distortion that school creates in the true roles of the teacher. As suggested above, these were exemplified in the pre-school era: in the Greek slave who safeguarded his young charges in their excursions about the city, in the disciplinarian who kept them at their practice of arms, in the master prepared to dispute with them in matters of politics, ethics, and philosophy. Of these only the disciplinarian survived without major distortion in the early schools. Drill with the pen rather than the sword involved only a change of instrument and the method was equally effective. Schools stopped being effective in teaching skills when this method was abandoned. The other two roles were totally distorted in their incorporation into school. The caretaker role depended completely, for its educational validity, upon not overstepping its bounds. The caretaker slave had nothing to say about place, time or activity except to keep his charges within the bounds of safety. The educational value of the activities depended upon student selection and conduct. The master was also transformed into his opposite when placed within the school. His true role was to be questioned and to answer in such a way as to provoke even deeper questions. In the school this role is reversed; the master becomes the questioner and is forced to propound orthodoxy rather than provoke exploration.

Children and teachers do not yet make a school. Without required attendance in specialized space, teachers and children could be a home, a nursery or a crusade. Required classroom attendance adds the time and space dimensions, which imply that knowledge can be processed and that children have an assigned time and place. During infancy they belong in the home. At kindergarten age they begin to belong, for a few hours a day, in school. The amount of school time increases with age, until college becomes Alma Mater, sacred or soul mother, the social womb in which the child develops and from which it is finally delivered into the adult world. Classrooms may be varied to include laboratory, workshop, gymnasium, and year abroad, but this is all scholastic space, that is, sanitized, sealed off from the unclean world, and made fit for children and for the transmission of knowledge. In this specialized environment, knowledge must be transmitted; it cannot merely be encountered, since in most instances it has been taken out of its natural habitat. It must also be processed, not only to clean it up but also to facilitate transmission.

The transmission of knowledge through teaching, and its processing to fit school and school children, seems perfectly natural in a technological age that engineers a product to fit every human need. Once knowledge becomes a product, the graded curriculum follows—an ordered array of packets of knowledge each with its time and space assignment, in proper sequence and juxtaposition with related packages. The graded curriculum is the fourth dimension of the school. As in the case of the other defining characteristics, its quantitative aspects are critically important. Childhood becomes a problem when extended over too many years and too many aspects of life. Teaching becomes a problem when students begin to depend upon it for most learning. Classroom attendance becomes a problem when it builds sterile walls around too much of normal life. Similarly, curriculum becomes a problem as it approaches international universality.

Recent international achievement studies demonstrate quite clearly that the universal international curriculum is now a fact. International norms for mathematics and science have been established. These are admittedly the areas of greatest uniformity but others are not far behind. Nor is the proliferation of vocational schools, Black studies, and life-adjustment classes a significant counter trend. These auxiliary curricula are either tied to the core curriculum, in terms of prerequisites and grade standards, or else the degrees they lead to are meaningless in the marketplace.

The graded curriculum may be the most significant single characteristic of the school, especially in terms of the school's role in society. This is, however, only because the curriculum is, in a sense, the keystone of a system based on institutionalized childhood, teaching, and classroom attendance. Curriculum gives structure to these other elements, uniting them in a way that determines the unique impact of school on students, teachers, and society.

In itself, the central idea of curriculum is both simple and inevitable. Learning must occur in some sequence and there must also be some correlation between different sequences of learning. These sequences and correlations could, of course, be different for each individual. To some extent they must be and every educator pays lip service to the idea. Almost no one, on the other hand, would insist upon avoiding all attempts to correlate the learning programs of different individuals.

For a teacher to impose a preferred order on his subject matter is natural and desirable. To adjust this order to the needs of each individual student would, at some point, become self-defeating. It is also desirable that teachers learn from each other and adjust their own order of teaching accordingly. But imposing upon teachers an order not of their own choosing is undesirable, and requiring students to follow a particular order, except in deference to a particular teacher, is self-defeating. Only people committed to the idea of a knowledge factory that must run on a prearranged schedule will disagree. The argument that students and teachers must be able to transfer from place to place without losing time, by repeating or being forced to catch up, is valid only if the synchronized knowledge factory is assumed.

Synchronized learning requires, however, not merely a standard order imposed on all students and teachers, but also the integration of the different orders of the various subject matters. This integration of curricular sequence creates the school system, which in turn constrains individual schools in all of their major characteristics. Thus the core curriculum of secondary schools is dictated by standard requirements for college entrance. Since the economic value of other curricula depends upon their relationship to the core curriculum, this curriculum directly or indirectly determines hours of attendance, classroom standards, teacher qualifications, and entrance requirements for the entire secondary school system. Schools that deviate significantly from any of these norms lose their accreditation and their ability to qualify students for college entrance. Even primary school reforms can survive only if they do not threaten the progression of their graduates through the higher reaches of the system.

It is by way of the standardized graded curriculum, therefore, that schools become a system that then acquires an international monopoly of access to jobs and to political and other social roles. It can be argued that this monopoly is not by any means complete: some corporations will still employ the unschooled genius, and Roosevelt and Churchill did not have to pay more than lip service to the schools they attended. But these are exceptions and, if the present trend continues, they will not exist for long.

Organization by grade is maintained principally because the supposed benefits of a standard curriculum would be lost in an ungraded system, especially ease of transfer and objective norms for promotion. The grading of students and the maintenance of grade standards are also involved here. One makes little sense without the other and neither makes sense in the absence of an integrated standard curriculum. Standardized intelligence and achievement testing, promotion within the system, and certification for employment, are all justified by a curriculum that determines the internal structure and operations of a school, relationships between schools, and relationships between school and other institutions.

Would an educational institution lacking one of the defining characteristics proposed above still be recognizable as a school? Perhaps theoretically an institution based on children, teachers, and classrooms, but without curriculum, might be called a school but it would have little resemblance to schools as we know them. Schools without children can be imagined but adults would not, for long, put up with teachers, classrooms, required attendance, and curriculum. Schools for children without teachers are hard to imagine, while a child, teacher, curriculum combination appears intrinsically unstable without the restraining influence of the classroom. Just teachers and children might work, but would be hard to recognize as an institution, let alone a school. It is easy, on the other hand, to see children, teachers, classroom attendance, and curriculum as created by and for each other. It is also easy to see schools as a stable element in a fully technological world. Schools treat people and knowledge the way a technological world treats everything: as if they could be processed. Anything can, of course, be processed but only at a price, part of which involves ignoring certain aspects of the thing and certain by-products of the process. The price of processing people is intrinsically high. They tend to resist. What has to be left unprocessed may be the most important part of the person. Some of the by-products of educational processing are already evident. The greatest danger, however, lies in the prospect of success. A successfully processed humanity would lose the little control of its destiny that has always distinguished man from the rest of the world.

. . .

THE REVOLUTIONARY ROLE OF EDUCATION

Effective alternatives to schools cannot occur without other widespread changes in society. But there is no point in waiting for other changes to bring about a change in education.

Unless educational alternatives are planned and pursued there is no assurance they will occur no matter what else happens. If they do not, the other changes are likely to be superficial and short-lived. Educational change, on the other hand, will bring other fundamental social changes in its wake.

True education is a basic social force. Present social structures could not survive an educated population even if only a substantial minority were educated. Something more than schooling is obviously in question here, more than a college degree, even a PhD; indeed, almost the opposite of schooling is meant. People are schooled to accept a society. They are educated to create or recreate one.

Education here has the meaning that serious students of education and of human nature have always given it. None has defined it better than Paulo Freire, the Brazilian educator who has taught peasant illiterates to read and write in just a few weeks, by helping them become conscious of their own real-life situation. Freire defines education in just these terms: becoming critically aware of one's reality in a manner that leads to effective action upon it. An educated man understands his world well enough to deal with it effectively. Such men, if they existed in sufficient numbers, would obviously not leave the absurdities of the present world unchanged.

Some such men do exist: men who understand reality well enough to deal with it effectively. But they exist today in small numbers, most of them engaged in running the world for their own convenience, a few in trying to alert others to what is going on. If, in any society, the proportion of persons so educated were 20% instead of 2%, or 30% instead of 3%, such a society could no longer be run by a few for their own purposes but would have to be run for the general welfare. The laurels of leadership lose their appeal if spread over more than a few and even an educated minority, above a certain size, would have to opt for justice and sanity. There just is not room for 20% of a population in the combined ranks of presidents and prophets. Imagine the Kennedys, De Gaulles, or Churchills sharing honors with ten times their number; or the Galbraiths, Sartres, or Gandhis. It wouldn't be worth the trouble. Whenever, as in pilgrim New England, ancient Athens, or early Rome, a reasonable proportion of the population have been educated, in the sense of knowing what the local score was, their societies have been run not by the few for their own interests, but by the many in the common interest.

One result of such widespread social participation is an open society, open to the outside and open on the inside. Nation-states as they exist today could not for long survive an educated population. Their boundaries would crumble. Nation-states are closed systems, striving for external and internal equilibrium; they require school systems for their continuing survival. Societies composed of educated citizens, or containing a substantial minority of such citizens, would be open societies, growing, changing, merging with other societies. This could, of course, happen within the nominal framework of the nation-state. Geographical boundaries would not have to change; if immigration and tariff restrictions change sufficiently, political frontiers become meaningless.

Class distinctions would also disappear in open societies; as indeed they have tended to do in certain periods of history when certain nations have, for a time, had some of the characteristics of open societies. This does not mean that individual differences of value position or privilege would disappear. In a changing society new differences would tend to occur as rapidly as old ones were equalized. It would be difficult, however, to identify differences resulting from fairly constant change either with class, race, or any other socially identifying label. An open society would become and remain highly pluralistic, with many loosely related, fluid hierarchies based on a large number of fairly independent value criteria. Some people would be rich, some powerful, others popular, still others loved or respected or strong, but not very many could be all of these for very long to a degree that would incur the envy of others.

An educated population would make not only their nations but also their specialized institutions open, that is, subject to change, responsive to the needs and desires of clients and workers rather than merely those of managers. An educated minority of any size would never put up with current health and education services, environmental pollution, political policy control by military-industrial cliques or advertiser control of mass media, to say nothing of traffic jams,

housing shortages, and the host of other absurdities that afflict modern societies.

No educational magic is implied. Not even educated people could solve these problems in their present context. What they could and would do is recognize an impossible context and change it. They would realize, for example, and make plain to others, that competitive consumption is an impossible way of life for more than short periods or small minorities. Once this fact was grasped, much of our present production and employment would be seen as not only unnecessary but actually harmful. War materials are an obvious case, but schooling, pretentious short-lived consumer durables, advertising, corporate and governmental junketing, and a host of other products and activities are scarcely less so.

What makes it so difficult to do anything about these matters is that the present way of life of so many privileged people depends upon keeping things as they are. Education alone cannot solve this problem. It can help people to see what shifting sand their present security rests upon. It can help them visualize feasible alternatives, although something more is required to realize them. This is merely to say that education alone cannot bring about revolutionary social change.

What would happen in a society with a sizable educated minority and an equally large minority afraid to let go of its current claims to privilege? It may be that no such situation could exist, that this amount of education could never occur in a society where the group clinging to privilege was equal in size to the educated group. But, if such a situation could come to pass, education would carry the day. The neutral part of the population would have everything to gain by siding with the educated minority, except the short-term security of their institutional chains. This sounds like the familiar formula for revolution, but no historical revolution has ever been preceded by an educated minority of any size. Equally, no historical revolution has failed to be stifled before real and permanent changes in popular education and public participation could take place. There are, of course, a few revolutions that still have the opportunity to become exceptions. Most past revolutions, however, have changed mainly the people in power and much less the lives of the majority of the people, who have remained without power. A revolution preceded by education, or made on behalf of educational opportunity, could be different. The process of change in an open society would be rational; alternatives would be openly discussed and decided on the basis of evidence. This is not as utopian a speculation as it seems. Such societies would have problems. People are not used to regular change, nor to rational decisions. Both have their price. One casualty might be cultural integrity, which is highly valued today by intellectual minorities. It is by no means certain that peasant, worker and welfare populations, deeply deprived of elementary necessities, place such a high value on cultural tradition. If rational means the greatest good of the greatest

number, many such traditions might be lost beyond recall. Cultural differences would not be in danger. A changing world would produce these in ample supply, but they might not be the cultural differences of the past.

Rationality might, in a more general sense, tend to disrupt historical loyalties. It might make sense to lower immigration barriers, except to certain people with an emotional stake in certain pieces of national real estate. Ecumenical movements might have everything in their favor, except to Catholics, Buddhists, or Hindus faithful to ancient traditions. Elimination of certain proprietary products might seem a good idea to everyone except some longtime users or producers. Rationality is a good thing, but so is loyalty. Change is necessary, but so is permanence. Freedom is desirable, but so is responsibility. Open societies and institutions —flexible, open to change based on rational criteria—would not be without problems. Rational decisions should, of course, take such values as tradition, loyalty, and responsibility into account, but even if they did these values would frequently come off second best. Education and rationality are not, then, utopian in the romantic sense. They may, nevertheless, offer substantially greater hope than the uninformed power struggles that up to now have been the major means of social change. Jefferson's counsel of periodic revolution is the best we have had, but not only has it been neglected, it is also hard to see how normal human beings could put it into practice. The only other alternatives are either the traditional one of allowing institutions to become obsolescent and die, or the one proposed here: keeping institutions continually in line with the needs of the people they serve.

Theories of political revolution provide some basis for a more general theory of institutional revolution, but important revisions and additions are needed. Political institutions are uniquely based upon power and the use of violence. In political matters, ideology, loyalty, and rationality tend to be subservient to the uses of power and violence. In the case of other institutions—including the religious—ideology, loyalty, and rationality are better balanced. This balance may not always be apparent in the declining days of decadent institutions bolstered by naked power. It is nevertheless true that people choose their markets, their schools, their hospitals and transport, somewhat less blindly, somewhat more in accordance with costs and benefits, including sentimental attachments, than they do in choosing and defending their citizenship. Changes in nonpolitical institutions are, at least on the surface, subject to rational discussion. Major changes in nonpolitical institutions are at times carried through without violence, although this might be less the case if legitimate violence were not a monopoly of political institutions. It is conceivable, at any rate, that revolutionary change in nonpolitical institutions could take place without violence, could be semirational, could be affected by analysis, research, debate, legislation, resource allocation, market behavior, and peaceful political participation. Socialization in the Scandinavian countries and Britain, the formation of the European Common Market, and some of the developments in Japan during the past century are supporting examples of changes that have taken place in relative peace, though certainly not without pressure.

Scientific and religious revolutions are worth looking at for ideas. Thomas Kuhn's account of scientific revolution, whether or not it is fully accepted in all its debatable aspects, illustrates how peaceful revolution can occur. He shows how in mature sciences one major theory controls research and teaching in the field until gradually its deficiencies become more and more widely recognized, it fails to satisfy an increasing set of requirements made upon it and is finally discarded in favor of a more successful rival. The necessary conditions for this kind of peaceful change are easy to identify. There is a common language that members of a branch of science use and jointly understand. There is regular communication among scientists. There is an ultimate court of appeal, namely, empirical evidence produced under controlled and published conditions. Finally, there are agreed upon canons of reason and logic. These conditions are hard to match outside the mature sciences but they provide useful objectives and have actually been adequately approximated in the examples of peaceful institutional change cited above. The records of the European Common Market document in detail how, in one case, this approximation was achieved.

Religious revolutions have not so commonly been peaceful, but some have been, and these illustrate an important principle. They show that something comparable to loss of faith in an old version of truth, like that that occurs in a scientific community at a time of paradigm change, also occurs among the rank and file of a population. New religious faiths have swept over large areas at a rapid rate, and the conditions under which this has happened have something in common, both with each other and with the conditions under which scientific revolutions have occurred. Sweeping religious movements have always occurred among miserable people, under deteriorating social conditions leading to disillusionment and despair. The other condition for their occurrence has been a powerful and attractive new revelation of truth. Sometimes, but not always, charismatic leaders and disciples have proclaimed the new truth. As in the case of science, common language, communication, and commonly accepted standards of reason and logic are necessary conditions for a religious revolution. The logical standards are not, of course, the same as those of science and the ultimate test of truth is very different. Not evidence for the senses but evidence for the emotions is the touchstone of religious truth. Deeply felt needs must be satisfied. Nevertheless, the parallels between scientific and religious conversion are much more impressive than the differences. Religious revolutions, too, may hold lessons for a theory of institutional revolution.

There is no assurance that institutional revolution can be peaceful. There is only a hope and not necessarily a very good one. Peaceful revolution is not, however, the only consideration. It is important partly because of its critical relation to an even more important criterion. This is that revolution be effective, that it achieve its purposes. The history of political revolution is a history of betrayal, both of the idealists who helped create the conditions for it, and even more of the common people on whose behalf it was made and who themselves made the major sacrifices. Revolution results in only those positive changes that are in the course of being made when the revolution occurs. If it consists in nothing but these changes, so much the better.

STRATEGY FOR A PEACEFUL REVOLUTION

Whether a peaceful revolution is possible only time will tell; it may be in some countries and not in others. The necessary conditions for it, however, are easy to state. It cannot occur unless most people are persuaded that it should, nor unless the verdict of this majority is accepted. Both conditions may appear unlikely. First, that a majority could be persuaded of the need for revolutionary change while control of the mass media and the powers of the state remained committed to the status quo. Second, that a minority holding these powers would yield them peacefully even if convinced of its minority status. Such possibilities seem less unlikely in Scandinavian and British societies than elsewhere, however, and are, clearly, totally unlikely unless people seek to bring them about.

An educated minority of substantial size could, under certain conditions, create a majority in favor of revolutionary change. The conditions are, first, deep disillusionment with existing institutions and, second, a compelling formulation of alternatives. The following attempt to show how these conditions might be brought about, in the area of education, is obviously no blueprint for revolution. It is merely a sketch of a possible series of preliminary steps.

The first step is already implied. Large numbers of people would have to become disillusioned with schools. While this disillusionment is currently happening, the numbers are not nearly large enough, nor is the disillusion deep enough. The basic contradictions of the school system must become publicly apparent: that schools are too expensive to serve as a universal system of education, that schools perpetrate inequality, that schools inoculate the vast majority against education by forcing unwanted learning upon them, that a schooled society is blinded to its own errors. The contradictions are there. To get them generally recognized is difficult, since the people most looked up to are the most schooled. It is always difficult to recognize what has been done to you, when the recognition is itself degrading. Unless this recognition occurs, however, nothing else can.

One way of exposing the contradictions of schooling is to first expose the hypocrisy of its pretensions. Schools pretend to offer universal access to education; yet, even in the richest country in the world, the average student attends only half as long as those who go all the way. In poor countries, this ratio is ten to one. Schools pretend that what is taught is learned; yet, achievement tests show that the average student learns a minute fraction of what is taught. Schools pretend to be educational institutions; yet 95% of school budgets are spent on non-educational activities. Schools pretend to liberate the mind; actually they produce pliable material that production and sales managers mold to their coordinated schedules. The already schooled have trouble seeing these hypocrisies. Fortunately, school does different things to different people, and it is not so difficult to see what they do to others. From there, insight can gradually come to focus on the more personal impact of school. For those who have been to school, personal memories help, if they can be stripped of the patina of romance.

The program described below assumes that the disillusionment described above will occur. If it does, the following proposals for legal, fiscal, institutional and educational programs will become progressively more feasible and these, if gradually carried out, will themselves help to speed the loss of faith in schools. People hang on to what they recognize as very faulty institutions until they see what else they can do. While they hang on, it is difficult for them not to rationalize their actions by hoping that things are not as bad as they seem.

On the legal front a two-part strategy is needed: the first consisting of action under existing laws, the second of proposals for new legislation. Some kinds of legal action already have a long history, especially the objections to compulsory schooling traditionally associated with dissident religious sects. More recently, such defense has been based upon nonreligious grounds, including the claim that children are not receiving the education that schools purport to give. In the United States suits claiming an equal share of public resources earmarked for education have also been filed, based on the promise of equal protection of the laws, contained in the fourteenth amendment. Further legal action possible under existing law may be suggested by the following legislative program.

We need legislation that would parallel the first amendment to the Constitution of the United States, prohibiting any law with respect to an "establishment of religion." Institutional monopoly of education, especially by the state, has all the evils of a state church, compounded by the fact that a secular school system can be made to seem neutral with respect to basic values. Since such a claim is obvious nonsense, the defense of a national school system falls back upon the overriding needs and prerogatives of the state. But this involves a contradiction with democratic theory, which holds the state to be the instrument and not the shaper of its citizens. The school, in

modern times, has become more powerful than the church of the Middle Ages. The career and, therefore, the life of the individual depend upon his success in school. The law makes him a criminal if he does not attend it. He is subject to its influence far more than medieval man was ever subject to the church. The case for a prohibition of educational monopoly is stronger than the case against a state church, which in times of crisis could oppose the state and claim heavenly authority for its position. The claim for academic freedom is the nearest schools can come to a similar role and we have now seen how relatively feeble it is. Churches did infinitely better against the Nazis and Fascists than did the universities. The school is an instrument of the state and creates subservience to it.

Along with prohibition of an established school we need to extend our antidiscrimination laws to include schooling. We must forbid favoritism based on schooling as well as on race or religion and for the same reasons. Where and how one has been schooled is as irrelevant to one's capacity to do a job as race or religion. All affect aspects of job performance that are of interest to the employer but that the law has decided, in the cases of race and religion, are not his legitimate concern. Neither is the school the job applicant went to, nor whether he went to school at all, if he can demonstrate the ability to do the job. We are so used to schools that this statement appears strange; yet the logic is simple and obviously parallel. We now reserve the best paid jobs for those whose training has cost the most. If schooling were privately financed this situation might make ethical sense, but its economics would still be ridiculous. The public has, indeed, been schooled to believe that a more expensive item must be better, but economists explain this on the assumption of price competition among suppliers. Schools have precisely the opposite basis for competition. Even Harvard would be suspect if it were cheap.

We would have to distribute educational resources in an inverse ratio to present privilege in order to equalize educational opportunity. The argument against such a policy is that it would spend the most money on those with the least aptitude and would produce the least total education. This argument, in turn, can be challenged since aptitude judgments are based on success in a school system that discriminates against the poor. In the end such arguments will not decide a political issue. Most people believe that public resources are equally shared and if not that they should be. A law requiring equal sharing of public educational resources is, thus, a third item in a legislative program. A system of individual educational accounts would be the only feasible way to enforce such a law.

These three laws would effectively disestablish the school system as an educational monopoly. They would not prevent the development of a new one. By creating an educational market they would open the way to already powerful economic institutions that might easily take advantage

of their power to establish a new educational monopoly.

Effective extension of anti-monopoly laws to the field of education would, therefore, be a necessary fourth legal step. Since such laws are now relatively ineffective in many other fields this step would be far from routine. More generally, however, no legislative program could, by itself, reform education but could only be part of a strategy including economic, institutional, and educational programs that are mutually supporting.

If the best way to establish an institution is to finance it, then one part of a strategy to replace schools is obvious. The obvious is not, however, always easy. We are, for one thing, talking about a great deal of money. The combined public school budgets of the world are close to a hundred billion dollars—almost as much as is spent on armaments and soldiers. This amount of money will not be liberated from its present channels unless very attractive alternatives can be found. Fortunately, not only educationally but politically attractive alternatives exist.

Public funds for education might be redirected to students, teachers, taxpayers, or businessmen.

Educational accounts would channel funds that now go directly to schools through the hands of students. Students might still spend them on schools, either because the law gave them no option or because the schools succeeded in hoodwinking them or because the schools, under the impact of necessity, succeeded in delivering the goods. In all probability, schools would get a steadily declining share of the educational dollar if it went directly to students.

Students would probably elect to spend some of their dollars directly on teachers, bypassing the schools, but there are also other ways in which teachers could profit at the expense of schools. Any significant weakening in the regulatory power of school would tend to have this effect —their power to compel attendance, for example, or to certify compliance with curriculum requirements. If students insisted upon receiving credit by examination without attending classes, teachers would be in increased demand as tutors, both by groups and individuals. For them to increase their earnings would, of course, require a transfer of the savings resulting from reduced school attendance to a tutorial account. Most school laws would not have to be changed to make this a possible option.

One way of transferring funds from schools to taxpayers is merely to reduce the resources earmarked for education. Another way, however, is to shift educational emphasis from children to adults. Since there are more taxpayers than parents, education distributed over the adult population would match educational benefits with tax liability. The taxpayer, of course, would get back a dollar earmarked for education in place of one with no strings attached, but this might have good educational by-products. The taxpayer would insist upon maximum control of his dollar and would spend it on education valued by him rather than dictated by another. He would thus get real education, regardless of what other people might think of it.

There are several ways to shift the educational dollar from schools to businessmen. Educational accounts are one. Performance contracts are another. Such contracts have recently been written by a number of schools with enterprisers who guarantee to teach a testable skill and who are not paid unless they do. Still another way to benefit business is to shift the burden of teaching from people to reproducible objects, be these books or computers.

There is an understandable reluctance on the part of educational liberals to make common cause with taxpayers and businessmen but the only other choice is to submit to an ever-waxing bureaucracy. If, on the other hand, education really resulted from this proposed unholy alliance this would in itself reduce the danger of a resurgent economic domination. In any case, responsibility is best divided between private and public interests if policy is made by those who do not stand to gain by its implementation and carried out by those who do. Taxpayers, businessmen, and educational liberals can be satisfactory allies if none are permitted to write the rules under which they will operate.

It would be a mistake, however, to conclude that a competitive market in educational resources would necessarily result in good education. If everyone were already educated it might, but this is to assume the end we are seeking. Starting from where we are, there would have to be at least partially subsidized educational institutions receiving economic and other kinds of preference. The following are merely examples of the kind of institution building a strategy for alternatives in education would have to include.

One of the most important tasks would be to induce parents and employers to reassume their proper educational responsibilities. Every thinking person knows that real education occurs primarily at home and at work, but a number of factors have conspired to rob this truth of its former general acceptance. The modern organization of society rewards both parents and employers, in the short run, for reducing their normal educational roles by offering free schooling. Schools also benefit politically potent parents and employers more than the less privileged, thus earning their support. The main thing, however, is that current rules for competition among employers reward any reduction in production costs. Similarly, the competitive consumption in which modern households engage induces them to save on costs for which there is nothing to display.

This kind of dominantly economic competition among employers and households is itself the product of a particular kind of legal structure. Until this is changed, some kind of special inducement, some kind of subsidy, is needed to put educational processes back where they occur most rationally and economically, in the home and on the job.

Another place where a great deal of effective education used to occur was in the practice of the arts. Before modern technology took over, all production involved the practice of art. What we now call the fine arts were integrated with the practice of other crafts, and people learned not only by working with more experienced masters but also from associates practicing related arts. In the early stages of industrialized labor, now rapidly passing, this kind of learning was disrupted. It could now be reestablished since the demand for industrial labor is rapidly declining, but only if people who learn, teach, and practice the various arts are given a dependable claim on the goods and services produced by modern technology. Unrestricted competition between men and machines is not a natural phenomenon but one that has been deliberately engineered in modern societies. Most countries of the world are currently frustrated in their efforts to bring this competition about. Modern countries may find it no less difficult to undo, but they must undo it if the arts are to reclaim an educational role that can in no other way be performed. There is no comparable way of teaching everyone the essential skills of hand and foot, ear and eye, mind and tongue.

A third traditional educational institution that must be reestablished is the teaching profession. Schools have robbed teachers of their authority, and equally of their role as raisers of questions rather than expounders of doctrines. They have also forced teachers to assume functions that destroy their educational effectiveness. The modern world requires an expanded teaching profession, largely independent of schools and other institutions, having as one of its functions the professional guidance of clients in the use of these institutions. Once well established, in a world that does not allow schools to monopolize its educational resources, such a profession could survive without subsidy, but it would require assistance in achieving professional independence.

In addition to the revival of traditional educational institutions, the modern world requires new ones, both to make available to learners the objects they require and also to make available the human assistance they need. Libraries, laboratories, and museums provide models for the first type of institution, but not very good ones. None have yet resolved the dilemma of whether to serve their clients or to preserve their objects, except in favor of the latter. There is less and less excuse for this solution, or even of remaining caught in the dilemma. It is becoming increasingly cheaper to give people many kinds of books, records, and experiences than it is to retain them or get them back. But existing libraries, laboratories, and museums are also hopelessly elitist. They offer mostly objects that their actual clients could afford to buy or rent and almost none of the kinds of objects and facilities that poor people need and want. Even the kinds of books, records, instruments, and artifacts available are of little interest to the poor, and there are whole classes of objects and services that are not available at all. Where are tools, for example, or machines to make things, or musical instruments,

sporting goods, playthings, bicycles, or automobiles? There is, of course, no end to this list since all objects including spaceships are educational. Now, however, there is not even a good beginning. The accumulated wealth of almost all societies is systematically locked up against the people who need it in order to learn.

To make fully available the human resources required for education, modern society needs an economical way of bringing together people whose educational skills and interests are supplementary. We already have the computer, uniquely capable of performing this task. To learn a skill, one usually only needs someone who has the skill and is willing to teach it. To practice a skill, in pursuit of further knowledge, one needs only others with a similar set of skills and interests. Matching people on skills, interests, and availability can increase educational choices and decrease educational costs in proportion to the size of the base population. Computer technology removes almost all limits on this size, while communication and transportation technologies steadily increase the possibility of realizing the matches that the computer could indicate. A public utility designed to match human educational resources to educational needs would probably be self-supporting, once established. It might even become established with minimum public investment, but some experimental operation and testing would probably be required for such a utility to reach its full potential.

The final and perhaps critical component of a strategy for peaceful educational revolution is education itself. People have been schooled to regard an unschooled world as fantasy. Alternatives that lack the familiar characteristics of schools have an unreal aspect to a schooled mind. From what kind of fulcrum, with what kind of lever, can the required change in perspective be achieved? One answer is the school system itself, and efforts to change it. Today's disillusioned students, teachers, taxpayers, and administrators include those who have tried and failed to change the system. The architects of educational revolution will be recruited from these ranks.

Paulo Freire provides the educational means by which the revolutionary rank and file can be assembled. Poor people, black and white, peasant and urban proletariat, can learn to see what schools so obviously do to their children. Taxpayers can learn to interpret the meaning of trends in the costs of schooling. Even the privileged, oppressed by the stink of pollution and their growing fear of the poor, may come to wonder why they did not learn about these things in school. If they do not, their children are likely to tell them. These children of the privileged may turn out to be the teachers of the educational revolution, though not all of them, for many seek inconsistent goals. Oppressed by the hypocrisy around them, they seek the truth. But they also seek the warm social womb that a technological world denies them. Some will find one, some the other, perhaps most neither. Since the total number of dissatisfied students can only increase, however, enough may find the truth.

One further component is needed, which current cynicism makes it easy to forget. Research today is so identified with physical science, military technology, and establishment support that its crucial role in education and revolution may be overlooked. It is obvious that people will never abandon schools in pursuit of alternatives so vaguely stated as above. It should be equally obvious that more concrete alternatives must be locally developed, all over the world, to fit specific time, place, and circumstance. This development will require the kind of hard, systematic intellectual work that can only be called research. Enough of this kind of work is a necessary, and might even be a sufficient, condition for a peaceful educational revolution.

SO YOU WANT TO CHANGE TO

○
○
○

Another educational wave is breaking on American shores. Whether termed "integrated day," "Leicestershire Plan," "informal classroom," or "open education," it promises new and radical methods of teaching, learning, and organizing the schools.[1] Many American educators who do not shy from promises of new solutions to old problems are preparing to ride the crest of the wave. In New York State, for instance, the commissioner of education, the chancellor of New York City schools, and the president of the state branch of the American Federation of Teachers have all expressed their intent to make the state's classrooms open classrooms. Schools of education in such varied places as North Dakota, Connecticut, Massachusetts, New York, and Ohio are tooling up to prepare the masses of teachers for these masses of anticipated open classrooms.

Some educators are disposed to search for the new, the different, the flashy, the radical, or the revolutionary. Once an idea or a practice, such as "team teaching," "nongrading," and (more recently) "differentiated staffing" and "performance contracting," has been so labeled by the Es-

tablishment, many teachers and administrators are quick to adopt it. More precisely, these educators are quick to assimilate new ideas into their cognitive and operational framework. But in so doing they often distort the original conception without recognizing either the distortion or the assumptions violated by the distortion. This seems to happen partly because the educator has taken on the verbal, superficial abstraction of a new idea without going through a concomitant personal reorientation of attitude and behavior. Vocabulary and rhetoric are easily changed; basic beliefs and institutions all too often remain little affected. If open education is to have a fundamental and positive effect on American edu-

[1] For a fuller description of this movement, see Roland S. Barth and Charles H. Rathbone, annotated bibliographies: "The Open School: A Way of Thinking About Children, Learning and Knowledge," *The Center Forum*, Vol. 3, No. 7, July, 1969, a publication of the Center for Urban Education, New York City; and "A Bibliography of Open Education, Early Childhood Education Study," jointly published by the Advisory for Open Education and the Education Development Center, Newton, Mass., 1971.

AN OPEN CLASSROOM

Roland S. Barth

cation, and if changes are to be consciously made, rhetoric and good intentions will not suffice.

There is no doubt that a climate potentially hospitable to fresh alternatives to our floundering educational system exists in this country. It is even possible that, in this brief moment in time, open education may have the opportunity to prove itself. However, a crash program is dangerous. Implementing foreign ideas and practices is a precarious business, and I fear the present opportunity will be abused or misused. Indeed, many attempts to implement open classrooms in America have already been buried with the epitaphs "sloppy permissivism," "neoprogressive," "Communist," "anarchical," or "laissez-faire." An even more discouraging although not surprising consequence has been to push educational practice further away from open education than was the case prior to the attempt at implementation.

Most educators who say they want open education are ready to change *appearances.* They install printing presses, tables in place of desks, classes in corridors, nature study. They adopt the *vocabulary:* "inte-grated day," "interest areas," "free choice," and "student initiated learning." However, few have understanding of, let alone commitment to, the philosophical, personal, and professional roots from which these practices and phrases have sprung, and upon which they depend so completely for their success. It is my belief that changing appearances to more closely resemble some British classrooms without understanding and accepting the rationale underlying these changes will lead inevitably to failure and conflict among children, teachers, administrators, and parents. American education can withstand no more failure, even in the name of reform or revolution.

I would like to suggest that before you jump on the open classroom surfboard, a precarious vehicle appropriate neither for all people nor for all situations, you pause long enough to consider the following statements and to examine your own reactions to them. Your reactions may reveal salient attitudes about children, learning, and knowledge. I have found that successful open educators in both England and America tend to take similar positions on these statements. Where do you stand?

assumptions about learning and knowledge[2]

I / ASSUMPTIONS ABOUT CHILDREN'S LEARNING

Motivation

Assumption 1: Children are innately curious and will explore their environment without adult intervention.

strongly agree	agree	no strong feeling	disagree	strongly disagree

Assumption 2: Exploratory behavior is self-perpetuating.

strongly agree	agree	no strong feeling	disagree	strongly disagree

Conditions for Learning

Assumption 3: The child will display natural exploratory behavior if he is not threatened.

strongly agree	agree	no strong feeling	disagree	strongly disagree

Assumption 4: Confidence in self is highly related to capacity for learning and for making important choices affecting one's learning.

strongly agree	agree	no strong feeling	disagree	strongly disagree

Assumption 5: Active exploration in a rich environment, offering a wide array of manipulative materials, will facilitate children's learning.

strongly agree	agree	no strong feeling	disagree	strongly disagree

Assumption 6: Play is not distinguished from work as the predominant mode of learning in early childhood.

strongly agree	agree	no strong feeling	disagree	strongly disagree

Assumption 7: Children have both the competence and the right to make significant decisions concerning their own learning.

strongly agree	agree	no strong feeling	disagree	strongly disagree

Assumption 8: Children will be likely to learn if they are given considerable choice in the selection of the materials they wish to work with and in the choice of questions they wish to pursue with respect to those materials.

strongly agree	agree	no strong feeling	disagree	strongly disagree

[2] From Roland S. Barth, *"Open Education,"* unpublished doctoral dissertation, Harvard Graduate School of Education, 1970.

Instructions: Make a mark somewhere along each line which best represents your own feelings about each statement.

Example: School serves the wishes and needs of adults better than it does the wishes and needs of children.

strongly agree	agree	no strong feeling	disagree	strongly disagree

Assumption 9: Given the opportunity, children will choose to engage in activities which will be of high interest to them.

strongly agree	agree	no strong feeling	disagree	strongly disagree

Assumption 10: If a child is fully involved in and is having fun with an activity, learning is taking place.

strongly agree	agree	no strong feeling	disagree	strongly disagree

Social Learning

Assumption 11: When two or more children are interested in exploring the same problem or the same materials, they will often choose to collaborate in some way.

strongly agree	agree	no strong feeling	disagree	strongly disagree

Assumption 12: When a child learns something which is important to him, he will wish to share it with others.

strongly agree	agree	no strong feeling	disagree	strongly disagree

Intellectual Development

Assumption 13: Concept formation proceeds very slowly.

strongly agree	agree	no strong feeling	disagree	strongly disagree

Assumption 14: Children learn and develop intellectually not only at their own rate but in their own style.

strongly agree	agree	no strong feeling	disagree	strongly disagree

Assumption 15: Children pass through similar stages of intellectual development, each in his own way and at his own rate and in his own time.

strongly agree	agree	no strong feeling	disagree	strongly disagree

Assumption 16: Intellectual growth and development take place through a sequence of concrete experiences followed by abstractions.

strongly agree	agree	no strong feeling	disagree	strongly disagree

Assumption 17: Verbal abstractions should follow direct experience with objects and ideas, not precede them or substitute for them.

strongly agree	agree	no strong feeling	disagree	strongly disagree

Evaluation

Assumption 18: The preferred source of verification for a child's solution to a problem comes through the materials he is working with.

strongly agree	agree	no strong feeling	disagree	strongly disagree

Assumption 19: Errors are necessarily a part of the learning process; they are to be expected and even desired, for they contain information essential for further learning.

strongly agree	agree	no strong feeling	disagree	strongly disagree

Assumption 20: Those qualities of a person's learning which can be carefully measured are not necessarily the most important.

strongly agree	agree	no strong feeling	disagree	strongly disagree

Assumption 21: Objective measures of performance may have a negative effect upon learning.

strongly agree	agree	no strong feeling	disagree	strongly disagree

Assumption 22: Learning is best assessed intuitively, by direct observation.

strongly agree	agree	no strong feeling	disagree	strongly disagree

Assumption 23: The best way of evaluating the effect of the school experience on the child is to observe him over a long period of time.

strongly agree	agree	no strong feeling	disagree	strongly disagree

Assumption 24: The best measure of a child's work is his work.

strongly agree	agree	no strong feeling	disagree	strongly disagree

II / ASSUMPTIONS ABOUT KNOWLEDGE

Assumption 25: The quality of being is more important than the quality of knowing; knowledge is a means of education, not its end. The final test of an education is what a man *is*, not what he *knows*.

strongly agree	agree	no strong feeling	disagree	strongly disagree

Assumption 26: Knowledge is a function of one's personal integration of experience and therefore does not fall into neatly separate categories or "disciplines."

strongly agree	agree	no strong feeling	disagree	strongly disagree

Assumption 27: The structure of knowledge is personal and idiosyncratic; it is a function of the synthesis of each individual's experience with the world.

strongly agree	agree	no strong feeling	disagree	strongly disagree

Assumption 28: Little or no knowledge exists which it is essential for everyone to acquire.

strongly agree	agree	no strong feeling	disagree	strongly disagree

Assumption 29: It is possible, even likely, that an individual may learn

and possess knowledge of a phenomenon and yet be unable to display it publicly. Knowledge resides with the knower, not in its public expression.

---

strongly agree	agree	no strong feeling	disagree	strongly disagree

Most open educators, British and American, "strongly agree" with most of these statements.[3] I think it is possible to learn a great deal both about open education and about oneself by taking a position with respect to these different statements. While it would be folly to argue that strong agreement assures success in developing an open classroom, or, on the other hand, that strong disagreement predicts failure, the assumptions are, I believe, closely related to open education practices. Consequently, I feel that for those sympathetic to the assumptions, success at a difficult job will be more likely. For the educator to attempt to adopt practices which depend for their success upon general adherence to these beliefs without actually adhering to them is, at the very least, dangerous.

At the same time, we must be careful not to assume that an "official" British or U.S. government-inspected type of open classroom or set of beliefs exists which is the standard for all others. Indeed, what is exciting about British open classrooms is the *diversity* in thinking and behavior for children and adults—from person to person, class to class, and school to school. The important point here is that the likelihood of successfully developing an open classroom increases as those concerned agree with the basic assumptions underlying open education practices. It is impossible to "role play" such a fundamentally distinct teaching responsibility.

For some people, then, drawing attention to these assumptions may terminate interest in open education. All to the good; a well-organized, consistent, teacher-directed classroom probably has a far less harmful influence upon children than a well-intentioned but sloppy, permissive, and chaotic attempt at an open classroom in which teacher and child must live with contradiction and conflict. For other people, awareness of these assumptions may stimulate confidence and competence in their attempts to change what happens to children in school.

In the final analysis, the success of a widespread movement toward open education in this country rests not upon agreement with any philosophical position but with satisfactory answers to several important questions: For what kinds of people—teachers, administrators, parents, children—is the open classroom appropriate and valuable? What happens to children in open classrooms? Can teachers be *trained* for open classrooms? How can the resistance from children, teachers, administrators, and parents—inevitable among those not committed to open education's assumptions and practices—be surmounted? And finally, should participation in an open classroom be *required* of teachers, children, parents, and administrators?

[3] Since these assumptions were assembled, I have "tested" them with several British primary teachers, headmasters, and inspectors and with an equal number of American proponents of open education. To date, although many qualifications in language have been suggested, there has not been a case where an individual has said of one of the assumptions, "No, that is contrary to what I believe about children, learning, or knowledge."

COMMUNICATION, EDUCATION, AND CHANGE

Charles Weingartner

The first hole ever dug on the moon by a man-made machine is now done. It's the most expensive hole in the history of the human race. But that *may* be incidental. The question comes up—what does that mean? What we're confronted with here, in this small hole, is a kind of a metaphor for the continuing human problem, the question, "what does it mean?" Who decides? How do they decide whether that hole is worth digging? What criteria do they employ? What priorities are established? And on the basis of what assumptions? How do we know whether this is one of man's most noble accomplishments or whether it's a game being played by a small group of lunatics for their own amusement?—and at our expense. This is one example of the most common problem we're all continually faced with, and it is intensified by the rate of change that characterizes the world today. The key question is "what does it mean?" and—for the first time, there's no place we can go to look it up—there's no reference book to turn to find out whether the hole on the moon is an accomplishment or a fraud. And that's the world we're all going to have to live in from now on. As we move into the future at supersonic speed we're not going to get much help in figuring out what it all means from looking, as Marshall McLuhan says, in the rear-view mirror. This is probably the first time in the history of the race that this has ever been true. Up until relatively recently there's always been a place to "look it up." But from here on there's no such place. *Everything* changes much too rapidly to make this feasible, even if it were possible. Maybe to try to illustrate this point I should ask that we have about two seconds of silence for the statistician who drowned while wading across a river with an average depth of three feet. You see, he got into trouble because the language in which he was codifying meanings insulated him from the reality he had to deal with. His metaphors were too static and too abstract and his failure to understand this had insured his self-termination. To a large extent the failure to recognize the effects of dead metaphors characterizes the business of education. The title, "Communication, Education, and Change," has education in the middle to suggest that education is the mediating process between developments in media of communication and the change that results from these developments. The primary function of education now has to be that of helping us to understand the meanings of media produced change. One way of looking at education is to say that the basic purpose of it is—and probably always has been—to help the group learn . . . to survive. That has always been the aim of education, and we should all be able to agree on that. The problem all educators face . . . , however, is that of developing a viable perspective on the processes of education in relation to the environment we must live in. We have to do this to make sure that the processes that comprise our education are relevant to our survival needs. Santayana wrote a line that is unfortunately apt as a description of the most common kind of educational decisions being made today. He said, "Fanaticism consists of redoubling your efforts after having forgotten your aim." Much dialogue in education today goes something like this—"If the amount of something doesn't work, . . . double it." This is commonly called enrichment. But it might more accurately be described as polishing up the rear-view mirror. Education, along with all the other traditional institutions in our culture, including of course the family and the church, needs to re-assess its efforts, after remembering its aim. And this is a very difficult task. It is one that most of us would rather avoid or leave to someone else, since it requires a rigorous reexamination of our fondest (and least conscious) assumptions. If we can agree that the basic aim of education is still that of enhancing the survival prospects of the group, then perhaps we can also agree that two of the most obvious conditions of the environment in which survival attempts must be made by all of us—now—are first, that of change—rapid, increasing, unceasing, accelerating, incomprehensible change, in everything; and second, that of the existence of media of communication which to a large degree cause this change. We are, as a matter of fact, trying to live and to make sense of our lives in the midst of several simultaneous revolutions —on which we have almost no perspective. McLuhan is trying to help us to develop a perspective on the most central revolution—that of the electronic media. Almost none of us seems to have any perspective on these things. It's quite curious: the person who is least equipped to describe a revolution seems to be the person who is in the middle of it and most affected by it. Most of us, when we're in the midst of a revolution—perhaps especially because it consists of several different revolutions at once— respond to the changes that result or that symptomize these revolutions by simple annoyance. We are irritated by the changes that occur and we hope . . . that they'll just go away. All of these revolutions stem from the central revolution that McLuhan is probing. Without this "communication revolution," the other revolutions, including the information explosion (a revolution directly affecting education), the civil rights movement (made possible by television), dramatic changes in traditional religious ritual (the jazz mass in the Catholic church, for example), the teen ager, the population explosion, and all the other symptoms of high-speed changes in human patterns of behavior, would not be possible. What's unique, unprecedented, about all these changes is the degree to which they are occurring. Well, you say, changes always occur—but the degree of change here is what's important. This degree of change simultaneously includes the speed of the change and the magnitude of the change. And what it means is almost incomprehensible. Lest we miss the point about the critical importance of this point about the degree of change in the world today, it's worth noting that Norbert Wiener reminded us that the difference between a fatal and a therapeutic dose of strychnine is "only a matter of degree."

Traditionally, education devoted itself largely to training students to become sophisticated in the use of the most contemporary means of communication. This, after all, is what the Trivium sprang from. As the basis for the seven liberal arts, the Trivium consisted of training in grammar, rhetoric, and logic. Because, at the time, the most important contemporary medium of communication was speech. The educational efforts engaged in under these names, grammar, rhetoric, and logic—were appropriate to the aim of education at the time. There were no textbooks—as a matter of fact, writing was considered a debasement of speech—at least by Socrates as he appears in the *Phaedrus*. There weren't any syllabi—no lesson plans—the focus was on the behavioral skill in this particular survival strategy that the student was to develop. The student and his survival and, contingently, that of the group was central. The aim was in sight.

A few things have changed since then. In an attempt to get a perspective on some of these changes—and the time in which they occurred—let us use a clock face as a metaphor. Let's have our clock face—the 60 minutes on it—stand just for the time man—at least some men—have had access to writing—but a very special kind of writing. Writing consisting of what we call a phonetic alphabet—of course our phonetic alphabet isn't phonetic, it's phonemic. But, again, a special kind of "phonetic" alphabet— one that's used on a portable surface—vellum, papyrus, or paper or whatever—this permits us to have our clock face represent something like three thousand years. If we can use this then we can have one minute on our clock stand for a fifty year period. Now on this scale, looking at our clock, we can see that as far as man-made change resulting from innovations in communication is concerned the environment was *relatively* stable until about nine minutes ago. About nine minutes ago on this clock movable type (the printing press) came into use in Western culture. Now the effects of the printing press in Europe were quite different from the effects of the printing press in Asia, even though both used movable type, because the characters on the type faces did entirely different things to people and so they produced entirely different results. The characters on the type faces in Europe were phonetic (as we erroneously call them) and the characters on the type faces in Asia were ideographic—and therein lies a fascinating tale that is too long to go into here—what phonetic writing does to meaning. The introduction of print in Western culture "merely" changed the form and substance of Western institutions, concepts, assumptions, and patterns of thought that had persisted for more than a thousand years. Print broke all kinds of monopolies. For example, the Protestant Reformation would not have been possible without print; neither would the American Revolution have been possible without print. Print produced a long series of interesting consequences, not all of them unmixed blessings. Technological change as we have yet to understand it resulting from man's invention of symbol, message, and information processing machines began, for all practical purposes, with the printing press. The first repeatable—virtually to infinity—man-made object, the first non-exclusively hand-made, non-unique, non-one-of-a-kind item in the history of the human race was the printed book. And this was the *fourth* stage in a process of revolution that we have yet to understand. If we don't soon understand this revolution and where it *now* has us, it may destroy us. The *first* stage in this revolution, of course, was the development of language—speech. The *second* stage was the development of writing. The *third* stage was the "phonetic" alphabet. What happened in

Europe after the introduction of the printing press was that the whole course of the world changed. New metaphors, new ideas, new patterns of perception and behavior exploded into being. The Cadmus myth was borne out. Lacking any precedent for what was happening—but nonetheless staring into the rear-view mirror—we interpreted these changes as if they were merely extensions of older processes and in so doing we missed the point—just as we're missing the point today. We're in the midst of trying to solve *right now* a number of problems that were caused by the introduction of printing into Western culture—but we're not very good at that either. It's interesting to note, incidentially, that 500 years after the introduction of print the biggest problem in the schools is reading.

Back to our clock now. About three minutes ago on our clock (150 years) the telegraph, the photograph, and the locomotive, all means of communication, came into being. It's worth noting that they could not have come into being without print.

About two minutes ago on our clock the telephone, the rotary press, the motion picture, the automobile, the airplane, the radio also came into use, all media of communication.

About one minute ago on our clock the talking picture was developed. Television has appeared in the last ten seconds; the computer in the last five, and communications satellites about a second ago. The laser beam— probably the most potent medium of communication yet—appeared only a fraction of a second ago.

Now as any ecologist will tell you, when you're studying the transactions between an organism and its environment you'll miss the point about how the organism survives if you see a change in the environment as being only additive or linear. This is to say that you never have an old environment

---

plus a new element—you don't have an old Europe plus the printing press —you always have—and we seem not to have learned what this difference means yet—*a totally new environment, requiring a wholly new repertoire of survival strategies.* This is really quite a new notion, as the compressed time on our clock is intended to indicate. For example, up until just the last generation, it was possible to be born, grow up, spend a life—with all that that means—the work, the family, the living, and so on—in the United States without moving more than 50 miles from home, without ever confronting serious questions about one's basic values, beliefs, and patterns of behavior. You could be born, grow up, and die virtually intact—staying in a single role, operating on a single set of beliefs, in a single pattern of behavior. You could spend a life free of change produced anxiety. Stability and consequent predictability—within natural cycles—was the characteristic mode. But then (less than two minutes ago on the clock) what's called the "conflict between generations" developed, where the younger generation grew up in an entirely different environment from the older generation and while media of communication improved, personal communication seemed to begin to break down between the older and younger generations. The new generation grew up in a different environment mostly as a result of developments in media of communication. The new generation grew up in a different set of assumptions, values, perceptions, patterns of behavior from the old and so serious conflict between generations resulted. And now, in just the last minute, we've reached the stage where change occurs so rapidly that each of us in the course of our lives has continuously to develop, continuously to work out a set of values, perceptions, beliefs, patterns of behavior that are viable, or seem viable, to each of us personally. And just as we think we've identified a workable system it turns out to be irrelevant because so much has changed, and so we have to begin working on another one and by that time we're beginning to get the feeling that this system isn't really going to work either because by the time we get it figured out changes will have occurred that require a new system. This kind of ultimately demoralizing frustration can be avoided, however, if we shift from dead concepts (embodied in dead metaphors and rhetoric) possibly relevant once to a static environment to new and live concepts relevant to a dynamic, changing environment.

The need to change traditional concepts, forms, and metaphors in order to survive in a rapidly changing environment produced the Ecumenical Council. The purpose of this council, as conceived by Pope John XXIII, was to effect changes in the traditional religious concepts, forms, and metaphors in order to increase the relevance of the Roman Catholic Church, as an institution, to the changed and changing lives of its constituents. Some of the changes resulting from this essentially conservative conclave have been truly revolutionary when viewed from old perspectives.

Education, also an essentially conservative institution, might well take some cues from the Catholic Church and its recent innovations resulting from its concern about being relevant. What might be the school analogue for a jazz mass for example? Possibly the inclusion of the study of film as seriously and intensively as print is now studied? Now some people, of course, are outraged by the idea of a jazz mass because they're not used to making a distinction between what is important and what is merely conventional. They are so preoccupied with form that they have forgotten, if they ever knew, that form is best when it follows function—as in nature. Despite all the changes in media of communication—especially since World War II—the schools proceed as if the printed word were the most recent, the most important, the most relevant—even the ONLY EXISTING form of human communication.

In an attempt to get some perspective on how ludicrous this is, imagine this experiment being done in your neighborhood. Imagine that your home is in a cordoned off area from which will be removed all the electric and electronic media of communication that have appeared in the last 50 years. These media will be subtracted in reverse order with the most recent going first. The first thing to leave your house then is the television set—and everybody will stand there as if they're at the funeral of a friend —wondering "What are we going to do tonight?" And all the furniture will be aimed at that blank space in the room. And it will be very difficult to think of something to do. How about "let's go to the movies?" But there won't be any movies either because they're out next, and there won't be any LP records, there won't be any tapes, there won't be any radio, and there won't be any telephone, or telegraph, or slick magazines. There won't even be an electric light, which is itself a medium of communication. All that stuff will be gone. Just think about that for a minute. Just think of all the differences in family behavior at home. How, in the absence of all these media, would the pattern of your life change? In what ways? With what consequences? Everybody might be forced to sit at the same table and talk to each other instead of scurrying off to their separate cubicles to turn on their private shows and eat their TV dinners. What would happen to TV dinners if there weren't any TV? How would life be different? Can you imagine the differences that would occur that would bother you personally? And how might most classrooms in most schools be affected by the subtraction of these media—this reversion to the old days? Would there be the same response as in our personal lives or might the feeling even be in the classrooms that removing all this communication potential that has been developed in the last 50 years would be a good thing? What about that? We wouldn't have to worry about the kids wasting so much time watching TV, or listening to records, when they should be doing "important" things like looking in some printed rear-view mirror. Perhaps you begin to get the feeling that we really have no idea, most of us, about what these media have done to us, what they mean to us, and what they mean for us. The curious inability to figure out what changes in media of communication mean (cf. Socrates' opposition to writing) might be one of the most durable achievements of conventional schooling. What would you guess the response was to print in Western culture? It was deplored. It was regarded by medieval scholastics as a debasement of the manuscript. Of course, the big question for schoolmen when the printed book came into existence was—"what are we going to do now?" The only reason anybody came to school in those days was to make their own handwritten copy of the book that the teacher was reading from. The printed book produced all kinds of annoying consequences for the schoolmen to contend with. For example, examinations, as we now know them, are a result of the introduction of print. The written examination was an attempt on the part of the teacher to confine the students' . . . attention to what he was talking about. The printed book made knowledge about all kinds of things accessible to students, including much that the professor did not know. And you know how annoying it is to have some student know more than you do. "I don't care how interesting that is, it's not going to be on the test!" Right? And we're still in about the same state the medieval schoolmen were when print first appeared. The printed book was regarded by them as simply . . . a kind of poorer version of a hand-produced manuscript. It took many years to figure out that if you put numbers on the pages you could find a specific place easier. Of course, with a manuscript you didn't need numbers on the pages—the manuscript was an oral form which meant that, among other things, it was completely memorized. It took many years to figure out that a printed book might be

---

read silently. And it was about the same time that numbered pages came into being. The reason for mentioning these little details is simply to illustrate the difficulty we have—have always had, apparently—in figuring out what changes in media of communication mean. Right up to the present moment. We are merely saying about TV today what Socrates said about writing and what medieval schoolmen said about print. It's an old story. We all seem to be slow learners in this regard. When, for example, radio came into existence, it was not taken seriously by anybody, except one man. And this story is a variation on the theme about seeing the new medium as merely doing the job of the preceding medium. When it first appeared, radio was generally regarded as being useful only for the job that the telegraph had done—business messages, diplomatic correspondence, etc. The appearance of the telegraph itself, of course, changed the patterns of diplomacy in Western culture. But there was one man, a telegraph operator, incidentally, who had notions about the use of radio that seemed not to occur to most other people. His name was David Sarnoff.

Another example: the LP record, which was invented by an engineer at CBS who happened to be a classical music fan, which, in turn, moved him to invent the LP record. It just annoyed him to have the music he loved interrupted every three minutes or so by a silence and a clack. So he said there must be another way. There was: you smallen up the groove and you longen out the music. Now what's interesting is, for the first several years after the appearance of the LP record—you see we're right up to a couple of seconds ago on our clock—it didn't occur to any of the sophisticated communicators at CBS that you could ever put anything but classical music on LP records. But just think of what the LP record has done. What's the humor students especially know and respond to? What's the poetry students know and respond to? The poetry is, of course, sung to the accompaniment of guitar music, but it's all on LP records. For all practical purposes, if you took the LP record out there wouldn't be any humor. Students meet in groups to listen to humorous commentaries on our tribal activities—recorded on LP's. Poetry is enjoying a renaissance among students—despite the feelings of many English teachers. If the size of the audience is any criterion for judging the value of poetry, it may be that Bob Dylan is one of the most important poets that we've ever had. And what's he saying?

He is saying . . . that the entire system of Western society, built upon Aristotelian logic, the Judeo-Christian ethic and upon a series of economic systems from Hobbes to Marx to Keynes, does not work.

What he is saying is getting an unbelievably intense reaction from a generation thirsting for answers other than those in the college textbooks. Students may very well learn more from Dylan today than from the obsolete educational system, structured by another epoch. "I know I am a better human being for reading Bob Dylan," a high school student wrote me, adding: "I would rather write poetry now than study science." In schools all over the country, students are copying down lyrics of Dylan songs from records and insisting that the English class study them. A Jesuit high school in Sacramento devoted most of an English class one semester last year to the study of Dylan as poetry, and the University of California, like numerous other colleges and universities, has seen students get together themselves to hold unofficial seminars on his poems.[1]

[1] Ralph J. Gleason, "The Children's Crusade," *Ramparts*, March 1966, p. 28.

The movies provide another example of myopia among the media-makers. The movie-makers themselves had no idea in the early stages that movies would ever be anything other than a kind of visual amusement to accompany oral gratification. They were seen as a novelty to accompany beer-drinking and ice-cream eating. The idea that the movies might change the course of the world is still not a widely-held notion. Sukarno, however, when he visited Hollywood, thanked American movie-makers for making possible the revolutions in Asia. American movies make revolutions in Asia possible because they develop needs and wants among viewers in many parts of the world where the existing system cannot fulfill those needs. The consequent frustration makes revolution not only possible but inevitable. More recently, television made possible—made inevitable—what we call the civil rights movement or the Negro revolution. Without TV this couldn't happen. Without television Martin Luther King, instead of winning a Nobel Peace Prize, would probably just have been beaten up, and would never have been heard or seen by anybody outside of Montgomery, Alabama. So, the whole texture of the world in which we live is changed by the appearance of each new medium of communication. One of the generalizations that it is possible to make about communication is that two media cannot exist at the same time to do the same thing. Now it might be easier to get a perspective on that if we think about the two most recent media to demonstrate that. It was only about 10–12 years ago that television began doing what up until that moment movies had done. And what happened to movies at that stage? . . . The movies lost their audience. After TV began to do what the movies had done up to that point, what did the movies have to do? Well, obviously something different, because two media cannot exist at the same time to do the same thing. It upset a lot of people—change upsets most people—when movies became . . . more realistic. Movies began to do about what the stage had done up to that point. They couldn't survive doing what they used to do because TV was doing that. Once film had found a new role for itself, its survival was assured. It had a new function and a new audience. The old movie audience stayed home and watched movies on TV. There is a new movie audience.

And there is a new student. . . . [I]f the school tries to persist in its old role (the school is a medium of communication) it will increasingly lose its audience. The question that is raised by change resulting from media developments is "what is the most appropriate role for the school?" The one thing that we know for sure is that the school cannot survive primarily as a medium to disseminate information. There are too many alternatives. There are too many other ways to do that, much more economically, much more efficiently. So the question is "what's the . . . function of the school . . . ?" Father John Culkin, following Marshall McLuhan, suggests that one function of the school is to train students to be literate in *all* of the media. He reminded us that:

A lot of things have happened since 1900 and most of them plug into walls. Today's six-year-old has already learned a lot of stuff by the time he shows up for the first day of school. Soon after his umbilical cord was cut he was planted in front of a TV set "to keep him quiet." He liked it enough there to stay for some 3,000 to 4,000 hours before he started the first grade. By the time he graduates from high school he has clocked 15,000 hours of TV time and 10,800 hours of school time. He lives in a world which bombards him from all sides with information from radios, films, telephones, magazines, recordings, and people. He learns more things from the windows of cars, trains, and even planes. Through travel and communications he has experienced the war in Vietnam, the wide world of sports, the civil rights movement, the death of a President, thousands of commercials, a walk in space, a thousand innocuous shows, and, one may hope, plenty of Captain Kangaroo.

This is all merely descriptive, an effort to lay out what *is,* not what should be. Today's student can hardly be described by any of the old educational analogies comparing him to an empty bucket or a blank page. He comes to the information machine called school and he is already brimming over with information. As he grows his standards for relevance are determined more by what he receives outside the school than what he receives inside. A recent Canadian film tells the story of a bright, articulate middle-class teen-ager who leaves school because there's "no reason to stay." He daydreams about Vietnam while his teacher drones on about the four reasons for the spread of Christianity and the five points such information is worth on the exam. Only the need for a diploma was holding him in school; learning wasn't, and he left. He decided the union ticket wasn't worth the gaff. He left. Some call him a dropout. Some call him a pushout.[2]

There are many indications of increasing student dissatisfaction with their schooling. It's probably more visible on the college level than it is else-where. Last summer [1966], for example, there was a student conference

[2] John M. Culkin, S.J., "A Schoolman's Guide to Marshall McLuhan," *Saturday Review,* March 18, 1967, pp. 71–72. Copyright 1967 Saturday Review, Inc. Reprinted with permission.

held in Washington, D.C. The purpose of the conference was to identify the concerns of the American college students. Among student concerns were such items as the pill, the bomb, the draft, and civil rights. But it turned out that the students were much more concerned about the relevance of their education than any of the other things. So we have a new kind of a student in schools today as a result of all these changes produced by media. The average American student of 1900 never saw a national political convention or a presidential candidate or a major league baseball game. He never saw an opera or a play or a presidential inauguration, or a Kentucky Derby. He never saw a war in process, or the earth from outer space. He had only a vague idea how a great singer sounded, or how a great prize-fighter hit. He never saw a steel mill. He had no picture of Congress in session, or of Negro children being screamed at, spat upon, and struck while trying just to go to school. But today all these things are routine for students and for adults alike. The capacity for observation of the world has increased remarkably—this is the extension of our perception that McLuhan is talking about. The student is simultaneously much more informed and *misinformed* than was his grandfather. And it's worth noting that the new knowledge vicariously and seemingly easily arrived at is not necessarily profound, meaningful or even accurate. The media then have produced a new kind of a society that we have yet to understand. We have a new kind of society and a very new kind of student to deal with in the school, so we need new strategies for survival. The old medium cannot . . . [survive] when the new one comes along and does its job better. It has to find a new job to do. What this means for education is that the school can't justify itself primarily as a medium designed to "impart information." Education needs to do something other than that, something more important than that. . . .

In order to survive we have to help young people in our culture learn a whole new way of thinking. The students we have in school now are going to live well past the year 2000. This should help us to understand that we need to focus on concepts that will be viable then rather than on facts which may not even be relevant now. This is especially true since we are now at a stage where facts are virtually self-obsolescing. We need to help students learn something other than facts—even if they are learnable. And, there's another problem: there's so much to know that human knowledge is rendered almost unknowable simply by volume. So education must do something else. Our educational system is still . . . [obsessed], however, with . . . the past. This is one part of the rear-view mirror tendency McLuhan talks about. . . .

The issue lies here—how do you help students learn to survive in a culture changing with enormous speed imposed on it largely by changes in the media of communication if all you have them do is regurgitate dead, unrelated "facts"? . . . Most of us are just beginning to experience future-shock, . . . as the irrelevance of almost everything we say we know and believe and hold dear and want to act out becomes inescapable.

What are we going to do in the face of all this? There've been some suggestions in an interesting book titled *Frontiers of Knowledge.* Lynn White, president of Mills College, writes about "the changing canons of culture." He simplifies the task for education, in a way, by suggesting that all these changes resulting from media of communication require our moving from what the four most common canons that we act on to four new canons of culture, if we're to survive. The first canon of culture that we have to abandon—and you may begin to see the sources of many of the now irrelevant assumptions that we make in education—is the Canon of the Occident. White suggests that this be replaced by the Canon of the

Globe. His reasons for this are not unlike those McLuhan embodies in his reference to the world as a "global village." The second canon he suggests we relinquish is the canon of logic and language, which needs to be replaced by the canon of symbols. The third canon, that of rationality, needs to be replaced by the canon of the unconscious. It is worth noting that most of the metaphors of the school are mechanistic. We talk as if the basic problems in education are merely in-put out-put problems, as if learning were merely rational. We talk about the logic of the subject. The canon of the unconsicous would require us to talk about the psycho-logic of the learner. . . . And, finally, White suggests that we need to shift from the canon of the hierarchy of values, a kind of vertical Victorian stratification, to the canon of the spectrum of values, where differences can be equally valuable. Almost all the criteria for judging whatever is happening in the school is based on a vertical hierarchy of values, with dismal consequences.

Complementing White, and extending his perception into the school curriculum specifically, McLuhan suggests that:

. . . all forms of mathematics and science as much as the changing modes of historiography and literature, offer instruments and models of perception. It follows that any existing "subject" in our curricula can now be taught as a more or less minor group of models of perception favored in some past or at present. Taught in this way any "subject" becomes an organic portion of almost any other "subject." Moreover, it also follows that "subject" taught structurally in this way offers innumerable opportunities for new perception and new insight even at elementary levels. The idea of the "content" of education as something to be lodged in the mind as a container thus belongs to the pre-electronic phase and to the era of Euclidean space and Newtonian mechanics. A structure cannot be contained. Any conceivable container is at once part of the structure, modifying the whole. The idea of "content" at once reveals a structure of perception and assumptions from which the artist and the poet have been trying to free us for a full century. But now the nuclear physicist has intervened on the side of the artists, and the pressure to heed the message of the artists has become more urgent. . . .

The nineteenth century discovery of the method of invention was the ultimate stage of the mechanical genius of our Western world that began with the alphabet and ended with the assembly line. To have isolated this process from its mere products, we owe to the artists and not to the scientists. However, we have now gone beyond the technique of the method of invention. It is the unique achievement of the twentieth century to have discovered the technique of the suspended judgment. That means the technique of understanding process in such a way as to avoid its consequences. We can now avoid "closure" because we understand it, in some areas at least. Perhaps this is akin to "weightlessness," the by-passing of gravitational consequences of a false step, as in a trick movie. And such understanding of process with the attendant means of evading its consequences is a natural feature of the simultaneous "field." For, in "field" awareness, the effects are seen at the moment as the cause.[3]

Here we have some cue as to what the role of the school as a medium of communication might be if it can no longer justify itself solely as a

[3] Marshall McLuhan, "We Need a New Picture of Knowledge," in Alexander Frazier, ed., *New Insights and the Curriculum*, 1963 Yearbook (Washington, D.C.: Association for Supervision and Curriculum Development, 1963), pp. 66–67. Reprinted with permission.

medium for disseminating information. All of this suggests that the most important function to which education can address itself is that of helping all of us to deal with the change that's presently occurring and that will increasingly occur from now on. That is to say, education has to help us to learn and to understand and to use the concepts necessary for survival in a nuclear-space-age environment of high speed.

But what concepts and attitudes does education as yet reflect and teach? The first, above all, is certainty. Absolutes. Fixed states. Most of the "curriculum" consists of the memorization of facts and everyone comes away with the deeply internalized concept that there's one right answer for every question. If this was ever true, it is no longer true. Most subjects are taxonomies—verbal classification systems—that are memorized, without any understanding of the degree to which the "subject" relates to anything else in the curriculum much less anything outside the curriculum. Another concept that education presently internalizes in students is that of the value of obedient passivity. The student who is best rewarded in school is the one who does what he is told, quickly and without question. All this produces personalities that are rigid, timid, and authoritarian. . . . [We] learn best, as Dewey said, what . . . [we] *do.* In a world of rapid change what can you predict about the survival prospects of someone who expects or demands absolute certainty, and absolute stability? And, consequently, who requires a "higher authority" to make decisions and choices for him? It would seem reasonable that education rather should focus on helping students to develop mastery of such concepts as relativity, probability, contingency, and process. These concepts foster personalities willing to formulate and act on tentative estimates. What can be more important to understand in an increasingly complex world than understanding that nothing occurs in isolation; that everything always depends on a number of other things; that there is no single cause for any effect? Students need to master the concept of function and relationships as process rather than as fixed states. And all the while the student must be at the center of the activity, through which these concepts are to be developed, in the role of the maker of knowledge rather than as a regurgitator of . . . [trivia]. The student needs practice in a role that requires knowing what questions to ask rather than merely that of memorizing somebody else's answers to somebody else's questions. Mastery of concepts such as these produces an individual who is flexible, who is courageous, who is tolerant, who can deal fruitfully with change. In his book, *Self-Renewal,* John Gardner addressed himself to the need for education to do this. He said:

> Education at its best will develop the individual's resources to the point where he can learn and will want to learn on his own. It will equip him to cope with unforeseen challenges and to survive as a versatile individual in an unpredictable world. Individuals so educated will help society itself to stay flexible, adaptive, and innovative.[4]

Education has a new role to play.
The times they are a changing.

---

[4] John Gardner, *Self-Renewal: The Individual and the Innovative Society.* Harper Colophon Books, Harper & Row, New York, 1965, p. 26.

new nation seed fund

   Our struggle for a better world takes many forms,
but none is more important than the rearing and educating of our children. We believe that children
raised in wholeness and natural pride will not grow
up to be slavish adults, nor agree to immoral politics and irresponsible technology.
   Our present system of public education, coercive
in its methods, is a symptom and major cause of our
unsatisfactory way of life. It ignores the requirements of normal growth, subordinates everything to
centralized administration, and undermines the very
best of our democratic ideals. Perhaps this system
can be changed from within. We hope so. But one thing
is clear: it cannot be changed without working models
of a better way, both as examples and as a competitive spur.
   Such models exist. They have been described in
dozens of books and hundreds of periodicals. They
are known as "free schools," and are what is meant
by the recurrent phrase "alternative education."
Everywhere in this country—and now in impressive
numbers—independent young adults are manning such
schools. Their methods are based on the observed
needs of children's growth, and on the philosophies
of Dewey, Tolstoy, Neill, and many others. The

schools are kept small so that persons can have access to one another. Relationships replace arbitrary discipline. The absence of coercion makes room for morality and ethics, and these in turn foster the humane relations which alone are the proper setting for the growth of the young.

There are documented examples of brilliant success with these methods. Yet the libertarian schools have no friends in government, industry, or the foundations, and are always short of funds. There is special difficulty for the poor, whose children must be enrolled free of charge.

The function of the NEW NATION SEED FUND is to help new schools get started, and existing ones stay alive. (We have seen excellent schools founder for want of a small sum.) We ask you to remember this fund by thinking of it on your own birthday, and we ask you to send it a gift at that time. Since it is easier to remember small gifts than large ones, we ask you to send one dollar. If you are a parent, and do agree with us, urge your own children and young people to ally themselves with other children by sending small presents on their birthdays, fifty cents, or a quarter. We cannot solve large problems with these sums, but we _can_ contribute to a large solution. Above all, we can keep alive one of our few working models of freedom.

The money will be used exclusively for children. It will be disbursed from the fund in consultation with reliable people in the field of education, including the sponsors named below. Priority will be given to schools enrolling significant numbers of the poor.

Checks may be made payable to: New Nation Seed Fund, Box 4026, Philadelphia, Pa. 19118

George Dennison, Paul Goodman, Nat Hentoff,
John Holt, and Jonathan Kozol

Joan Baez is equally well-known as a folksinger and pacifist. Joan is the mother of a young son, Gabriel, and author of a poignant autobiography, *Daybreak*.

Roland S. Barth has been an elementary school teacher in New Jersey and California, Assistant to the Dean at the Harvard Graduate School of Education, and is currently principal of the Angier School in Newton, Massachusetts. He is the author of many articles and a new book entitled *Open Education*.

Richard Brautigan is a poet whose writings have appeared in *The Pill Versus the Springhill Mine Disaster* and other volumes.

James Cass is the education editor of *Saturday Review*.

Walter R. Coppedge is Assistant Vice President for Academic Affairs at Virginia Commonwealth University in Richmond, Virginia.

Alice de Rivera is now a student at Clark University in Massachusetts. Since her fight at New York's Stuyvesant High the school has been coeducational.

Connie Dvorkin is an unemployed high school dropout now living in Brooklyn. She is not involved in organized politics since she discovered that it usually means "a lot of ego-tripping." She still believes in the ideas of women's liberation and tries to raise consciousness among women wherever she goes.

Herbert J. Gans is a Professor of Sociology at Columbia University and Senior Research Associate at the Center for Policy Research. He is the author of *The Levittowners, People and Plans,* and the *Urban Villagers.*

Ira Glasser is Executive Director of the New York Civil Liberties Union.

James D. Greenberg is Director of the Office of Laboratory Experiences at the University of Maryland's College of Education.

Beatrice and Ronald Gross. Ronald Gross is currently an Adjunct Associate Professor of Social Thought at New York University, on leave from his position as Vice President of the Academy for Educational Development. Books he has written or edited include *High School, Radical School Reform, The Teacher and the Taught,* and *Pop Poems*. Beatrice Gross has been a teacher, consultant, and reporter on educational innovations. She coedited *Radical School Reform*.

John Guernsey is education editor of the *Portland Oregonian*.

Carol Stolley Hastie was five years old in 1940 and spent the next eighteen years being taught—finally acquiring a masters' degree in social work from Columbia University as proof of her rite of passage through the educational system. Her real education came at home during her childhood and in New York's Harlem and Lower East Side, rural southern

Indiana, and Pittsburgh's black ghettos, where she has worked with the children and families of the poor and oppressed. She currently works in a residential treatment center for drug addicts in California.

Ivan Illich is the Director of the Center for Intercultural Documentation (CIDOC) in Cuernavaca, Mexico. He was born in Vienna, and was ordained a priest and later named a monsignor. He voluntarily renounced his priestly functions and now devotes most of his time to CIDOC. One of the most radical thinkers in education today, he is the author of *Celebration of Awareness: A Call for Institutional Revolution* and *De-Schooling Society.*

Christopher Jencks is an Associate Professor at the Harvard School of Education, a contributing editor of the *New Republic,* and coauthor with David Reisman of *The Academic Revolution.*

Jonathan Kozol is a Harvard graduate and a Rhodes scholar. His book *Death at an Early Age,* an exposé on conditions in the Boston public schools, brought him national attention. A former trustee of the community-controlled Store-Front Learning Center, Kozol has lived and worked in Boston's black ghetto for over seven years. His articles have appeared in *Esquire, New Republic,* and *Harvard Educational Review.* He is also the author of a new book, *Free Schools.*

Peter Marin is a former editor of the *New Schools Exchange Newsletter.* Before that, he was a Fellow at the Center for the Study of Democratic Institutions, and was the director of Pacific High School. With Dr. Allan Cohen, he coauthored *Understanding Drug Abuse.*

Richard Martin is a staff reporter for *The Wall Street Journal.*

New Schools Exchange Newsletter is published monthly by the New Schools Exchange in Santa Barbara, California. The Exchange is a clearing house for persons involved in educational alternatives. It is one of the leading journals which speaks for the "free school movement."

Neil Postman is a Professor of Education at New York University, is on the faculty of Harlem Preparatory School, and with Charles Weingartner coauthored *Teaching as a Subversive Activity* and *The Soft Revolution.*

Everett Reimer has been director of the ongoing seminar on "Alternatives in Education" at CIDOC since 1968. A close friend of Ivan Illich, he is the author of *School Is Dead: Alternatives in Education.*

Wallace Roberts is the former associate education editor of *Saturday Review* and the American editor of *The Little Red Schoolbook.* He has also been a teacher and newspaper reporter, and is now living in Vermont dividing his time between carpentry and writing.

Michael Rossman once wrote that readers might recognize him "as a maniac dope fiend anarchist freak" since he has no institutional identity. He does have a B.A. from Berkeley (1963) plus four years of graduate work. His articles have appeared in *The American Scholar, Commonweal, Saturday Review,* and *New Schools Exchange Newsletter.* His books include *The Wedding Within the War* and *On Learning and Social Change.*

Robert E. Roush is the Director of the Center for Allied Health Manpower Development at Baylor College of Medicine in Houston, Texas.

Arthur E. Salz is an Assistant Professor of Education at Queens College where he coordinates a program that trains teachers for the open classroom. His articles on collective bargaining have appeared in *The Urban Review* and *Phi Delta Kappan.*

Peter Schrag is a reporter whose writings have appeared in *Commonweal, New Republic,* and *Saturday Review.* His books include *Voices in the Classroom* and *Out of Place in America.*

Harvey B. Scribner was Education Commissioner of Vermont from 1968 to 1970. He is now the first chancellor of the New York City public schools. Outspoken and controversial, he is dedicated to educational reform.

Mark R. Shedd became superintendent of the Philadelphia public schools in 1967 at the age of forty. Among the innovations for which he is responsible are the Pennsylvania Advancement School, an experimental laboratory for curriculum development and teacher training, and the Parkway Program, Philadelphia's "school without walls." On December 9, 1971, Shedd was forced to resign by a conservative school board appointed by the new mayor, Frank Rizzo, who had promised Shedd's ouster if he were elected.

Harold W. Sobel is an Assistant Professor of Education at Queens College. His articles on educational reform have appeared in *Phi Delta Kappan* and *Education Digest.* He is the editor of the *Open Education Newsletter.*

Bonnie Barrett Stretch was the associate education editor of *Saturday Review.*

Arthur J. Tobier is the editor of *The Center Forum,* a publication of the Center for Urban Education in New York City.

Charles Weingartner is an Associate Professor of Education on leave from Queens College. He is coauthor with Neil Postman of *Teaching as a Subversive Activity* and *The Soft Revolution.*